The Oromo Movement
and Imperial Politics

The Oromo Movement and Imperial Politics

Culture and Ideology in Oromia and Ethiopia

Asafa Jalata

LEXINGTON BOOKS
Lanham • Boulder • New York • London

Published by Lexington Books
An imprint of The Rowman & Littlefield Publishing Group, Inc.
4501 Forbes Boulevard, Suite 200, Lanham, Maryland 20706
www.rowman.com

6 Tinworth Street, London SE11 5AL

Copyright © 2020 by The Rowman & Littlefield Publishing Group, Inc.

All rights reserved. No part of this book may be reproduced in any form or by any electronic or mechanical means, including information storage and retrieval systems, without written permission from the publisher, except by a reviewer who may quote passages in a review.

British Library Cataloguing in Publication Information Available

Library of Congress Control Number: 2019956284

ISBN 978-1-7936-0337-1 (cloth : alk. paper)
ISBN 978-1-7936-0339-5 (pbk : alk. paper)
ISBN 978-1-7936-0338-8 (electronic)

Dedicated to all Oromo nationalists who have made us proud by sacrificing their precious lives for the Oromo liberation and Democracy

Contents

Preface		ix
Acknowledgments		xi
1	Introduction	1
2	The Oromo Epistemology, Agency, and Movement	13
3	The Oromo Nation: Toward Mental Liberation and Empowerment *With Harwood Schaffer*	31
4	The Oromo National Movement and Gross Human Rights Violations	53
5	Theorizing *Oromummaa*	75
6	*Gadaa/Siqqee* as the Fountain of *Oromummaa* and the Theoretical Base of Oromo Liberation *With Harwood Schaffer*	99
7	The Oromo Movement: The Effects of State Terrorism and Globalization in Oromia and Ethiopia	119
8	Politico-Cultural Prerequisites for Protecting the Oromo National Interest	137
9	The Challenges of Building Oromo National Institutions	153
References		177
Index		187
About the Author		197

Preface

This book on *Oromummaa* or Oromo nationalism and the Oromo national movement reflects my many years of political and intellectual experiences. I entered into political activism when I was a high school and college student in Oromia and Ethiopia. I made a serious commitment to focus on Oromo and Ethiopian studies when I was in a graduate school in the United States because of my love for freedom, democracy, and the knowledge for liberation. The political, cultural, economic, and social crimes that have been committed on my people, the Oromo, and other oppressed peoples, and by extension on my life and psychology have had a deep impact on my political and intellectual commitment. This commitment has involved the development of liberation knowledge, democracy of knowledge, and the demystification of the knowledge for domination, exploitation, and dehumanization. After I was forced to live in exile in the United States by fleeing from the repression and control of the Ethiopian government, which could have imprisoned or killed me, I decided to continue higher education in order to further develop and sharpen my intellectual capacity to contribute to the Oromo national struggle on the intellectual front.

Despite the fact that several of my professors and fellow graduate students in the Department of Sociology at the State University of New York, Binghamton, advised me that specializing in Oromo studies was tantamount to committing professional suicide because the Oromo people were not or little known in global history in the late 1980s, my commitment to engage in Oromo studies only increased. In fact, I have continued to accumulate more knowledge and experience in the fields of Africana and global studies. As demonstrated by my numerous scholarly publications, my research and productivity have been expanding and increasing over the years. This book is the continuation of these efforts. It demonstrates the essence, complexity, and characteristics of Oromo nationalism, which I call national *Oromummaa*.

National *Oromummaa* reflects Oromo culture, history, knowledge, institutions, identity, and ideology, and opposes the mainstream Ethiopianism. Ethiopianism as the main ideology of the Amhara-Tigrayan ethno-nations explains and justifies an ethno-national hierarchy and Ethiopian colonialism over the Oromo and other colonized nations in the Ethiopian Empire. Furthermore, there is an Oromo collaborator class that has been domesticated by Ethiopian institutions to promote and practice Ethiopianism at the cost of the larger Oromo nation. Therefore, the external and internal oppressors of the Oromo have never recognized and appreciated Oromo nationalism and the Oromo national movement. This book is written to challenge the oppressor nationalism of Ethiopianism and to advance the Oromo national struggle for national self-determination, statehood, and an egalitarian multinational confederal or federal democracy in which all peoples will be able to fully participate.

The successive Amhara, Tigrayan, and Somali state elites and others have attacked the Oromo national movement from all directions to keep the Oromo in a subordinate position and to expropriate their lands and other resources. It is a miracle that Oromo nationalism has survived and recently has blossomed and changed into a mass movement, decomposing the Tigrayan-led Ethiopian government and engaging in reconstructing of Oromo national institutions in order to rebuild a democratic Oromia state that will either be independent or an integral part of egalitarian multinational confederal or federal democracy. This book unravels these complex processes in an unprecedented way.

However, the issues addressed in this book on Oromo nationalism and the Oromo national movement are limited, and a comprehensive study of national *Oromummaa* and the Oromo national struggle can be done when the Oromo people will have total control on their destiny and political economy. Unfortunately, the Oromo are still under the control of the Ethiopian state and its collaborators, who have little or no commitment for the interest of the Oromo nation. Still Oromo economic resources are primarily used to build and maintain the colonial institutions, which are determined to keep the Oromo people in a subordinate position because of the fear of their size and potential.

I thank many people who directly or indirectly contributed to this book by reading and commenting on a chapter or a few chapters of this book so that I would clarify my points and arguments. Harwood Schaffer was one of these people. I also thank my wife, Zeituna Kalil, and my children, Beka and Kulani, for emotionally, psychologically, and intellectually standing with me and supporting me in my commitment of studying and promoting the Oromo national movement.

Asafa Jalata
Knoxville, Tennessee
August 2019

Acknowledgments

I am grateful to the publishers of *Sociology Mind* for allowing me to reprint my article entitled "Politico-cultural Prerequisites for Protecting the Oromo National Interest," 2019, Vol. 9, pp. 95–113. I also thank *The European Scientific Journal* for granting me permission to reprint "The Oromo National Movement and Gross Human Rights Violations, Vol. 12, Number 5: 177–204; and *Social Justice: A Journal of Crime, Conflict & World Order* for allowing me to reprint, "The Oromo Movement: The Effects of Globalization and Terrorism on Oromia and Ethiopia" Vol. 44, No. 4, Issue 150, pp. 83–105.

ONE
Introduction

The book deals with the issues of Oromo nationalism and the Oromo national movement, which have been exposing and struggling against Ethiopian colonialism and global imperialism for almost five decades. It critically examines how the Ethiopian colonial state has denied structural assimilation (equal accesses to valued resources) and citizenship rights to the Oromo based on the ideology of Ethiopianism (chauvinism and racism) and other factors and contributed to the development of the collective political consciousness of national *Oromummaa* (Oromo national culture, identity, and nationalism). It also explains how oppressor Ethiopian nationalism rationalizes and justifies the hierarchical organization of various peoples or nations and how oppressed Oromo nationalism provides an ideology or a vision and a program for seeking self-determination, sovereignty, and multinational confederal or federal democracy by radically transforming the Ethiopian colonial state and its racist political structures. Overall, this chapter explains the essence and characteristics of the Oromo national struggle by providing theoretical insights of social movements in general, and that of the Oromo, in particular.

The "modern" Ethiopian state that emerged through the expansion of the European-dominated capitalist world system to the Horn of Africa during the last decades of the nineteenth century (Jalata 1997) had created a system that has perpetuated exploitation and oppression by establishing racist policies and practices and by denying civil equality to the Oromo and others. The Oromo national movement developed to challenge the Ethiopian colonial state and change the subordinate position of the Oromo nation. At the beginning of the twenty-first century, the intensifications of globalization and the proliferation of nationalisms are the two main global social processes shaping world history. The nature and the role of the colonial state are being challenged and changed by the globalizing structures, technological transformation, the revolution in international communication and transformation of information, and by forces of national diversity and multiculturalism.

THE ORIGIN AND ESSENCE OF THE OROMO NATIONAL MOVEMENT

The Oromo national movement began to develop in the 1960s by challenging the policies and practices of the Ethiopian colonial state (Jalata 1993a, 1993b). Despite the fact that the Oromo people are the largest national group in the Ethiopian Empire and estimated at 50 million, they are a political minority and the colonial subjects of Ethiopia. The Oromo movement was produced by social structural and momentous factors, such as the dynamic interplay of social structures, ideologies, political consciousness, human agencies, and actions. The inability of the colonizers to control totally or crush human spirit, individual and collective resistance to colonial or racial/national domination, the immortality of certain cultural memories, transformations in social structures because of economic and political changes, urbanization and community formation, the development of institutions, the emergence of an educated class, politicized collective grievances, and the dissemination of social scientific and political knowledge through global and local networks have interplayed and facilitated the development of the Oromo movement.

The Oromo national movement has gained political legitimacy because it politicized the grievances of collective memory and appealed to a common oppression and ancestry to regain for the Oromo people cultural, political, and economic rights by rejecting subordination and cultural supremacy of their oppressors. However, collective identities are not automatically given, but "essential outcomes of the mobilization process and crucial prerequisites to movement success" (Buechler 1993, 228). Although the struggle of the Oromo people embodies the continuation and culmination of the previous resistance, it emerged from certain historical and socioeconomic factors and momentous events. Colonial capitalism produced new class forces and social groups, such as workers, the military, intellectuals, and students in the Oromo society during and after the mid-twentieth century. Some revolutionary and nationalist elements from these social forces had transformed a peaceful opposition movement to a peasant-based guerrilla-armed struggle. The Ethiopian colonial government and society have effectively excluded these emerging social forces and the masses from equal access to political power and cultural and economic gains.

Political disfranchisement and exclusion, repression, and massive human rights violations had stimulated the development the Oromo national movement. This movement only developed into a mass movement recently (Jalata 1997). This development occurred after a long period of resistance and struggle. Initially the Oromo resisted slavery and colonization without systematically organizing themselves. The Oromo cultural and political resistance continued after their colonization because they were assigned to the status of slaves and colonial subjects and second-class citizens by the Ethiopian colonial state. Various Oromo groups continued to challenge Ethiopian settler colonialism to regain their freedom and independence. There were numerous local uprisings in different parts of Oromia (the Oromo country). Sometimes these local groups expelled the Ethiopian colonial settlers from their country (Jalata 1993a, 152–153). The search for freedom and decolonization was clearly manifested when thirty-three Oromo chiefs held meetings in 1936 and decided to establish a Western Oromo Confederacy. The document they signed to establish this confederacy expressed the desire of the people of Western Oromia to become a League of Nations protectorate with the help of the British government until the Oromo could achieve self-government.

Despite the fact that Oromo individuals and groups resisted and fought against the combined forces of Ethiopian settler colonialism and global imperialism, a few Oromo elites and urbanites started to develop and manifest Oromo collective consciousness and to create and develop the Oromo national movement only in the early 1960s. Before this decade, the destruction "of Oromo national leadership, the tight control of the government, the meagerness of a modern educational establishment, lack of transport and communication systems and mass media, [and] the absence of written literature in the Oromo language . . . may have contributed to retarding the growth of an Oromo national consciousness" (Hassen 1998, 193). For long periods, Oromo lacked formally trained and culturally minded intellectuals. While the Ethiopian elites "feared Oromo nationalism as a major threat to the disintegration of the Ethiopian Empire, Somali ruling elites regarded it as a dangerous movement that would abort the realization of the dream of greater Somalia" (Hassen 1998, 189). Overall, the development of colonial capitalism in Oromia, the emergence of a few conscious Oromo intellectuals and bureaucrats, the cumulative experiences of struggle, and politicized collective and individual grievances had facilitated the development of the Oromo national movement (Jalata 1993b, 1998).

It was not only the Oromo masses, which were mistreated by the Ethiopian colonizers. Those Oromo elites who joined the Ethiopian colonial institutions were not treated as equal citizens. Since the colonial government ignored them, those few Oromo individuals who joined the colonial institutions (such as schools, parliament, the army, and the administration) and Oromo merchants began to think about ways to improve the Oromo living standard. Despite their relative achievements, these individuals had inferior status to the Ethiopian ruling elites due to their Oromo national identity. Paradoxically, the idea of developing the collective consciousness of Oromo peoplehood and Oromo nationalism was initiated by a few Oromo who were educated to be members of an Ethiopianized Oromo collaborator class, but who were not treated as equals with members of the Ethiopian ruling elites. Since there has been a fundamental contradiction between the Ethiopian colonizing structures and the colonized Oromo, the Ethiopian society could not culturally and structurally assimilate the Oromo elites. The formation of the Macha-Tulama Self-Help Association in the year 1963–1964 marked the public rise of Oromo nationalism (Jalata 1993a, 1998). Since the Ethiopian Constitution did not allow establishing a political organization, emerging Oromo leaders formed this association as a civilian self-help association in accordance with Article 45 of his Imperial Majesty's 1955 Revised Constitution and Article 14, Number 505 of the Civil Code.

The Oromo nationalist elites through forming this association in Fifinnee (Addis Ababa), the capital city of the Ethiopian Empire, started to articulate the collective grievances of the Oromo people, by formulating programs to solve some economic, cultural, social, and educational problems of the Oromo society. According to Mohammed Hassen (1998, 183), within a short time, the association "transformed itself from a self-help development association in the Shawa administrative region, into pan-Oromo movement that coordinated peaceful resistance, and in turn gave birth to Oromo political awareness. This means that since their conquest in the 1880s, the Oromo developed a single leadership." When the Ethiopian government and the Ethiopian elites continued to mistreat these Oromo elites and conspired to deny Oromo educational and professional opportunities, and even attempted to destroy the leadership of the association, the association under its charismatic leader, General Taddasa Biru, unsuccessfully attempted in 1966 to take over the control of the Ethiopian state (Zoga 1993, 118–133).

The Oromo nationalist elements of the 1960s recognized what C. Geertz (1994, 30) describes: "The one aim is to be noticed; it is a search for identity, and a demand that identity be publicly acknowledged. . . . The other aim is practical: it is a demand for progress for a rising standard of living, more effective political order, great social justice, and beyond that of 'playing a part in the larger arena of world politics,' of exercising influence among the nations." The Ethiopian colonial state and the Ethiopian settlers in Oromia did not tolerate any manifestation of Oromo consciousness. The Haile Selassie government banned the association in 1967, and its leaders were imprisoned or killed. Since the association started "to articulate the dissatisfaction of the Oromo with the government and particularly with their position in society," it was not tolerated (Wood 1983, 516). The Ethiopian government did not even tolerate the existence of the Arffan Qallo and the Biftu Ganamo musical groups in Hararghe because they manifested themselves in the Oromo language and culture. They were banned like the association. Similarly, the Bale

Oromo armed struggle that started in the early 1960s was suppressed with the assistance of Great Britain, the United States, and Israel between 1968 and 1970 (Gilkes 1975, 217–218). The banning of the Macha-Tulama Self-Help Association, the destruction of the Arffan Qallo and Biftu Ganamo musical groups, and the suppression of the Bale Oromo armed struggle forced Oromo nationalism to go underground.

The Macha-Tulama "movement marked the beginning of a new political experience that was crucial to the growth of Oromo nationalism in the 1970s, an experience that taught the Oromo elites that they needed a liberation movement that would marshal the resources of their people, harmonize their actions and channel their creative activities and innovation against the oppressive Ethiopian system" (Hassen 1998, 196). The suppression of Oromo reform nationalism forced some Oromo nationalists to go underground and others went to Somalia, the Middle East, and other countries to continue the Oromo national movement. When the Oromo were denied the right to express themselves in the late 1960s and the early 1970s, a few Oromo militant elements produced political pamphlets, such as *Kana Bekta* (Do you know this?), and historical documents, such as *The Oromos: Voice against Tyranny*. The authors of this document were Magarsa Bari, Dima (Yohanis) Noggo, Addisu Tolosa, Nagasso Gidada, Tsegaye Namarra, and Boru Xadacha. Also, Baro Tumasa, Gudina Tumsa, and Abiyu Galata were indirectly involved, and probably edited its final version. For the first time the original name of the people, Oromo, was used in the publication by rejecting the derogatory name, *Galla*. *The Oromos: Voice against Tyranny* (1980, 23) raised the Oromo question as a colonial one and defined the future direction of the Oromo national struggle. In the late 1970s, publications such as *Bakalcha* and its youth wing, *Warraqa*, and *Oromia* and its youth wing, *Gucaa Dargaagoo*, appeared in Finfinnee to explain and promote the Oromo national cause. Lydia Namarra, Abraham Mosisa, Kifile Ummata, Lagasse Barki, and I were the founders and members of *Gucaa Dargaagoo*.

The denial of individual, civil, and collective rights and the suppression of all forms of Oromo organizations and movements forced Oromo nationalists to engage in the Oromo national struggle in clandestine forms. These nationalists formed the Ethiopian National Liberation Front (ENLF) in 1971 and the Oromo Liberation Front (OLF) in 1974, As Bonnie Holcomb and Sisai Ibssa (1990, 299) note, "intellectuals who had survived the banning of Macha-Tulama had gone underground to find a new approach. Those who had been able to leave the country were also searching together for alternative tactics and strategies to achieve the objective they had espoused and to find a new model for effective organization." The ENLF's main objectives were to reform Ethiopia, introduce democracy, and to bring civil and political equality for all peoples by removing the imperial nature of Ethiopia (Jalata 1994, 5–7). However, most Oromo nationalists did not endorse these objectives recognizing the nature of the

Ethiopian state and elites, but rather determined to develop revolutionary nationalism that attempts to dismantle Ethiopian settler colonialism and to establish a people's democratic republic of Oromia as an independent or as an autonomous state within a federated multinational democratic society (*The Oromo Liberation Front Program* 1976). The more Oromo have intensified their national struggle, the more the crisis of the Ethiopian state and its terrorism have increased.

A few Oromo revolutionary elements established an underground political movement and transformed reform nationalism into a revolutionary one because the Ethiopian colonial government totally denied Oromo any channel through which to express their individual and collective interests. These revolutionary elements understood from the beginning the significance of the reconstruction of Oromo culture and history for the survival of the Oromo national identity and the development of Oromo nationalism. The revolutionary Oromo leaders produced political pamphlets and expanded their sphere of influence by organizing different political circles in different sectors of the Oromo society, such as students, professionals, workers, farmers, and the army. As soon as the OLF began to challenge Ethiopian colonial domination ideologically, intellectually, politically, and militarily, the Ethiopian state initiated terrorism against Oromo nationalists and the Oromo people. Due to the lack of international support and sanctuary, Ethiopian terrorism, Somali opposition to Oromo nationalism, and internal disagreement and competition within the Oromo elites, the growth of Oromo nationalism was slow in the 1970s and 1980s.

In the late 1970s, almost all members of the OLF executive committee were wiped out on their way to Somalia to attend an important organizational meeting. Also, the Ethiopian regime targeted prominent Oromo nationalists and assassinated veteran leaders like Tadassa Biru and Hailu Ragassa. In 1980, it imprisoned or murdered top OLF leaders and activists. Because of all these factors, the Oromo movement played a secondary role in overthrowing the Ethiopian military regime headed by Mengistu Haile Mariam in May 1991. With the demise of this regime the Ethiopian People's Revolutionary Democratic Front (EPRDF), created and dominated by the Tigrayan People's Liberation Front (TPLF), came to power with the support and endorsement of the US government and the Eritrean People's Liberation Front, and then later established a minority Tigrayan-based authoritarian-terrorist government. To obtain political legitimacy, at the beginning the new regime invited different liberation fronts, most prominent of which was the OLF, and other political organizations and established a transitional government. The new regime persuaded these fronts and organizations that it would prepare a ground for the formation of a multinational federal democratic government of Ethiopia.

However, in less than a year, the regime expelled all coalition partners by using intimidation, terrorism, and war, and established an ethnic-based party dictatorship without any opposition from the United States and other Western countries (Trueman 1997; Pollock 1997). The United States, other Western countries, and the Organization of African Unity called the sham elections this regime used to legitimize its power satisfactory, fair, and free (see *Reuters Business Briefing*, July 5, 1994; *Reuters*, May 15, 1995). The feat was accomplished through systematic intimidation and outright terrorism. The development of the Oromo national movement representing the largest national group had become an obstacle for the establishment of Tigrayan hegemony. Therefore, the Oromo were the main target of Ethiopian state terrorism. The Tigrayan-led Ethiopian government accepted state violence against the Oromo and others as a legitimate means of establishing political stability and order. The regime practiced state terrorism with the support of global capitalist elites against the Oromo because they have ideologically, culturally, and intellectually challenged Ethiopian cultural and ideological domination and also redefined the relationship between the Oromo and the Habashas.

In April 2018, the Oromo peaceful movement led by *Qerroo/Qarree* (Oromo youth) forced the Tigrayan-dominated colonial government called the Ethiopian Peoples' Revolutionary Democratic Front (EPRDF) to reorganize itself under the leadership of Prime Minster Abyi Ahmed who has promised to transit Ethiopia to democracy. The popular uprising did not yet accomplish its revolutionary transformation because of the lack of national organizational/institutional capacity. Despite the fact that the Oromo national movement has been transformed into a mass movement, the result of this change is not yet known. But, the EPRDF's army has already started to terrorize the Oromo in Gujii and Wallaga claiming that it fights against the Oromo Liberation Army. Generally speaking, the development of the Oromo national movement is considered as an aspect of the worldwide struggle for cultural/national identity, multiculturalism, economic freedom, social justice, and inalienable political and cultural rights. This book considers the Oromo national struggle in relation to broader theoretical perspectives, which are explored below.

THEORETICAL INSIGHTS

While colonial states, nation-states, dominant classes, powerful racial/ethnonational groups, corporations, and patriarchal institutions have engaged in producing false or biased knowledge, theories, and narratives in order to naturalize and justify all forms of inequalities and injustices, various progressive social movements—national/indigenous movements, women's movements and labor unions—have struggled to expose and discredit such knowledge by producing alternative narratives, theories, knowledge, and worldviews. Critical studies, such as subaltern studies, assist to confront and expose the false claims of universalism, dominant ideology, and worldviews that attempt to hide colonial history and imperialist practices in Africa and other places (Mbembe 2008). Consequently, there are two forms of contradictory processes of theory and knowledge production, narratives, and modes of thought in the capitalist world system: one form is associated with a dominant narrative and knowledge for domination, exploitation, and maintaining the status quo while the other is associated with subaltern narratives and knowledge for liberation, social justice, and egalitarian democracy (Jalata 1996). Despite the fact that various social movements, including the Oromo national movement, have introduced some social reforms, they have yet to develop a necessary critical theory of human liberation that invigorates the struggle to overthrow the dominant worldview in order to produce a new politico-economic paradigm—one which will facilitate the emergence of a participatory and egalitarian democracy for all peoples.

Most often, subaltern movements and social revolutions have been about the capturing of state power and have subsequently become an integral part of the capitalist world system. As a result, social movements and social revolutions have only been successful in introducing limited changes and reforms that are confined by the parameters of global capitalism (Arrighi, Hopkins, and Wallerstein 1989). Nevertheless, the increasing crises of the capitalist world-system—the possible depletion of the world's valuable resources, global financial and ecological crises, growing social inequality, the intensification of terrorism from above and below, and the declining of material resources for ordinary people—indicate possible paradigmatic shifts that could shape the prospects for advancing new and system-transformative modes of thought, knowledge, and action. Learning from the past limitations of various social movements and social revolutions, critical scholars who engage in Oromo studies, progressive Oromo forces, and the Oromo national movement, need to develop an alternative knowledge and a critical ideology that are encapsulated in Oromo nationalism or national *Oromummaa*. This development can help in reimagining a new Oromo worldview beyond domination and exploitation. Similarly, the movements of other colonized and oppressed nations should also develop a critical knowledge and ideology based on their democratic and egalitarian traditions that promote horizontal relations within their societies and in relationship to other societies that struggle for freedom, self-determination, and egalitarian multinational democracy.

Mainstream classical scholars of collective behavior, such as Neil J. Smelser (1962) and modernization theorists, such as W. W. Rostow (1960, 4–16), wrongly considered social or national movements as abnormal and irrational or deviant. These theorists believed that the collective behavior of social revolutions and movements are caused by factors such as social breakdown, strain, deprivation, discontent, cognitive dissonance, ambiguity, and psychological frustration (Buechler 2011, 91–106.) Such theorists blamed the victims for struggling for their own emancipation. The mainstream theoretical approaches of social movements have failed to explain how the politicized collective grievances lead to collective action. In the 1960s, resource mobilization theory emerged, challenging the classical model of collective behavior and social movements (McCarthy and Zaid 2001, 553–566). Progressive movement scholars and activists started to use neo-Marxism and conflict theory as alternative theories to explain the relationship among political power, conflict, and domination. Resources mobilization theory as a theoretical paradigm shift challenged the collective behavior approach. This theory primarily depended on political, sociological, and economic theories and pay less attention to political interests, social psychology, and other issues (Tilly 1978; McAdam 1982, 42–43). Criticizing resource mobilization theory, political process theory emerged in the 1970s by explaining social movements in relation to capitalism, industrialization, urbanization, and state formation.

The political process model criticized resources mobilization for: (1) downplaying politics and political interests; (2) deemphasizing the role of grievances, ignoring ideology, and exaggerating rationalistic roles of movement actors; and (3) ignoring group solidarity as well as social psychology (Buechler 2011, 123–140). Combining the traditions of Karl Marx, Max Weber, and John Stuart Mill, Charles Tilly emphasized the importance of ideology, grievances, aspects of rationality, the importance of social solidarity and common interests, and the availability of political opportunities for social movements to emerge and develop (Tilly 1978). Tilly integrated the Marxian tradition that recognizes conflicting interests, the existence of conflict, and the importance of organization with the Weberian tradition that stresses commitment to belief systems (Tilly 1978). Political process theory recognizes factors such as the availability of material, intellectual, and cultural resources, the capacity of mobilizing these resources for collective action, the importance of the existence of preexisting social networks, organizations, and institutions, and the rationality of participants in weighing costs and benefits for engaging in collective action of social movements (Tilly 1978).

Similarly, criticizing resource mobilization theory, Doug McAdam further developed political process theory (McAdam 1982, 42–43). He identified that mobilization theory blurs the difference between the oppressed classes and groups and the established polity members, over exaggerates elite's financial support for social movements, minimizes the role of the masses in movements, lacks clarity on the concept of resources, and glosses over the issue of grievances. McAdam identified two necessary conditions for social movements to challenge the established political system. These two conditions are the structure of political opportunities such as political and economic crises and the strength of indigenous political organizations that are equipped by cognitive liberation. Cognitive liberation has three dimensions, namely the recognition of the illegitimacy of the established system, the capacity to overcome fatalism among the populace in order to believe in changing a social system, and the ability to believe that introducing social change is possible. Furthermore, another theory called framing and social construction emerged to criticize political process theory for giving a secondary role for collective grievances in the emergence and development of social movements (Buechler 2011, 141–143). This theory focuses on micro-level social dynamics and emphasizes framing, signification, media, and social psychology. It also pays attention to both symbolic interaction and cultural theories that help in the construction of meaning and understanding of grievances, motivations, recruitment process, and identity formation.

Framing and construction theory identifies three categories and focuses on them. These three categories are: (1) the process through which social movements frame grievances as injustice and illegitimate and require a collective challenge; (2) the recognition of movements such as status and identity politics, religious movements, lifestyle interests, and environmental concerns; and (3) the necessity to understand the role of meaning and signification (Buechler 2011, 145–159). By focusing on micro-level analysis, framing and social construction theory emphasizes the importance of cognitive liberation for politicizing grievances. Cognitive liberation allows people to integrate individual interests, values, and beliefs with the activities, goals, and ideology of social movements. When there is cognitive liberation or the transformation of consciousness and behavior, movements emerge. The process of the transformation of political consciousness indicates that when movement actors do not recognize the legitimacy of a given establishment, they may organize and engage in collective action. Most political process theorists focus on structural factors of political opportunity and organization and pay less attention to subjective factors such as cognitive liberation (Tilly 1978; McAdam 1982). William Gamson (1982, 6–9) recognized the importance of micro-mobilization and cognitive liberation, and identified the role of ideas and political consciousness in shaping collective action.

In micro-mobilization, know-how is very important, and it includes "a repertoire of knowledge about how to engage in collective action along with the skills to apply that knowledge" (Buechler 2011, 144). Micro-level analyzing and convincing people to mobilize and organize require building loyalty, managing the logistics of collective action, mediating internal conflict, and framing and politicizing grievances in relation to structural factors (Gamson 1982, 6–9). Referring to this theoretical framework of Ervin Goffman, Steven M. Buechler (2011, 146) defines framing as an "interpretive schemata that people use to identify, label, and render meaningful events in their lives. Frames allow people to organize experiences and guide actions, both in everyday life and in social movements."

The dominant classes and groups in the capitalist world system can control and exploit oppressed classes and subaltern groups because they have the know-hows, skills, and knowledge as well as economic resources for developing central organizing ideologies that can be translated into organizational capacity (Jalata 1996). Overall, the critical integration of the theories of resource mobilization, political process, and framing and social construction is necessary to understand how the Oromo national movement and other movements emerged in the Ethiopian Empire. These movements have also continued to develop political consciousness through developing the knowledge for liberation to expose the fallacy and irrationality of Ethiopianist knowledge for domination, control, and exploitation. Therefore, as this book demonstrates, the Oromo national movement has emerged and developed through such processes.

CONCLUSION

Studies of social and national movements are complicated by competing ideologies and interpretations. Edward Said (1993, 327) admires those scholars who submit to the method of critical approach, and comments that "What one finds in their work is always, first of all, a direct sensitivity to the material before them, and then a continual self-examination of their methodology and practice, a constant attempt to keep their work responsive to the material and not to a doctrinal preconception." In studying movements, we need to go beyond the artificial boundaries of the social sciences and intellectual paradigms by employing interdisciplinary, multidimensional, and historical and comparative methods, and critical approaches that include political economy, multiculturalism, and critical theoretical and historical methodology. Furthermore, introducing participatory research methods to studies of nationalism and national movements is also highly essential so that the indigenous peoples tell their stories without distortion and misinterpretation.

Participatory research emerged as part of the resistance to colonial or neocolonial research practices in peripheral parts of the world and adopted by activist scholars in core countries "as part of a larger discourse on emancipatory . . . or transformative practice" (Hall 1993, xiv). Scholars need to allow the subjugated peoples or nations to actively participate in their research since their experiences are more valuable than a number of learned speculations. Participatory research approaches can help scholars better understand the question of movements by supplementing other methods of enquiry through assisting them to identify the weaknesses of their own concepts, theories, and assumptions by learning from the actual experiences of the indigenous peoples. As an activist Oromo scholar, I have been participating in and studying the Oromo national movement starting from the late 1970s to the present, and this book immensely reflects my accumulated theoretical and practical knowledge.

TWO

The Oromo Epistemology, Agency, and Movement

This chapter critically explores how Ethiopian colonialism and global imperialism through the suppression of an Oromo epistemology, the denial of formal education, the practice of physical and mental genocide, the destruction of institutions and leadership, and the denial of the rights for self-expression and organization have slowed the development of Oromo agency in the form of institutional and organizational capacity. By denying the Oromo the freedom of knowledge production and dissemination and by preventing them from building their own independent institutions, organizations, and leadership, Ethiopian colonialism and global capitalism have kept the Oromo people in the darkness of ignorance and abject poverty for more than a century. Under these conditions, Oromo activists, nationalists, and democrats have faced monumental challenges in learning about the Oromo epistemology for developing liberation knowledge. Hence, the Oromo national struggle has not yet achieved its full institutional and organizational capacity in order to fulfill its political objectives of national self-determination, statehood, and egalitarian democracy despite the fact that it emerged in the 1960s with other African national liberation struggles, which at least gained "flag independence."

Nevertheless, the Oromo national movement is slowly and surely progressing and mobilizing the wider Oromo society in general and Oromo students in particular. The Oromo protest movement led by Oromo students popularly know as *Qeerroo/Qaree* (Oromo youth) between 2015 and 2018 clearly demonstrated how the Oromo people were mobilized all over Oromia and beyond to oppose the policy and practice of land grabbing in the name of the so-called Addis Ababa Master Plan and other colonial policies. In critically analyzing and understanding the complexity of the Oromo national struggle in relation to the issues of knowledge and agency, I ask the following four interrelated questions and answer them: First, what are the cultural, epistemological, and institutional factors that facilitate the progress or stagnation of a society? Second, why did Ethiopian colonialism and global capitalism destroy or repress the epistemology and cultural knowledge of the Oromo? Third, what are the major factors that delayed the achievement of Oromo political objectives? Finally, what should be done to hasten the development of the organizational capacity of the Oromo national movement in order to totally mobilize the Oromo nation and to achieve its political objectives?

THEORETICAL AND METHODOLOGICAL CONSIDERATIONS

Every society has its unique epistemology and civilization. This shows that the world is epistemologically diverse and culturally plural. As Boaventura de Sousa Santos (2007, xlvii) notes, "*There is no ignorance or knowledge in general. All ignorance is ignorant of . . . certain knowledge, and all knowledge is the overcoming of a particular ignorance. There is no complete knowledge*" (emphasis in the original). Colonized peoples such as the Oromo had their epistemologies that helped them in producing and disseminating their cultural-centric knowledge and wisdom before their domination and subjugation. So, the Oromo had their unique epistemology and cultural knowledge manifested mainly through their democratic governance called the *gadaa/siqqee* system, their indigenous religion known as *Waaqeffannaa*, their practices of farming, cattle herding, environmental protection, and their techniques of military organization and warfare for national self-defense before they were colonized by the alliance of European imperialism and Ethiopian colonialism. Since colonization, the Oromo have been prevented from freely developing the cultural, political, military, religious, and educational institutions that they used to produce and disseminate their authentic knowledge.

Generally speaking, all colonialists sought to destroy "every last remnant of alternative ways of knowing and living to obliterate collective identities and memories and to impose a new order" (Smith 1999, 69). Colonialism and imperialism oppose the plurality of cultures and diversity of knowledge, and modern sciences, more or less, are the tool of colonial and imperial institutions. "The epistemological privilege granted to modern science from the seventeenth century onwards, which made possible the technological revolutions that consolidated Western supremacy, was . . . instrumental in suppressing other [forms] of knowledges and, at the same time, the subaltern social groups whose social practices were informed by such knowledges" (Santos 2007, xix). The suppression of indigenous knowledge is a form of "epistemicide . . . the other side of genocide" (de Santos 2007, xix). Mainstream scholars call the modern sciences, both natural and social sciences, universalistic; I call these kinds of sciences knowledge for domination and exploitation. There are scholars who call such sciences colonial knowledge that must be decolonized (Smith 1999). Mainstream academic, religious, and other institutions have promoted the knowledge for domination and corrupted the minds of the colonized in general and that of the educated elites in particular. According to Linda T. Smith (1999, 23), "The reach of imperialism into 'our heads' challenges those who belong to colonized communities to understand how this occurred partly because we perceive a need to decolonize our minds, to recover ourselves, to claim a space in which to develop a sense of authentic humanity."

Until the intellectuals of the colonized communities develop critical knowledge for human liberation by decolonizing their minds and the modern sciences, which help perpetuate domination and exploitation, there cannot be a true human liberation because mainstream knowledge cannot facilitate human freedom and justice. Realizing this reality, Audre Lorde (1979, 98–101) states, "*The master's tools will never dismantle the master's house*" (emphasis in the original). Counter-hegemonic interpretive and political frames, indigenous theories and forms of knowledge (rather, modes of knowing) highlight the fallacies of hegemonic theories and knowledge that naturalize, rationalize, justify, and promote social hierarchies in the name of scientific rigor. Mainstream theories and forms of knowledge do have little room or incentive to address the fundamental problems of indigenous peoples such as the Oromo and other subaltern groups due to their self-contained nature and the self-referential thrust of modern concerns despite their claim to universality. Scientific knowledge—including social-scientific knowledge—is not value-neutral, but based on standards that are (or reflect) social constructions, and it frequently enforces and perpetuates related perspectives that result from and inform the socio-historical context that generates and sustains those standards. According to Third World Network (1993, 485), "Scientists are strongly committed to beliefs and certain cultural ethos, which compel them to convert diversity and complexity into uniformity. In addition to this belief system and cultural ethos—which manifest themselves in the propositions that scientists embrace—science has its own power structure, reward systems and peer groups. All of these [factors] combine to ensure that [mainstream] science is closely correlated with the existing, dominant and unjust, political, economic and social order of the world."

Mainstream as well as oppositional critical social theories and knowledge embody Europe- and North America–centric and other dominant perspectives and notions, which at the same time constitute their horizon of concern and inquiry. As Sandra Harding (1993, 2) characterizes, Eurocentrism adheres to "the assumption that Europe functions autonomously from other parts of the world; that Europe is its own origin, final end, and agent; and that Europe and people of European descent in the Americas and elsewhere owe nothing to the rest of the world." Consequently, in the name of modernity, progress, civilization, and cultural universalism, dominant theories and scholarship have suppressed, or at least implicitly and/or explicitly distorted the cultures, traditions, and knowledge of indigenous peoples (McGregor 2004). These dominant theories and knowledge have presented the destructive capacities of more than 500 years of global capitalism and colonialism as beneficial to indigenous peoples. As S. McGovern (1999, 27) observes, indigenous "knowledge systems have been represented by adjectives such as 'primitive', 'unscientific', and 'backwards', while the '[dominant] system' is assumed to be uniquely 'scientific and universal' and superior to local forms of knowledge. . . . The modern knowledge system 'is merely the globalized version of a very local and parochial tradition' arising with 'commercial capitalism' and 'a set of values based on power.'" Hegemonic theories, scholarship, and the ruling ideas have ignored that the colonized peoples have been "a data mine for social theory" (Connell, 2007, 369) and the source of objective knowledge production. The hegemonic and state-centric knowledge limits our understanding of humanity as a whole by ignoring the geo-cultures of indigenous and other subaltern groups.

Of course, there have been critical and leftist scholars who have labored to expose the exploitative and oppressive aspects of global capitalism by focusing on hierarchies based on gender, class, and race/ethnonation. However, due to the confining horizon of dominant thinking, their limited knowledge of indigenous societies, and proclivity toward versions of evolutionary and modernist thinking, most critical scholars have glossed over the problem of indigenous peoples like that of the Oromo. Furthermore, with the exception of a few instances, their works on indigenous peoples have been contradictory, incomplete, or distorted. Because of the rejection or neglect of multicultural knowledge and wisdom, and the tradition of abyssal thinking (Santos, 2007), the dominant theoretical and intellectual knowledge from right and left has been prone to disregarding the humanity of indigenous peoples. To a greater or lesser extent, these intellectual traditions have tended to see indigenous peoples as organized socially in forms that are unable to withstand the onslaught of the process of modernization. Mainstream political and social theories and approaches to social research have supported or promoted colonial and neo-colonial agendas, explicitly or implicitly, or have neglected to engage in the requisite critical reflexivity, thus promulgating suppositions about indigenous peoples that originated in ideological definitions of societal reality. "If the success of these sciences required the military and political defeat of non-Western peoples," Sandra Harding (1993, 8) writes, "we are entitled to skepticism about claims that the history of these sciences is unmitigated the history of human progress; progress for some has been at the expense of disempowerment, impoverishment, and sometimes genocide for many others."

I employ a social-constructionist model of making societies (Roy 2001), and critical comparative political economic and sociocultural approaches to demonstrate the deficiencies of dominant social theories and systems of knowledge production. Social theories, as all forms of knowledge, are socially constructed. Hence, I reject the essentialist theoretical perspective that assumes that "things are the way they are by nature" (Roy 2001, 8). Since the beginning of the modern age, the capitalist class and its intellectual supporters have utilized liberal Enlightenment's claim to universality as the ideology of promoting human equality in order to overthrow the feudal order. Yet, later on, liberal Enlightenment philosophers and other scholars "naturalized" the capitalist order, thus impeding, if not undercutting entirely, the project of emancipating ordinary people in order to defend positions of power and influence through the creation and perpetuation of private property via dispossession and exploitation. Mainstream scholars constructed theories, concepts, and ideologies of race and racism, and further consolidated gender and class hierarchies, to facilitate and intensify the ongoing accumulation of capital and wealth (Jalata 2012 [2001]).

In reality, there is historical evidence of an extensive period in human history when racial and class categories and gender hierarchies did not exist, and when all human groups were non-hierarchical and non-exploitative (Trigger 2006, 21–28). Elites began to construct and maintain social hierarchies of gender, class, and race/ethnonation through the invention and establishment of institutions: "What becomes socially constructed is disproportionally the result of dominant institutions in society. Institutions are groups of organizations, categories, and ways of doing things that do something important in society" (Roy 2001, 22). Hence, it ought to be the purpose of my analytical tools, concepts, and categories to enable us to demystify ideological constructions of social, political, cultural, and economic forms that naturalize inequalities in a society, as well as all those theoretical paradigms and methodologies that, either by default or intent, legitimate and perpetuate forms of injustice and exploitation that benefit the rich, powerful racial/ethnonational groups, patriarchy, and dominant classes, and to focus on the development of an emancipatory project for humanity as a whole. My research and methodological stance confirms the need for scientific methods to be enlarged toward such demystification in order to overcome the pitfalls of traditional research methods and theoretical approaches that justify the destruction of the Oromo epistemology and original culture.

CULTURE, EPISTEMOLOGY, INSTITUTIONS, TECHNOLOGY, AND SOCIAL CHANGE

Societal formations and transformations have been taking place through social innovations, technological advances in forms of the techniques of production and exchange, and through organizational capacity building in the forms of educational, political, and religious institutions and ideologies since early periods in human history. When people were hunters and gatherers, all human groups started their slow development with stone tools until they engaged in copper, bronze, and iron production successively to improve their weapons initially for hunting animals and for fighting their competitors for control of resources and later for increasing economic productivity. With the use of metal tools, technological improvements, and development of agriculture in the forms of cattle herding and production of grains, the emerging elites of certain societies developed religious and political institutions that organized societies within and beyond an ethnonational boundary. Starting from the Middle East, both Christianity and Islam and the need for commercial expansion and empire-building played decisive roles in expanding spheres of influence through the spread of religions, wars, slavery, conquest, and reorganization of societies on local, regional, and global levels. The development of Christianity and Islam cannot be seen beyond this reality although most followers of these religions do not know these historical facts. For instance, the history of north, east, and west Africa from ancient times to the arrival of European slavers and colonizers demonstrate the effective roles of commerce, empire-building, and Christianity and Islam in hierarchically organizing and legitimizing colonialism, slavery, cultural destruction, and dehumanization of various indigenous Africans (Shillington 2005).

So a society developed or stagnated or destroyed through the introduction of new ideas such as religions and technology, which are forms of knowledge that help in building or undermining an institutional or organizational capacity of a given society. Furthermore, the innovative ideas of Christianity and Islam that focus on life after death while empowering elites on the earth and the liberal ideology of capitalism and the oppositional ideology of the so-called socialism have played great roles in large-scale and long-term social transformations or destruction beyond a single society. Indigenous Africans in general and the Oromo in particular have been negatively affected by these ideological, religious, and political orientations. Furthermore, technological advancements and scientific and organizational knowledge and skills that emerged with global capitalism have also undermined the interests of indigenous peoples in general and that of the Oromo in particular. As Smith (1999, 63) states, "The globalization of Knowledge and Western culture constantly reaffirms the West's view of itself as the center of legitimate knowledge, the arbiter of what counts as knowledge and the source of 'civilized' knowledge. This form of knowledge is generally referred to as 'universal' knowledge, available to all and not really 'owned' by anyone . . ." The Ethiopian state and knowledge and religious elites have benefited from Western and Eastern knowledge and civilization by becoming agents of global imperialism in the Horn of Africa. Under these conditions how can the Oromo benefit from these ideological, religious, and technological phenomena that work as forms of knowledge and human agency in the current era of globalization?

When capitalism was developing in Western Europe in the late fifteenth century, the Oromo and Abyssinians started to confront each other on the issues of land, religion, and power in the Horn of Africa without dominating each other (Jalata 2005; Holcomb and Ibssa 1990). Until the late nineteenth century the Abyssinians/Ethiopians were on the defensive side because of the institutional capacity of the *gadaa* system and its military structure (Jalata 2005). In almost three and a half centuries (i.e., from the sixteenth to the mid-nineteenth centuries), the Oromo people established their homeland that they called *Biyyaa Oromoo*, later Oromia, even sometimes penetrated into the heartland of Abyssinia by joining the Oromo who were already there (Hassen 2015). The balance of power started to change in the last decades of the nineteenth century, when Europeans, particularly England, France, and Italy initiated the partition of the Horn of Africa. As history demonstrates, using Christianity the Abyssinians established linkage with Christian Europe, specifically with Portugal, that saved them from total destruction by an Islamic Jihad war led by Gran (Ahmad ibn Ibrahim) in 1529 (Shillington 2005). Again, during the second half of the nineteenth century, Christianity and the willingness to collaborate with European colonial powers empowered the Abyssinians under the leadership of Menelik to receive military skills, firepower, and diplomatic assistance to defeat and colonize the Oromo that Abyssinians had considered the dangerous enemy that must be destroyed forever. Despite the fact that elements of Oromo society under the leadership of Gobana Dache and others collaborated with the Abyssinian colonial project, most Oromo resisted and later engaged in cultural revitalization, resistance, and civic movements. Starting in the early 1960s, a few elements of the Oromo society initiated a self-help association because forming a political organization was prevented in the Ethiopian Empire; in the same decade cultural movements and armed resistance struggles emerged. Because of the repression of these efforts, a few Oromo nationalists created the Oromo Liberation Front (OLF) in the 1970s to engage in the protracted political and armed struggle to achieve national self-determination for the colonized Oromo nation.

However, after almost a half century, the Oromo national struggle has yet to achieve its organizational capacity to defeat Ethiopian colonialism by empowering the Oromo people. The replacement of the Amhara colonial state by that of Tigray has intensified the processes of state terrorism, genocidal massacres, and gross human rights violations in the Oromo society as the Oromo national movement has gained momentum by galvanizing the society since the early 1990s. In order to clearly understand the challenges of the Oromo national struggle and how to overcome them, we need to critically explore the effects of Ethiopian colonialism on the Oromo society and how the Ethiopian colonial state has continued to control the minds of its colonial subjects. By killing Oromo political, cultural, and religious leaders during the colonization of the Oromo people and their country and by creating submissive and less informed or ignorant leaders for the Oromo society, the Ethiopian colonial state committed physical and mental genocide. Also, by expanding its religious and colonial institutions in the Oromo country, the colonial state, more or less, deleted or suppressed the Oromo cultural knowledge and epistemology from the minds of the Oromo people. Only a few Oromo nationalists understood what was going on and initiated the Oromo cultural renaissance and the development of national *Oromummaa* or Oromo nationalism. Such farsighted organic intellectuals have been targeted for elimination by successive Ethiopian colonial regimes, and some of them have been killed or imprisoned or forced into exile. The transformation of the Oromo national movement and the building of its national organizational capacity requires knowledge and retrieval of the Oromo epistemology that had empowered the Oromo nation before its colonization.

THE DESTRUCTION OR SUPPRESSION OF THE OROMO EPISTEMOLOGY

When the Oromo society was free and independent, it had its own authentic ways of producing and disseminating knowledge that were based on Oromo-centric culture and worldview. Consequently, Oromo family, cultural, political, and religious institutions were informed and framed by the Oromo epistemology that is explored in this section. The Oromo have a theoretical concept of social and cultural development known as *finna*, which has explained phases and features of development in the Oromo society by embodying the cumulative historical and recent changes that have taken place to produce a new social order. *Finna* "represents the legacy of the past which each generation inherits from its forefathers [and foremothers] and which it transforms; it is the fertile patrimony held in trust by the present generation which it will enrich and bequeath to future generations . . . it describes a movement emanating from the inside, a developing of the inner potential of society based on the cultural roots it has already laid down" (Kassam 1994, 19–40). It has seven interconnected cumulative development phases, namely *guddina* (growth), *gabbina* (enrichment), *baliina* (broadening), *badhadha* (abundance), *hoormaataa* (reproduction and rejuvenation), *dagaaga* (development with sustainability), and *dagaa-hoora* (reciprocity, sharing and cultural borrowing with neighboring communities).

Guddina is a concept that explains how the Oromo society improves itself by creating new experiences and adding them to its existing cultural life. *Gabbina* is the next concept that explains the enrichment of cultural experiences by integrating the cumulative past experiences with the contemporary ones through broadening and deepening the systems of the production and dissemination of knowledge and worldview. According to Aneesa Kassam (1994, 19–40),

> [*Gabbina*] can only be achieved through the full knowledge, consent and active participation of all members of the community. This implies the existence of a political organization, the forum for debate and the democratic means of reaching consensus on all decisions affecting the common good. This should be obtained without force and coercion, without excluding the interests of any group, within the Oromo society and outside it, in the broader context of the national or international arena. To this end, the Oromo evolved a political process of power sharing reputed for its highly egalitarian nature: *Gadaa*.

The Oromo people believed in democracy, consensus, *nagaa* (peace), fairness, and social justice. They also believed that without Oromo democracy, there is no sustainable and egalitarian sociocultural development. These characteristics are not marks of backwardness as mainstream theories and knowledge have tried to label them. *Baliina* refers to the expansion of enriched cultural experiences from one society to another through the reciprocity of cultural borrowing, based on the principles of social equality, fairness, and social justice.

The cumulative experiences of *guddina*, *gabbina*, and *baliina* lead to the stage of *badhadha*. This phase is the stage of wholeness and peace. According to the Oromo tradition, this stage indicates the maintenance of peace among *Waaqa* (God), nature, and society; theoretically speaking, there is no conflict, poverty, disease, or natural calamity because of the balance among *Waaqa*, nature, and society is maintained. The development of *badhadha* leads to the stage of *hoormata*. In this stage, people, animal, and other living things reproduce and multiply because of the availability of conditions such as rain, resources, and peace. The next stage is *dagaaga*, which is the phase of development cycle that is integrated to maintain an even and sustainable development of society. The final phase is *daga-hoora* in which full development takes place in the Oromo society and expands to neighboring societies through reciprocity, sharing, and cultural borrowing. As the destruction and/or suppression of the Oromo epistemology, culture, and knowledge were aspects of colonial mental genocide, the destruction of Oromo lives and institutions were aspects of colonial terrorism and genocide. The surviving Oromo who used to enjoy egalitarian democracy known as the *gadaa/siqqee* system were forced to face state terrorism, political repression, and impoverished life. Alexander Bulatovich (2000, 68) explains about *gadaa/siqqee* and notes: "The peaceful free way of life, which could have become the ideal for philosophers and writers of the eighteenth century, if they had known it, was completely changed. Their peaceful way of life is broken; freedom is lost; and the independent, freedom loving [Oromo] find themselves under the severe authority of the Abyssinian conquerors."

Once the Abyssinians effectively colonized the Oromo with the help of European colonial powers, they started to propagate their ruling ideas and mythology in the discourse of Orthodox Christianity. The document known as the *Kebra Nagast* (*The Glory of the Kings*) rationalized and legitimized the monarchy using the Solomonic narrative (Budge 1932) and, by extension, related the Abyssinians to the chosen people of Israel. According to the *Kebra Nagast*: "God has appointed all these rulers and given them authority; one that opposes the ruler and is against him, rebels against the ordinances of God, his creator. Those who rebel against the rulers secure their condemnation" (Strauss 1968, 29). Menelik sought to stamp out the democratic tradition of the Oromo. He and his followers destroyed the political function of the *gadaa/siqqee* institution and officially abolished all pilgrimages to the *Abbaa Muuda*, the spiritual leader of the Oromo who among other roles was the person responsible for maintaining the democratic nature of Oromo society (Legesse 2000/2006). Menelik took all these and other actions to prevent the possibility of these pilgrimages developing into an Oromo insurrection and to eliminate any memory of a democratic tradition among the Oromo (Hassen 2005). The *gadaa* system had the principles of checks and balances (such as periodic transfer of power every eight years and division of power among executive, legislative, and judiciary branches), balanced opposition (among five *gadaa* grades), and power sharing between higher and lower administrative organs to prevent power from falling into the hands of despots.

Other principles of the system have included balanced representation of all clans, lineages, regions and confederacies, the protection of women from abuse, the protection of women's economic resources, accountability of leaders, the settlement of disputes through reconciliation and the respect for basic rights and liberties. In the *gadaa* system, there are age-sets and generation-sets (*gadaa* class). Male children join age-sets as newly born infants. Males born in the same eight-year period belong to an age-set, but they enter into the *luba* class 40 years after their fathers, and since one grade is eight years, fathers and sons are five grades apart. Male children also join generation-sets at birth, joining men or old men who are considered to be members of their genealogical generations. In these cross-cutting generation-sets, older men mentor young males in teaching rules and rituals, but the former treat the latter as equals since there is no status difference between the two groups in a *gadaa* class (or grades). Between the third and fourth *gadaa* grades, boys become adolescent and initiated into taking serious social responsibilities. The ruling group has responsibility to assign senior leaders and experts to instruct and council these young men in the importance of leadership, organization, and warfare. Young men are also trained to become junior warriors by taking part in war campaigns and hunting large animals; they learn the practical skills of warfare, military organization, and fighting so that they can engage in battle to defend their country and economic resources. As Paul T. Baxter (1978, 177) notes, the Oromo have used age-sets for war because generation-sets "cannot be an efficient means to mobilize troops, and a quite distinct organisation based on closeness of age . . . exists for that purpose." The rule of law is the key element of the *gadaa* system; those leaders who violated the law of the land or whose families could not maintain the required standard of the system were recalled before the end of their tenure in the office. Leaders selected or elected under *gadaa* implemented the laws that were made by male representatives of the people (though women undoubtedly had informal/indirect influence). Oromo democracy had allowed the Oromo people through their representatives to formulate change or amend laws and rules every eight years. The *siqqee/gadaa* system accepted the Oromo people as the ultimate source of authority, and believed nobody was above the rule of law.

Gadaa officials were elected by established criteria by the people and received rigorous training in Oromo democratic philosophy and governance for eight years before they entered the *luba* grade (administrative grade); the main criteria for election or selection to office included bravery, knowledge, honesty, demonstrated ability to govern, etc. Today, aspects of *siqqee/gadaa* still exist in some Oromo regions. In the Boorana Oromo community, for example, the *Gumii Gaayyo* (assembly of multitudes) brings together almost all important leaders, such as living *Abbaa Gadaas* (presidents of the assembly), the *qaallus* (spiritual leaders), age-set councilors, clan leaders and *gadaa* councilors, and other concerned individuals to make or amend or change laws and rules every eight years. In August 1996, the 37th *Gumii Gaayyo* Assembly, reflecting a tradition that began in 1708, was held to make, amend, or change three kinds of laws that the Boorana Oromo classify as cardinal, customary, and supplementary laws (Huqqa 1998). The *Gumii Gaayyo* assembly has a higher degree of ritual and political authority than the *gadaa* class and other assemblies because it "assembles representatives of the entire society in conjunction with any individual who has the initiative to the ceremonial grounds," and "what *Gumii* decides cannot be reversed by any other assembly" (Legesse 1973, 93). However, under the Ethiopian colonial system, the surviving *gadaa/siqqee* and the *Gumii Gaayyo* do not have the sovereignty it used to have. The Oromo claim that the understanding of the laws of *Waaqa*, nature, and society both morally and ethically and living accordingly are necessary. They believe in God's law and the law of society that they establish through the *gadaa/siqqee* system of democracy to maintain *nagaa* (peace) and *safuu* (moral and ethical order) among *Waaqa* (God), society and nature to achieve the full human destiny known as *kao* or *kayyo* (Hinnant 1978, 210).

Respect for the laws of *Waaqa* and the institution of *siqqee/gadaa* have been essential to maintain *nagaa* Oromo (Oromo peace) and *safuu* in society (Hinnant 1978, 207–208). Most Oromo believe that they had full *kao* before their colonization because they had freedom to develop their independent political, economic, cultural, and religious institutions. Emphasizing the centrality of an Oromo religious institution to democracy H. A. Kelly (1992, 166) notes the following:

> *Qaallus* have had a moral authority and the social obligation to oppose tyrants and support popular Oromo democracy and *gadaa* leaders, and to encourage harmonious and democratic relations based on the principles of *safuu, kao, Waaqa* and *uumaa*. The *qaallu* is thought to possess sacred characteristics that enable him to act as intermediary between the people and ... [God] ... he had no administrative power, but could bless or withhold blessings from *gadaa* leadership, and had an extraordinary power to curse anyone who threatened the wellbeing of the entire community by deviating from ... [God's] order.

The *qaallu* institution had been committed to social justice, the laws of God, the rule of law, and fair deliberation; the *qaallu* "residence was considered politically neutral ground, suitable for debating controversial issues and for adjudicating highly charged disputes, although he himself might not take a prominent role in proceedings" (Kelly 1992, 166). The *qaallu* institution had played an important role in protecting original Oromo culture, religion, worldview, and identity. When those Oromo who were influenced by this institution kept their indigenous Oromo names, most Oromo who were converted to Islam or Christianity willingly or by force abandoned their Oromo names and adopted Arab or Habasha or Jews or European names depending on their borrowed religions. The *qaallu* can be credited with having played an indirect role in the preservation of the Oromo identity and the remnants of the Oromo political system. The leader of all *qaallus* was known as the *Abbaa Muuda* (father of the anointment and original Oromo religious leader) who was considered to be the prophet and spiritual leader of Oromo society.

The *Abbaa Muuda* served as the spiritual center and symbol of Oromo unity and enabled all Oromo branches to keep in touch with one another over the centuries: "As the Jews believe in Moses and the Muslims in Muhammad, the Oromo believe in their Abbaa Muuda" (Hassen 1991, 90–106). The *Abbaa Muuda*, like other *qaallu* leaders, encouraged harmonious and democratic relations in the Oromo society. According to the *qaallu* mythology, the *Abbaa Muuda* was descended from heaven (Golocha 1988; Knutsson 1967). Oromo representatives travelled to the highlands of the mid-south Oromia to honor the *Abbaa Muuda* and to receive his blessing and anointment that qualified them as pilgrims, known as *jilas*, to be ritual experts in their respective areas (Knutsson 1967, 148). When Oromo representatives went to him from far and near places to receive his blessings, the *Abbaa Muuda* commanded them "not to cut their hair and to be righteous, not to recognize any leader who tries to get absolute power, and not to fight among themselves" (Knutsson 1967, 148). In its modified form, the *qaallu* institution still exists in some parts of Oromia such as in the Guji and Boorana areas. It still protects an Oromo way of life, such as dispensing of local justice based on Oromo customs and providing solutions to problems created by a changing social condition (Knutsson 1967, 133–135). The *qaallus* of Guji and Boorana are ritual leaders, advisors, and ritual experts in the *gadaa/siqqee* system. The *qaallus* "possess the exclusive prerogative of legitimizing the different *gadaaa* officials, when a new *gadaa* group is initiated into the politically active class" (Knutsson 1967, 142). The Oromo still practice some elements of Oromo democratic values in the areas where the *siqqee/gadaa* system was suppressed a century ago. This system is still practiced in the Boorana and Guji regions under the control of the Ethiopian colonial system. In its modified form, it helps maintain peace, exchange knowledge, and practice rituals among some clans and regional groups (Van de Loo 1991, 25). The current *siqqee/gadaa* of Boorana and Guji cannot fully reflect its original political culture under Ethiopian colonialism. Theoretically, most Oromo, including those intermediaries who are collaborating with the enemies of the Oromo, recognize the importance of *gadaa/siqqee*, and some Oromo nationalists struggle to restore genuine Oromo democracy.

The Oromo culture, identity, and epistemology have been distorted or suppressed by Christianity and Islam, too. The suppression of *gadaa/siqqee* by Ethiopian colonialism allowed other societies to impose their Christianity and Islam by force and/or persuasion on the Oromo society. These religions are wrapped by the cultures of Jews, Arabs, and Habashas; consequently, these religious negatively affected Oromo culture, identity, as well as names. The main challenge that faces Christian and Muslim Oromo today is to reconcile the epistemologies of these religions with that of the Oromo, to restore their original culture, identity, and humanity while maintaining their Christian or Islam religion, and to develop their national *Oromummaa* (national culture, identity, and ideology) on diverse religious experiences. Furthermore, the serious question Oromo Christians and Muslims need to ask themselves is the following: Can we be Christians or Muslims without culturally and ideologically imitating Habashas, Jews and Euro-Americans, or Arabs? This is a serious question that Oromo religious scholars of these religions must answer through religious and interfaith dialogues in order to build national *Oromummaa* that will reflect the multi-religious Oromo society. Today, there are a few Oromo extremists in these religions who are attacking and undermining an indigenous Oromo religion and authentic Oromo culture by directly imitating fundamentalist Christians or Muslims. Oromo religious scholars, priests, Sheiks, and Imams can learn a lot from notable religious scholars like Abba Gamachis, Bakiri Saphalo, Gudina Tumsa, Muhammad Rashid, Martin Luther King, Malcolm X, Desmond Tutu, and others.

DISCUSSION AND CONCLUSION

At the turn of the twenty-first century, the Oromo national movement is at a crossroads just at the moment when capitalist globalization and the Ethiopian empire state are facing their deepest crises. Despite the fact that national *Oromummaa* has been developing and that the Oromo national struggle has achieved an ideological and moral victory over Ethiopian colonialism and the Tigrayan-led Ethiopian government, the Oromo national movement still lacks organizational capacity to defeat its enemy. Although the Oromo nation has been mobilized to protest against the Addis Ababa Master Plan starting November 2015 under the leadership of school children, because of lack of organizational capacity and military power, thousands of people have been gunned down, beaten, tortured, and imprisoned by the Tigrayan-led government and its security apparatus, the army and the police. The regime has also organized mercenary groups such as Special Police (Liyu Police) from Somali-speaking people to terrorize, kill, or expel different Oromo groups from the borders of Hararghe, Bale, Boorana, Guji, and Wallo. These tragic events have happened mainly because of the lack of organizational capacity to defend the Oromo people from their external and internal enemies. So what should be done?

The priority is to restore the Oromo epistemology and original culture that empowered the Oromo people during the age of the Oromo *gadaa* civilization. The knowledge and ideology that the Oromo elites have borrowed from Ethiopian institutions, foreign religious institutions, and Western and Eastern civilizations are deficient to develop liberation knowledge and to build independent institutions and organizations for liberating Oromo society and building a free and egalitarian democratic society. The second priority is to liberate the minds of the Oromo elites who worship colonial and imperial knowledge and who are serving the interests the enemies of Oromo society at the cost of their people. These elites include both the servants of the enemy and those who are not committed to participate in the Oromo national struggle because of their opportunism and/or lack of Oromo knowledge, culture, and history. The defeating of the collaborator class by any means is absolutely necessary. This is not possible without overcoming the regional and religious affiliation these collaborators have used to divide our people and empower the enemies over them. Furthermore, the lack of ideological clarity, political confusion, and organizational and leadership shortcomings in the Oromo national movement are some of the internal problems that hinder the movement from building strong national political leadership and organizational capacity.

These weaknesses of leadership and organizations have allowed the Tigrayan-led government to terrorize and repress Oromo society and loot their resources despite the fact that there are several millions of Oromo who are determined to fight and die for the liberation of their people and country. Specifically, with the mobilization the entire Oromo society to oppose the so-called Addis Ababa Master Plan in particular and the land grab policy in general, the Tigrayan-led regime was intensifying genocidal massacres, beatings, imprisonments, and torture of Oromo school children and others starting in November 2015. The saving of the Oromo people from extermination requires being serious about solving the problems of leadership and organizational crises through the total mobilization of the human, intellectual, and cultural resources at the grassroots and national level. So, Oromo activists and nationalists must be able to mobilize every self-respecting Oromo to engage in self- and national emancipation. All Oromo must realize that it is necessary to have state power to make sure that the Oromo nation and Oromia survive forever. Critically comprehending these complex problems and solving them require developing and applying liberation knowledge and avoiding commonsense politics. Oromo nationalists in general and the Oromo political leadership in particular have yet to fulfill their national obligations of enabling the Oromo nation to liberate itself from all forms oppression, state terrorism, degradation, and abject poverty.

The Oromo national movement cannot solve its ideological, leadership, and organizational problems without coordinating and consolidating the movement and without mobilizing all Oromo intellectual, cultural, financial, and human resources. The persistent failure of Oromo leaders and movement to overcome their ideological, organizational, and behavioral problems have allowed the strengthening of the internal enemies of the Oromo people, which in turn has strengthened the power of the Ethiopian state. If the Oromo cannot stop the genocidal policy of the colonial elites by their struggle, the survival of the Oromo nation and Oromia is going to be questionable. The colonial regime has completed the forced removal of the Oromo from the areas surrounding Finfinnee. It has settled millions of armed settlers in Oromia by removing the Oromo from their ancestral homelands. Furthermore, it has already leased several million hectares of Oromo lands to so-called investors such as the Chinese government as well as Arab, Indian, Malaysian, Jews, and European business people and local capitalists by evicting Oromo farmers from their lands. To achieve its political and economic objectives, the Ethiopian regime engages in political repression, state terrorism, genocidal massacres, and gross human rights violations in Oromia and beyond. The regime has engaged in these crimes with little or no opposition from Western powers, particularly the United States as well as China, an emerging imperialist power. All these crimes against humanity are committed in the names of democracy, human rights, and development.

Without developing the Oromo liberation knowledge based on the Oromo indigenous epistemology and clearly articulating the ideology of national *Oromummaa* based on diverse Oromo experiences and solving the incoherence of the Oromo national leadership through concrete policies and actions, Oromo activists and nationalists cannot solve the internal and external structural problems of the Oromo national struggle. The survival of the Oromo nation and national movement without strong organizational and military power is impossible. Accepting these realities will help Oromo nationalists and their political organizations as they seek a paradigm shift in the Oromo national movement. Since the Oromo national movement is facing danger from all directions, its formal and informal leaders and all nationalists must take pragmatic collective actions to save their nation from total humiliation and destruction. The activists and nationalists should take practical steps for building ideological and organizational coherence and leadership effectiveness and for coordinating and consolidating the Oromo national movement. If Oromo nationalists are truly concerned about their people and if they want to achieve a true liberation, they should show respect for the Oromo epistemology and democratic traditions and practice civility and engage in democratic political and ideological deliberations. Such responsible and courageous actions require taking accountability seriously and using a single standard for evaluating behavior and measuring performance in relation to the Oromo national struggle.

As the recent Oromo earth-shaking peaceful protests demonstrate, national *Oromummaa* and the Oromo agency have developed in the entire Oromo society. Oromo Diaspora communities are gradually overcoming their backward-looking worldviews that divided and made them powerless, and most of them have started to be united to support Oromo protest movements and the Oromo national struggle. These are great victories that must be built upon to defeat the enemy by facilitating the development of Oromo organizational capacity in order to create Oromo national power that will contribute toward achieving the objectives of the Oromo national movement. The Oromo society should avoid the pitfalls of other national movements that only achieved flag independence that replaces external tyranny with an internal one. While focusing on dismantling Ethiopian colonialism and ethnocracy, Oromo movements at a grassroots level should also start to discuss how to construct their state on the foundation of the Oromo democratic tradition that would empower the Oromo people to achieve true liberation by restoring *kayyo* and *saafu* that reactionary forces try to destroy. Similarly, Oromo religious institutions, while participating in mobilizing their nation for liberation from Ethiopian colonialism, have other obligations. It is their historical obligations to struggle to restore authentic Oromo culture, identity, history, names and the Oromo personality that have been attacked and undermined by imperial and colonial cultures and worldviews in the name of borrowed religions.

As Jews, Habasha, and Euro-American cultures should be separated from Christianity, Arab culture must be separated from Islam. Both Oromo Muslims and Christians can build their respective religions based on authentic Oromo culture that help in overcoming inferiority complex and developing Oromo dignity and personality that cannot be adulterated by colonial and imperial cultures. While maintaining their respective religions, Christian and Muslim Oromo can learn many lessons from the indigenous Oromo religion that protected the Oromo democratic tradition from tyranny by teaching the people to disobey leaders who would like to undermine *gadaa*. All Oromo who follow different religions have national obligations to participate in the Oromo national struggle to liberate their country and society in order to freely build their institutions such as mosques, churches, and other religious centers in their country, and to work for improving the living conditions of their society while teaching about life after death. Oromo followers of *Waqqefanna*, Islam, and Christianity need to engage in an interfaith dialogue without being religious chauvinists and extremists, and also need to start developing national *Oromummaa* that would reflect the diversity of Oromo society. All the efforts of Oromo political organizations and civic and religious institutions cannot be fully realized without restoring the Oromo epistemology, agency, and building liberation knowledge.

THREE

The Oromo Nation

Toward Mental Liberation and Empowerment

With Harwood Schaffer

In the second decade of the twenty-first century, the Oromo people face a monumental national crisis that requires their urgent recognition and resolution. The Ethiopian government has clearly recognized the potential of the Oromo nation and is determined to destroy and/or suppress it by engaging in state terrorism and genocidal massacres, conducting mass arrests, violating human rights, and eliminating opposition leaders and their potential successors while replacing them with *Afaan* Oromo-speaking *nafxanyas* (colonial settlers) and Oromo collaborators. The current regime continues to expropriate Oromo economic resources—including land—and transfer them to Tigrayan and Amhara elites and their regional and global capitalist supporters. This regime has also begun the practice of enslaving and selling young Oromo girls and girls of other nationalities to Arab countries that have no respect for human dignity and rights. All these have occurred in the era of globalization or transnational capitalism, as global, regional, and local forces have been integrated through the intensification of globalizing processes known as deepening and broadening (Robinson 2004, 2008). As a result, with the financial, military, diplomatic, and intelligence support of global and regional powers, the Ethiopian regime has been focused on dismantling and destroying the Oromo Liberation Front (OLF)—the hallmark, symbol, pride, and hope of the Oromo nation—and other independent Oromo civic and political organizations (Jalata 2010b, 47–82).

The attack on independent Oromo political and civic organizations and institutions was intensified before the Oromo national movement managed to achieve maturity. The consolidation of the Oromo national leadership and the maturation of *Oromummaa* (Oromo nationalism) are still incomplete. As such, the movement's ability to defend itself from internal and external enemies has been significantly compromised. These challenges confronted the Oromo national struggle before the Oromo leadership was able to develop the ideological coherence and organizational capacity to catapult the Oromo national movement to an advanced stage. The crisis of the Oromo national leadership has emerged from both external and internal sources and Oromo nationalists urgently need to address both in order to find an appropriate solution. The impacts of external forces (e.g., Amhara-Tigray colonial structures and global capitalism) have been adequately addressed in books and scholarly articles. We now need to focus on the internal crises facing the movement's leadership.

In our attempt to examine this internal dilemma, we address four major interrelated issues. First, we provide historical and cultural background to contextualize the problem in question. Second, we explore how Ethiopian colonialism has affected the process of the formation of Oromo elites and leaders. Third, we identify and examine the connections between liberation knowledge, the inferiority complex, and mental liberation in the development of a revolutionary consciousness. Fourth, we share some ideas on how to promote the development of mental liberation as a means of constructing a revolutionary consciousness. In addition, we suggest ways to cultivate national *Oromummaa* (culture, identity, and nationalism) so that a united Oromo national leadership may be forged—from the bottom up—around a common denominator, thus ensuring the survival and liberation of the Oromo nation and other captive nations from the yoke of Ethiopian colonialism and global imperialism.[1]

CONQUEST AND COLONIAL SUBJUGATION WITHIN THE ETHIOPIAN EMPIRE

Before Abyssinia/Ethiopia colonized the Oromo and other nations in the Horn of Africa with the help of European powers in the late nineteenth century, the Oromo presided over a form of republican government known as the *gadaa/siqqee* system (Jalata and Schaffer 2013). From the fifteenth until the mid-seventeenth century, the *gadaa/siqqee* government was organized on three levels: national, regional, and local. According to Lemmu Baissa (2004, 101), the Oromo government "was led by an elected *luba* council formed from representatives of the major Oromo moieties . . . under the presidency of the *Abbaa Gadaa* and his two deputies. . . . The national leadership was responsible for such important matters as legislation and enforcement of general laws, handling issues of war and peace and coordinating the nation's defense, management of intra-Oromo clan conflicts and dealing with non-Oromo peoples."

However, due to the geographical size of the Oromo territory and an increasing population, the central *gadaa/siqqee* government declined beginning in the mid-seventeenth century and autonomous regional and local republics took its place. These regional and local governments formed pan-Oromo confederations to defend themselves from external enemies (Etefa 2008; 2010). The rule of law and social equality were the guiding principles of the *gadaa/siqqee* system (Luling 1965; Legesse 1973). Although we have limited knowledge of Oromo history before the sixteenth century, it is reasonable to think that these people did not invent the *gadaa/siqqee* system while they were establishing *Biyyaa Oromoo* (what we now call Oromia). Historical studies suggest that during the sixteenth and seventeenth centuries, while various peoples were fighting over economic resources in the Horn of Africa, the Oromo were effectively organized under the national *gadaa* government for both offensive and defensive wars. According to Virginia Luling (1965, 191), "from the mid-16th to the mid-nineteenth century the [Oromo] were dominant on their own territories; no people of other cultures were in a position to exercise compulsion over them."

The *gadaa/siqqee* government organized and ordered society around political, economic, social, cultural, and religious institutions (Legesse 1973). Bonnie Holcomb (1991, 1–10) notes that the *gadaa* system "organized the Oromo people in an all-encompassing democratic republic even before the few European pilgrims arrived from England on the shores of North America and only later built a democracy." This system exhibits the principles of checks and balances (through periodic succession of leaders every eight years), division of power (among executive, legislative, and judicial branches), balanced opposition (among five parties), and power sharing between higher and lower administrative organs to prevent power from falling into the hands of despots (Legesse 1973). Other principles of the system included balanced representation of all clans, lineages, regions and confederacies; the accountability of leaders; the settlement of disputes through reconciliation; and respect for basic rights and liberties (Baissa 1971, 1993). There were five *miseensas* (parties) in *gadaa*; these parties have different names in different parts of Oromia (Lepisa 1975; Ibssa 1992). All *gadaa* officials were elected for eight years by universal adult male suffrage.

Chapter 3

COLONIALISM AND THE UNDERDEVELOPMENT OF OROMO LEADERSHIP

The Ethiopian colonial state destroyed the leaders of the conquered nations in the Horn of Africa who fought against Abyssinian/Ethiopian colonialism, co-opting those leaders who would collaborate with the system as intermediaries (Jalata 2010b). Abyssinian access to European guns, cannons, technology, diplomacy, and administrative skills were utilized in colonizing these various nations, the largest of which was the Oromo. This chapter focuses on the experience of the Oromo as a case study of the ways the Abyssinian/Ethiopian rulers have systematically destroyed the leadership capacity of the conquered peoples.

The Abyssinians systematically engaged in massacring and repressing Oromo while reorganizing Oromo society in order to control and exploit the Oromo people and their resources. Since the colonization of the Oromo people (as we shall see below), one of the goals of the Ethiopian state has been the destruction and underdevelopment of the Oromo people and their leadership; the Amhara-Tigray state has used both violent and institutional mechanisms to ensure that the Oromo people remain leaderless while it continues to repress and exploit them. To ensure its colonial domination, the Ethiopian state destroyed and/or suppressed Oromo institutions (e.g., the aforementioned *gadaa/siqqee* system, as well as an indigenous Oromo religion known as *Waaqeefata*) while glorifying, establishing, and expanding the Amhara-Tigray government and Orthodox Christianity. The state also sought to suppress Oromo history, culture, and language while promoting that of the Abyssinians.

Ethiopian settler colonialism was firmly established in Oromia through the imposition of five institutional arrangements in order to tightly control Oromo society and intensify its exploitation: (1) garrison cities and towns, (2) slavery, (3) the colonial landholding system, (4) the *nafxanya-gabbar* system (semi-slavery), and (5) the Oromo collaborator class (Jalata 2005 [1993]. The colonialists have been concentrated in garrison cities and towns and formulated political, economic, and ideological programs that they used to oppress their colonial subjects (Jalata 2005 [1993]). The settlers expropriated almost all Oromo lands, and forced most Oromo to work on these lands without payment. The Oromo intermediaries have been used in subordinating the Oromo people to the colonial society. Many people were enslaved and forced to provide free labor to the colonial ruling class, while others were reduced to the status of semi-slaves so they could provide agricultural and commercial products and free labor for their colonizers. As a consequence of these efforts, the Ethiopian state successfully destroyed and/or suppressed Oromo institutions and independent leaders and replaced them with its own leaders and political, religious, and educational institutions; colonialism also fractured Oromo culture and identity.

The Ethiopian state targeted any sense of Oromoness (*Oromummaa*) for destruction and established colonial administrative regions to suppress the Oromo people and exploit their resources. As a result, Oromo relational identities were localized and disconnected from the collective identity of national *Oromummaa*. On a national level, the Oromo were separated from one another and prevented from exchanging goods and information for more than a century. As a result, their identities were localized into clan families and colonial regions. They were also exposed to different cultures (i.e., languages, customs, values, etc.) and religions and have adopted some elements of these cultures and religions because of the inferiority complex that Ethiopian colonialism sought to create in them. Consequently, until Oromo nationalism emerged, Oromoness primarily remained on the personal and the interpersonal levels since the Oromo were denied the opportunity to form national institutions. In addition, today there are members of Oromo society and elites who have internalized clan and externally imposed regional and/or religious identities because of their low level of political consciousness or because of opportunism on their part, exhibiting the lack of a clear understanding of *Oromummaa* or Oromo nationalism.

Overcoming several obstacles, the founding fathers and mothers of *Oromummaa* created two pioneering organizations in the 1960s and 1970s: the Macha-Tulama Self-Help Association and the Oromo Liberation Front respectively. These organizations acted as a roadmap for the burgeoning Oromo national movement. Unfortunately, the national movement has since been confronted externally by the forces of Ethiopian colonialism—with assistance from their global supporters—and internally by an Oromo collaborator class that serves the interests of the oppressor of the Oromo people. Some Oromo elites have become raw materials for the Ethiopian regime and have implemented its terrorist and genocidal policies in the puppet parliament, the administration, and the army, and have participated in imprisoning and killing Oromo nationalists. These internal agents of the Ethiopian government have also participated in robbing Oromo economic resources. As Frantz Fanon (1963 [1961], 38) notes, "The intermediary does not lighten the oppression, nor seek to hide the domination . . . he is the bringer of violence into the home and into the mind of the native." The Oromo national struggle has to solve the internal problem of Oromo society before it can fully confront and defeat its joined external enemies.

It is estimated that the Oromo intermediary elites are the numerical majority at the lower echelons of the Ethiopian colonial institutions. These intermediaries have joined the Tigrayan-created and -led organization known as the Oromo People's Democratic Organization (OPDO) to satisfy their personal interests at the cost of the Oromo nation. It is true that every colonized nation has a collaborator class that fulfills its interests and the interest of its colonial masters. However, a few elements of this class clandestinely defend the interest of their people. For example, some Eritrean and Tigrayan intermediaries under the Amhara-led Ethiopia protected the interests of their respective people. What makes the Oromo collaborator class different, however, is its total commitment to serve the oppressor (except in a few cases) without being sympathetic to their own people. Ethiopian history demonstrates that key Oromo collaborators have been king makers and have protected the Ethiopian Empire without seeking authority for themselves and their people. "The oppressed learn to wear many masks for different occasions," Frantz Fanon notes, "they develop skills to detect the moods and wishes of those in authority, learn to present acceptable public behaviors while repressing many incongruent private feelings" (Bulhan 1985, 123).

Most Oromo members of the OPDO clearly exhibit such public behaviors. In every colonized society, those who collaborate with the dominant society are less competent and less accomplished, and yet they are "rewarded extravagantly with fame, fortune and celebrity status simply by their confirmation that the master's consciousness and his reality is the correct way to think" (Akbar 1996, 41). While imprisoning or killing independent Oromo leaders, the successive Ethiopian regimes have promoted to positions of authority less competent Oromo collaborators who have internalized and manifested their masters' worldviews. The Oromo collaborator elites are politically ignorant and harbor an inferiority complex that has been imposed on them by the Amhara-Tigray colonial institutions. According to Hussein Abdilahi Bulhan (1996, 41), "Prolonged oppression reduces the oppressed into mere individuals without a community or a history, fostering a tendency to privatize a shared victimization." Since they have been cut from their individual biographies and the collective Oromo history, members of the Oromo collaborator class only know what Amhara or Tigrayans have taught them and, as a result, they constantly wear "Ethiopian masks" that have damaged their psyches.

The colonizer was never content with occupying the land of indigenous peoples and expropriating their labor; he also declared war on the psyches of the oppressed (Fanon 1967 [1965], 65). By introducing an inferiority complex, the Amhara-Tigray state attacked the Oromo culture and worldview in order to alter the perspective of the colonized Oromo from independence to dependence; consequently, every colonized Oromo subject who has not yet liberated his/her mind wears an Ethiopian mask by associating his/herself with Ethiopian culture and identity. As Fanon (2008 [1952], 2–3) asserts, "All colonized people—in other words, people in whom an inferiority complex has taken root, whose local cultural originality has been committed to the grave—position themselves in relation to the civilizing language. . . . The more the colonized has assimilated the cultural values of [the colonizer], the more he [or she] will have" imitated his/her masters. As European colonialists did, the Amhara-Tigrayan colonizers have manufactured the Oromo collaborator elites in order to use them in their colonial projects. According to Bulhan (1985, 125–126), "in prolonged oppression, the oppressed group willy-nilly internalizes the oppressor without. They adopt his guidelines and prohibitions, they assimilate his image and his social behavior, and they become agents of their own oppression. The oppressor without becomes . . . an oppressor within. . . . They become *auto-oppressor* as they engage in self-destructive behavior injurious to themselves, their loved ones, and their neighbors." It is no wonder that some members of the OPDO, from ordinary individuals to high officials, engage in imprisoning, killing, and robbing members of Oromo society, particularly those whom they suspect of sympathizing with or supporting the Oromo national struggle.

The Oromo self has been attacked and distorted by Ethiopian colonial institutions. The attack on Oromo selves at personal, interpersonal, and collective levels has undermined the self-confidence of some Oromo individuals by creating an inferiority complex within them. Consequently, the manufactured Oromo elites are abusive to their people and they confuse their individual ambitions and interest with those of the Oromo nation. What Fanon (1963 [1961], 7) says about other colonial intermediary native elites applies to the Oromo elites: "The European elite undertook to manufacture native elite. They picked out promising adolescents; they branded them, as with a red-hot iron, with the principles of Western culture; they stuffed their mouths full with high-sounding phrases, grand glutinous words that stuck to the teeth." Since most Oromo elites who have passed through Ethiopian colonial institutions have not yet achieved psychological liberation, they consciously or unconsciously prefer to work for their colonial masters rather than work as a team on the Oromo liberation project.

What Walter Rodney (1972, 241) says about the consequences of the colonial educational system in Africa also applies to the situation of Oromo intermediaries: "The colonial school system educated far too many fools and clowns, fascinated by the ideas and way of life of the European capitalist class. . . . Some reached a point of total estrangement from African conditions and the African way of life. . . . 'Colonial education corrupted the thinking and sensibilities of the African and filled him with abnormal complexes.'" Similarly, some Oromo intermediaries who have passed through the Ethiopian colonial education system have been de-Oromized and Ethiopianized, and have opposed the Oromo struggle for national liberation. Colonial education creates submissive leaders who facilitate underdevelopment through subordination and exploitation (Rodney 1972, 241). Considering the similar condition of the African Americans in the first half of the twentieth century, Carter G. Woodson (1999 [1933], 2), characterized the educated Black as "a hopeless liability of the race," and schools for Blacks as "places where they must be convinced of their inferiority." He demonstrated how White oppressors controlled the minds of Blacks through education: "When you control a man's [or a woman's thinking] you do not have to worry about his [or her] actions. You do not have to tell him [her] not to stand here or go yonder. He [or she] will find his [or her] 'proper place' and will stay in it" (Woodson 1999 [1933], 2). The behaviors and actions of the educated Oromo intermediaries parallel what Woodson claims about the educated African Americans. But, starting in the mid-twentieth century, most African American elites developed nationalist political consciousness by overcoming their inferiority complex and participating in their national struggle for liberation.

There are also biologically and culturally assimilated elements that like to disassociate themselves from anything related to the Oromo. Most biologically and culturally assimilated former Oromo, like their Habasha masters, are the defenders of Habasha culture, religion, and the Amharic language and the haters of Oromo history, culture, institutions, and *Afaan Oromoo*. Explaining similar circumstances, Fanon notes, "The individual who *climbs up* into white, civilized society tends to reject his black, uncivilized family at the level of the imagination." The slave psychology of such assimilated Oromo has caused them also to prefer the leadership of the Amhara or Tigrayan oppressor. Through his seven years of experimentation and observation in Martinique, Frantz Fanon concluded that the dominated "black man's behavior is similar to an obsession neurosis.... There is an attempt by the colored man to escape his individuality, to reduce his being in the world to nothing. . . . The [psychologically affected] black man goes from humiliating insecurity to self-accusation and even despair."

These conditions apply to all colonized, repressed, and exploited peoples. Therefore, some Oromo also face similar problems. Furthermore, the attack on Oromo families and national structures introduced psychological disorientations to Oromo individuals, and incapacitated their collective personality. The family—as a basic institution of any society—provides guidance in values, norms, and worldviews and acts as the educational and training ground for entry into that society (Woodson 1999 [1933], 127). Because Oromo families have lived for more than a century under colonial occupation and because Oromo national institutions were intentionally destroyed or disfigured by Ethiopian colonial institutions, the Oromo people lack the educational, cultural, ideological, and experiential resources to guide their children in the process of building national institutions and organizational capacity. Oromo individuals who have lived under such conditions face social, cultural, and psychological crises and become conflict-ridden.

Due to these complex problems, the low level of political consciousness, and an imposed inferiority complex, those who claim that they are nationalists sometimes confuse their sub-identities with the Oromo national identity or with Ethiopian identity. According to Fanon, "The neurotic structure of an individual is precisely the elaboration, the formation, and the birth of conflicting knots in the ego, stemming on the one hand from the environment and on the other from the entirely personal way this individual reacts to these influences." The Ethiopian colonial system—as well as cultural and religious identities—was imposed on the Oromo creating regional and religious boundaries. Under these conditions, personal identities (e.g., religious affiliation) replaced Oromoness—with its unique values and self-schemas—and Ethiopianism replaced *Oromummaa*. Colonial rulers saw Oromoness as a source of raw material that was ready to be transformed into other identities. Since most of these individuals are psychologically damaged, they run away from the Oromo national identity. Are genuine Oromo nationalists free of these psychological crises?

THE PSYCHOLOGICAL LEGACY OF ETHIOPIAN COLONIALISM

Through political, educational, and religious institutions and the media, the Ethiopian colonial elites and their successive governments have continuously created and perpetuated negative stereotypes and racist values regarding the Oromo people[2] and have led some Oromo to think negatively about themselves. That is why some Oromo parents reject Oromo names and give Amhara or Arab names to their children in order to assimilate them into the cultures they consider superior. Some educated Oromo also develop self-hatred and self-contempt and wear the masks of other people. Ethiopian colonialism and racism have made some Oromo elites hate their culture and language and avoid self-discovery. The process of de-Oromization creates alienation among some Oromo and imbues them with distorted perceptions of their own people. Everything Amhara-Tigray is praised and everything Oromo is rejected and denigrated; the colonialists have depicted the Oromo as barbaric, ignorant, evil, pagan, backward, and superstitious.

In order to avoid these perceived characteristics, some Oromo elites who pass through the Ethiopian colonial education system are Amharized and Ethipianized. The colonization of the Oromo mind has indoctrinated Oromo students in order to isolate them from their families and communities and distort their identities by disconnecting them from their heritage, culture, and history (Dugassa 2011, 55–64). Oppressors don't just want to control the body of the oppressed; they also want to control their minds, thus ensuring the effectiveness of domination and exploitation. Na'im Akbar (1996, v–vi) succinctly explains how the mental control of the oppressed causes personal and collective damage: "The slavery that captures the mind and imprisons the motivation, perception, aspiration and identity in a web of anti-self-images, generating a personal and collective self-destruction, is [more cruel] than shackles on the wrists and ankles. The slavery that feeds on the mind, invading the soul of man [or woman], destroying his [or her] loyalties to himself [or herself] and establishing allegiance to forces which destroys him [or her], is an even worse form of capture."

The mental enslavement of most Oromo elites is the major reason why the Oromo, who comprise the majority of the population, are brutalized, murdered, and terrorized by the minority Tigrayan elites. What about the Oromo nationalist elites who are struggling for Oromo national self-determination? Are they mentally free? Why have they failed to build a united Oromo national leadership? There is no question that most of the founding fathers and mothers of *Oromummaa* or Oromo nationalism were mentally liberated heroes and heroines; that was why they created the Macha-Tulama Self-Help Association and the Oromo Liberation Front and paid the ultimate sacrifice. There have been thousands of Oromo nationalists who have followed in their footsteps and paid dearly. What about other Oromo nationalists (particularly leaders) who have partitioned the Oromo national movement by dividing it into different political factions? Oromo nationalists have failed to unite Oromo divided communities, which have been easily infiltrated by the enemies through clan and/or religious bonds. In addition, because of the inferiority complex that the enemies have inculcated in the Oromo mind, some Oromo have failed to respect Oromo leadership, just as Oromo leaders have failed to respect their followers. The nationalist Oromo elites, by failing to overcome the deeply entrenched divisions that the enemies of the Oromo created, have drastically failed to establish a united national movement.

Generally speaking, the necessity of liberating the Oromo mind from psychological oppression through liberation knowledge and consciousness-raising is totally ignored or unrecognized. Due to their political ignorance and ineptitude, Oromo intellectuals and political leaders have failed to organize the masses into a grassroots movement. As a result of psychological crises and oppressive institutions, Oromo collective norms and organizational culture are at a rudimentary level at this historical moment. Therefore, the enemies of the Oromo have found ample political opportunity to mobilize some Oromo against the Oromo national movement. Without the emancipation of Oromo individuals from the inferiority complex and without overcoming the ignorance and the worldviews that the enemies of the Oromo have imposed on them, the Oromo cannot have the self-confidence necessary to facilitate individual liberation and Oromo emancipation. Although it is uncomfortable to recognize the impacts of the psychology of oppression on the Oromo minds, the Oromo national struggle must engage in mental liberation by building liberation knowledge and political consciousness.

LIBERATION KNOWLEDGE, CONSCIOUSNESS-BUILDING, AND THE POLITICS OF EMPOWERMENT

In order to achieve psychological liberation via the development of political consciousness, it is essential to understand the process of oppression by learning about the bankruptcy of assimilated Oromo elites and the crises in both individual Oromo biographies and collective Oromo history. As Bulhan (1985, 55) asserts, "The experience of victimization in oppression produces, on the one hand, tendencies toward rebellion and a search for autonomy and, on the other, tendencies toward compliance and accommodation. Often, the two tendencies coexist among the oppressed, although a predominant orientation can be identified for any person or generation at a given time." The oppressed are chained physically, socially, culturally, politically, and psychologically; hence it is difficult to learn about these problems and search for ways to overcome them. A conscious element of the oppressed "opts for an introspective approach and emphasizes the need to come to terms with one's self—a self historically tormented by a formidable and oppressive social structure" (Bulhan 1985, 55).

As the current national crisis unfolds, Oromo nationalists in general and leaders in particular should start to engage in critical self-evaluation in order to identify the impact of oppressive and destructive values and behaviors on the Oromo political performance. Psychological liberation from ideological confusion and oppression requires fighting against the external oppressor and the internalized oppressive values. Most oppressed individuals understand what the oppressor does to them from outside, but it is difficult to comprehend how the worldviews of the oppressor are imposed on them and control them from within. As Bulhan (1985, 123) explains, "institutionalization of oppression in daily living . . . entails an internalization of the oppressor's values, norms, and prohibitions. Internalized oppression is most resistant to change, since this would require a battle on two fronts: the oppressor without and the oppressor within."

The Ethiopian colonial system has denied education to almost all the Oromo in order to keep them ignorant and submissive. Even those few who have received colonial education have not been provided with a critical education and knowledge for liberation. As Woodson (1990 [1993], 96) says, colonial education is "a perfect device for control from without." So, it has been difficult and challenging for most Oromo elites to engage in a struggle—liberating themselves from the values and worldviews of Ethiopians and Ethiopian colonial institutions and structures. Because of the lack of political consciousness, the oppressed individuals and groups learn the behavior of the oppressor, engage in conflict, and abuse one another. Attaining a critical political consciousness enables the oppressed individuals and groups to regain their identity, reclaim their history and culture, and regain self-respect internally while fighting against the oppressor externally. Those people who are disconnected from their social and cultural bonds are disorganized, disoriented, and alienated; lacking a critical understanding of individual biographies and collective history, they cannot effectively organize and fight against the values and institutions of their oppressors.

> If the occupation of land . . . entailed the occupation of psyches, then the war for liberation had to be waged on two fronts: The colonizer residing not only *without*, but also *within* had to be confronted on both fronts. Otherwise, the vicious cycle of domination would continue. To battle the colonizer *without* first assumes a degree of self-respect and self-validation, a conviction that one is at least as good and as human as he is. It also assumes the existence of a bond with others, a sharing of similar experiences and determination . . . . The colonized had been reduced to individuals without an anchor in history, alienated from themselves and others. So as long as this alienation prevailed, the colonizer *without* could not be challenged. His abuses, humiliations, and suffocating repression permeated everyday living, further undermining the colonized [person's] self-respect and collective bonds. (Woodson 1990 [1933], 139)

Colonialism attacks the individual psyche and biography, as well as the collective history, of a given people. These damaging processes occur through various forms of violence, including colonial terrorism. "*Violence is any relation, process, or condition by which an individual or a group violates the physical, social, and/or psychological integrity of another person or group.* From this perspective, violence inhibits human growth, negates inherent potential, limits productive living, and causes death" [emphasis given in original] (Woodson 1990 [1933], 135). Nationalist projects of the oppressed emerge to deal with these complex problems. A few Oromo nationalists who gained political consciousness and self-respect by overcoming the psychological and cultural impacts of Ethiopian colonialism in the 1960s and the 1970s began to engage in Oromo nationalist projects by creating a self-help association, a musical group, and a liberation front, while most Oromo elites were serving their own interests and the interests of their colonial masters.

When some elements of the colonized people develop political consciousness, organize, and engage in the struggle for freedom, they turn their internalized anger, hostility, and violence that destroyed relationships among them against the colonizers. The nascent Oromo nationalists faced monumental political problems as the result of the decadent Ethiopian political system. In addition to brutal violence and repression, the oppressor uses various methods of social control. "The oppressed is made a prisoner within a narrow circle of tamed ideas, a wrecked ecology, and a social network strewn with prohibitions. Their family and community life is infiltrated in order to limit his capacity for bonding and trust. His past is obliterated and his history falsified to render him without an origin or a future. A system of reward and punishment based on loyalty to the oppressor is instituted to foster competition and conflict among the oppressed" (Woodson 1990 [1933], 123). The Oromo have been living under political slavery for more than a century; they have been denied the freedom of self-expression, organization, and assembly. The colonialists and their collaborators have committed various crimes against Oromo culture, history, language, and psychology. The founding fathers and mothers of Oromo nationalism understood these complex problems and tried to solve them by developing social, economic, cultural, and political projects.

Human beings have basic attributes that Bulhan (1985, 262) characterizes as "essential human *needs* and essential human *powers*," both of which are necessary in order to survive and fully develop. The people who were colonized and dominated cannot adequately satisfy their basic needs and access their self-actualizing powers. These include "(a) biological needs, (b) sociability and rootedness, (c) clarity and integrity of self, (d) longevity and symbolic immortality, (e) self-reproduction in praxis, and (f) maximum self-determination" (Bulhan 1985, 262). Human beings must satisfy their basic biological needs, such as food, sex, clothing, and shelter in order to survive. However, these biological needs can only be satisfied in a culture that provides sociability and rootedness. Those people whose culture has been attacked and disfigured by colonialism are underdeveloped; their basic needs are not satisfactorily met and their self-actualizing powers are stagnated; "For to acquire culture presupposes not only a remarkable power of learning and teaching, but also an enduring capacity for interdependence and inter-subjectivity. Not only the development of our higher power of cognition and affect, but also the development of our basic senses rest on the fact that we are social beings" (Bulhan 1985, 263).

Colonialism can be maintained by committing genocide or ethnocide and/or by organized cultural destruction or mental genocide and the assimilation of a sector of the colonized population. Ethiopian colonialists expropriated Oromo economic resources and destroyed Oromo institutions and cultural experts and leaders; they have also denied the Oromo the opportunity to develop the Oromo system of knowledge by preventing the transmission of Oromo cultural experiences from generation to generation. All these colonial policies were designed to uproot the Oromo cultural identity and to produce individuals who lack self-respect and are submissive and ready to serve the colonialists. Under these conditions, the Oromo basic needs and self-actualizing powers have not been fulfilled. In other words, the Oromo biological and social needs have been frustrated. "If failure to satisfy biological needs leads to disease and physical death," Bulhan (1985, 263) notes, "then denial of human contact, communication, and affirmation . . . leads to a social and psychological 'starvation' or 'death' no less devastating than, and conditioning, physical death."

The Ethiopian colonialists—having caused the physical death of millions—have further attempted to introduce social and cultural death to the Oromo people. Both the Amhara and Tigrayan elites have attempted to destroy or control the Oromo selfhood in order to deny the Oromo both individual and national self-determination. From all angles, the Habasha have tried their best to prevent the Oromo from achieving clarity and integrity of the Oromo self; they have prevented the Oromo from establishing cultural and historical immortality through the reproduction and recreation of their history, culture and worldview, and from achieving maximum self-determination. "The pursuit of self-clarity is . . . intimately bound with the clarity developed first about one's body, the body's boundary and attributes, and later one's larger world. This pursuit of clarity has survival, developmental, and organizing value. It entails both a differentiation from as well as integration with others and with one's past. Without some clarity of the self, however tentative and tenuous, there can be no meaningful relating with others, no expression of inherent human potentials, no gratification of essential needs" (Bulhan 1985, 264).

The founding fathers and mothers of Oromo nationalism purposely engaged in political praxis to save the Oromo from psychological, social, cultural, and physical death. Without a measure of self-determination, a person cannot fully satisfy his/her biological and social needs, self-actualize, and engage in praxis as an active agent to transform society and oneself. "*Self-determination* refers to the process and capacity to choose among alternatives, to determine one's behavior, and to affect one's destiny. As such, self-determination assumes a consciousness of human possibilities, an awareness of necessary constraints, and a willed, self-motivated engagement with one's world" (Bulhan 1985, 265). As individuals and groups, the Oromo must struggle to achieve their personal and national self-determination. The Oromo have the internal power to make their choices from the best possible alternatives and to have control over what they do. The Ethiopian colonialists have assumed almost complete control over the Oromo in an attempt to deny them the right of self-determination, both individually and collectively.

Unfortunately, the oppression is not limited to national borders. Ethiopian colonialists have had psychological impacts on some Oromo in the diaspora, and have infiltrated diaspora communities and their organizations in order to dismantle them. Oromo individuals and groups who do not clearly comprehend the essence of self-determination and who do not struggle for it are doomed to both psychological and cultural death. "History and social conditions present [not only] alternatives but also constraints. We can choose to act or not act. But even when we lack alternatives in the world as we find it, we do possess the capacity to interpret and reinterpret, to adopt one attitude and not another. Without the right of self-determination, we are reduced to rigid and automatic behaviors, to a life and destiny shorn of human will and freedom" (Bulhan 1985, 265–266). At this historical moment, most of the Oromo in the diaspora are passive; they do not struggle effectively for their individual and national self-determination. This has left their communities vulnerable to infiltration by Oromo collaborators, who then attempt to turn Oromo against one another.

The founding fathers and mothers of Oromo nationalism as a social group reclaimed their individual authentic biographies and Oromo collective history and defined the Oromo national problem; they sought the political solution of national self-determination. In order to continue the policy of social, cultural, psychological, and physical death and control the Oromo society, the Ethiopian colonial state killed or destroyed these leaders. The Tigrayan-led regime of Ethiopia had continued the same policy. Without psychological liberation and organized, conscious, and collective action, the Oromo people cannot fulfill the objectives of the Oromo national movement. Currently, most Oromo elites and leaders do not realize the problems they are causing for the Oromo national struggle because of their socio-cultural and psychological crises and their failure to critically understand the national crisis. The continuation of this crisis and the absence of a united Oromo national leadership allow the continuation of the psychological, social, cultural, and physical death of the Oromo people.

> Physical, social, or psychological death is too heavy a price for an accustomed passivity, a corrosive apathy, self-defeating individualism, and predictability of stagnation. Psychological work with the oppressed must give priority to organized and collective activity to regain power and liberty. One critical focus of intervention has to do with unraveling, through active involvement and demonstrations in the social world, the self-defeating patterns of relating, the tendency toward betrayal of the self and/or others, the internalized script for failure and disaster, as well as the conditioned fear of taking a stand or even fear of freedom—all of which derive from a contrived system of socialization, and elaborate formula to produce willing victim. Another crucial focus is the comprehension and refinement of strategies as well as tactics for regaining power and liberty. (Bulhan 1985, 276)

In the capitalist world system, might is right. Those people who cannot empower themselves through liberation knowledge, psychological recovery, and the will to organize and defend themselves in a united movement cannot survive as a people. We know that one of the major reasons why the colonialists were able to destroy most indigenous peoples in the world was the result of these peoples' lack of unity and strong organization. It is not enough to know about the impact of colonialism without recognizing and solving the internal crises of the colonized or the oppressed. "A psychology of liberation would give primacy to the empowerment of the oppressed through organized and socialized activity with the aim of restoring individual biographies and a collective history derailed, stunted, and/or made appendage to those of others. Life indeed takes on morbid qualities and sanity becomes tenuous so long as one's space, time, energy, mobility, and identity are usurped by dint of violence" (Bulhan 1985, 277). The Oromo elites and leaders must realize that the Oromo cannot achieve the liberation objectives without understanding and overcoming the internalized values that they have learned from their oppressors and the inferiority complex that they are suffering from: "To transform a situation of oppression requires at once a relentless confrontation of oppressors *without*, who are often impervious to appeals, to reasons or compassion, and an equally determined confrontation of the oppressor *within*, whose violence can unleash a vicious cycle of auto-destruction to the self as well as to the group" (Bulhan 1985, 277–278).

For instance, vicious cycles of auto-destruction recently arose in the Oromo diaspora communities due to clan and regional politics, as some Oromo groups engaged in the destruction of the OLF from a distance. This was the result of a failure on the part of the Oromo leadership to confront the oppressor within. Without using the tool of liberation knowledge to build political consciousness and restore their usurped biographies and history, the Oromo cannot confront and defeat the oppressor within. The Oromo national movement is still suffering from the oppressor within and the lack of effective leadership. Since the Oromo masses are not organized and educated in the politics and psychology of liberation, they have been passive participants in the Oromo national movement. They have been waiting to receive their liberation as a gift from Oromo political organizations. This is a serious mistake. Oromo liberation can only be achieved by the active participation of an effective portion of the Oromo people. As Gilly Adolfo (1967 [1965], 2) states, "Liberation does not come as a gift from anybody; it is seized by the masses with their own hands. And by seizing it they themselves are transformed; confidence in their own strength soars, and they turn their energy and their experience to the tasks of building, governing, and deciding their own lives for themselves." Developing *Oromummaa* or Oromo nationalism among the Oromo elites and masses is required to increase Oromo self-discovery and self-acceptance through liberation education. Without overcoming the political ignorance and inferiority complex among all sectors of the Oromo people, the Oromo national movement continues to face multi-faceted problems. The Oromo can challenge and overcome multiple levels of domination and dehumanization through multiple approaches and actions. As Patricia Hill Collins (1990, 227) puts it, "People experience and resist oppression on three levels: the level of personal biography; the group or community level of the cultural context . . . and the systematic level of social institutions." Developing individual political consciousness through liberation knowledge generates social change. This is essential to the creation of a sphere of freedom by increasing the power of self-definition, which is absolutely necessary for the liberation of the mind. Without the liberated and free mind, we cannot resist oppression on multiple levels.

The dominant groups are against mental liberation, and they use institutions such as schools, churches or mosques, the media, and other formal organizations to inculcate their oppressive worldviews in our minds. According to Collins (1990, 229), "Domination operates by seducing, pressuring, or forcing . . . members of subordinated groups to replace individual and cultural ways of knowing with the dominant group's specialized thought. As a result . . . 'the true focus of revolutionary change is never merely the oppressive situation which we seek to escape, but that piece of the oppressor which is planted deep within each of us.' Or . . . 'revolution begins with the self, in the self.'" Every Oromo must be educated and acquire liberation knowledge to fight for his/her individual freedom and empowerment. Without the liberation and empowerment of the individual, we cannot overcome the docility and passivity of our people and empower them to revolt and liberate themselves. "Empowerment involves rejecting the dimensions of knowledge, whether personal, cultural, or institutional, that perpetuate objectification and dehumanization . . . individuals in subordinate groups become empowered when we understand and use those dimensions of our individual, group, and disciplinary ways of knowing that foster our humanity as fully human subjects" (Collins 1990, 230). The Oromo have been objectified and made raw materials for others who have state power. How much longer will we tolerate such deplorable conditions?

DISCUSSION AND CONCLUSION

The only way the Amhara-Tigrayan state elites continue their colonial domination and exploitation of our people is by controlling our mental power and preventing our mental liberation. They have continued to disrupt our consciousness-building process through different mechanisms, particularly by infiltrating our communities and organizations and dividing and turning us against one another. These colonial elites have imprisoned and tortured or killed our self-conscious individuals and bribed and promoted those Oromo who are not politically conscious or those opportunists who cannot see beyond their individual self-interests. According to Akbar (1996, 30), "Human beings have consistently worked to create the circumstances to maximize their consciousness and to insure that each subsequent generation will know fully who and what they are. On the other hand, whenever human beings chose to oppress or capture other human beings, they also did all that they could do to undermine any expansion of consciousness by the oppressed. . . . They understand that ultimately the control of the people was in the control of their thinking, in control of their minds, in control of their consciousness."

By preventing the restoration of the Oromo heritage, culture, history, and institutions, the colonialists have limited the expansion of Oromo consciousness and self-knowledge. These colonialists have also continued to disseminate lies or distorted information to the Oromo people and others using the media, education, and religion, leading to their continued acceptance of the worldviews of their oppressor. Every Oromo must know and understand Oromo history, culture, heritage, worldview, and religion from antiquity to the present time in order to build his/her national consciousness and self-knowledge. We also need to learn about all of our heroes and heroines and Oromo accomplishments throughout history. People who do not know their culture and history are mentally dead, and any group that has military power and knowledge can easily impose its worldview on those who do not.

We must teach our people and children the correct information about their conditions. Explaining the conditions of African Americans, Akbar (1996, 39) notes, "It is through self-celebration that we heal our damaged self-esteem. Yes, feeling good about oneself is a legitimate activity of cultures. In fact, any culture, which does not make its adherents feel good about them, is a failure as a culture. It is through the energy of self-worth that humans are motivated to improve and perpetuate themselves." The process of mental liberation requires courage, hard work, discipline, and commitment; it involves individual, family, and community. "Since the new consciousness can take a lifetime to begin to show tangible results," Akbar (1996, 4) writes, "it takes a great deal of courage to persist in breaking the chains of the old consciousness and developing a new consciousness." Those of us who are a part of the diaspora beyond Ethiopian political slavery must not waste our time and energy on trivial and unproductive issues; we must build our brains and communities to overcome the lonely and ill-equipped road to freedom. We do not need to wait for activists or politicians to engage us in mental liberation and community building since they are not any better than we are. Every Oromo nationalist has a moral and national obligation to promote and engage in consciousness-building projects. Colonialists use community divisions to keep mental shackles on their subjects, even in the diaspora. They use divide-and-conquer strategies, replete with tricks and deceit, in order to destroy Oromo community life. This is one of the reasons why many Oromo communities in the diaspora face substantial problems and are overwhelmed by perpetual conflicts.

Most Oromo—despite the fact that they brag about it—forget their *gadaa/siqqee* tradition, which was based on democracy, solidarity, and collectivity. We must realize that there is strength in democracy, solidarity, and unity, and there is weakness in loneliness and fragmentation. "As we gain greater knowledge and information, many of those divisions will disappear because they cannot stand under the light of Truth and correct information" (Akbar 1996, 42). In the capitalist world system, the less informed are the less organized. The less organized are the ones who are physically and mentally controlled by those who are organized. In forming solidarity and building our communities, we do not need to agree on everything; our unity must be built on our common denominator. As Akbar (1996, 43) states, "In the process of liberation, it is important to recognize that *unity does not require uniformity*. We can stand together and preserve our separate qualities which serve to enhance further the objectives of freeing ourselves and all of our people."

We need to have faith in ourselves, both individually and collectively. We have many talented individuals in many areas, which can play central roles in the process of mental liberation and consciousness- and community-building. "We must work to re-educate ourselves and our young people by seeking and studying new *information*. We must find every opportunity to celebrate ourselves and we must challenge the fear that causes us to hesitate in taking the chains out of our minds. We must work together and we must have faith that our struggle will be successful, regardless of the opposition" (Akbar 1996, 46). We must also stand with our heroes and heroines who have broken the Ethiopian physical and psychological prison house by shedding their blood and sacrificing their precious lives to send us around the world as Oromo diplomats to contribute toward the liberation of the politically enslaved, psychologically chained, and economically impoverished Oromo.

At this historical moment, we the Oromo in the Diaspora should overcome our passivity, political ignorance, individualism, naiveté, anarchism, fatalism, perceived inferiority, and community divisions by actively engaging in our psychological and mental liberation. How can we accomplish all these urgent tasks? We must attack the internalization of oppression and victimization by rejecting the worldview of our oppressors through un-brainwashing our entire people. This can be made possible by promoting quality informal and formal education through establishing alternative schools, study circles, cultural centers, and related institutions for engaging in small group workshops, discussion groups, seminars, lectures, etc. These kinds of engagements help us in overcoming our weaknesses and in fighting the basis of our powerlessness through participating in political actions that can be demonstrated every day. This array of activities can facilitate the further mobilization of our material, cultural, and intellectual resources to further develop Oromo communities. Once our communities are internally built and consolidated, it will be possible to disempower the agents of our oppressors who stand among us.

If we continue to allow these agents to divide and demobilize us, we will remain a weak society that always serves the interests of others. On the contrary, if we build strong communities, we can easily build alliances with progressive individuals and communities based on our political and social objectives. This is an important step forward for securing recognition for our nation and national movement from the international community. Furthermore, our political activism and actions must be expanded. We, the Oromo in the diaspora, must immediately take the following concrete steps to contribute to the survival and liberation of our people:

First, we must initiate town hall meetings in every town where an Oromo community lives and discuss the fate of the Oromo people, focusing on their achievements, failures, challenges, opportunities, and constraints as a nation. This is not openly possible in Oromia because the Oromo people are denied the freedom of self-expression, organization, and the media.

Second, the Oromo in the diaspora must stop the politics of self-destruction by refusing to engage in inter-clan, inter-religious, and inter-regional politics, and by isolating the Oromo mercenaries from every Oromo community. Since the Oromo mercenaries use clan, religious, and regional politics to divide the Oromo people and turn them against one another, the Oromo community must reject them and their politics. The Oromo community must disempower them by maintaining a sense of the unity of the Oromo community across clan, religious and regional identities in the face of their self-destructive ideologies. The Oromo must achieve a sense of *Oromummaa* at the deepest level (see chapter 5) so that they are not distracted from the task of achieving psychological and physical liberation.

Third, the Oromo Diaspora must challenge the Oromo activists, who have built their separate organizations, to break down barriers among different Oromo organizations and unite them—around a common denominator under one structured organization and leadership.

Fourth, Oromo youth and women should be encouraged to actively participate in national dialogues and town hall meetings. They must play a leading role, since they are less corrupted by the ideologies of egoism, clan, religious and regional politics.

Fifth, Oromo nationalists must establish a rule of law based on the principles of *gadaa/siqqee* and other democratic traditions and use them in the administration of their community and national affairs.

Sixth, since unconscious people cannot liberate themselves from the internalization of the inferiority complex, victimization, and colonial domination, the Oromo Diaspora should cultivate liberation knowledge through regular dialogues, seminars, conferences, workshops, lectures, and study circles. We must learn about our history, culture, language, and traditions from antiquity to the present, and about the world around us. At this historical moment, the number one enemy of our people is political ignorance; Oromo nationalists must smash this enemy. By building our political consciousness and organizing ourselves, we are going to play a historic role commensurate with our number. When our sleeping giant nation is awakened, others cannot use us as raw material. One of the main reasons why the fifty million Oromo are terrorized and ruled by the Habasha elites is the low level of our political consciousness. A low level of political consciousness results in passivism and fatalism.

Seventh, every self-respecting Oromo must realize that he or she has the power to determine the destiny of Oromia. Every Oromo must be educated about his or her potential power and what he or she must do to translate it to real power.

Eighth, the Oromo Diaspora movement must start building from bottom-up a confederation of Oromo political, religious, community, and self-help organizations to create a *Global Gumii Oromiyaa* that will contribute ideological, organizational, and financial resources for consolidating the Oromo struggle, the Oromo Liberation Army, and self-defense militias in Oromia. The *Global Gumii Oromiyaa* will play a fundamental preparatory role in creating and building an *Oromiyaa* state fashioned after our *gadaa/siqqee* system. This state will be a key element of a democratic, confederated or federated multinational state in the Horn of Africa. In order to do this, the Oromo national movement needs to retrieve, refine, adapt, and practice the principles of our *gadaa/siqqe* system.

The idea of creating and building a national *Gumii Oromiyaa* must be given top priority by all progressive and revolutionary Oromo in order to revitalize, centralize, and coordinate the Oromo national movement. All nationalist Oromo should be encouraged and invited to participate in a united Oromo national movement and to own their movement. All Oromo activists and nationalist leaders should begin to search for ways of enabling Oromo to participate in the united Oromo national movement by providing ideas, resources, expertise, and labor. Although the fire of Oromo nationalism was lit by a few determined revolutionary elements, the Oromo national struggle has reached a level where mass mobilization and participation is required. In this mobilization, the united Oromo national movement should use the ideology and principles of democracy which must be enshrined in *Oromummaa* in order to mobilize the entire nation spiritually, financially, intellectually, ideologically, militarily, and organizationally to take a centralized and coordinated political and military action.

Ninth, most members of the Oromo Diaspora must engage in public diplomacy by introducing the Oromo and their plight to the international community. In order to successfully do this, every Oromo in the diaspora must adequately learn about Oromo history, culture, and civilization and be able to teach others by refuting the lies and propaganda of the colonialists and their supporters.

Tenth, Oromo nationalists in the diaspora must start to build a well-regulated system that can provide support and security for individual Oromo who are determined to advance the Oromo national interest whenever they face hardship beyond their control.

Finally, the Oromo must believe that they will liberate themselves. There is no doubt that, despite hardships and sacrifices, the Oromo "social volcano" that is fermenting will soon burn down the Ethiopian colonial structures that perpetuate terrorism, genocide, disease, absolute poverty, and malnutrition in Oromia and beyond. The Oromo people and their leaders must intensify their commitment, hard work, and determination, and be ready to make the necessary sacrifices to restore Oromo democracy and to achieve national self-determination, sovereignty, statehood, and multinational democracy.

NOTES

1. The liberation of the Oromo is inextricably intertwined with the liberation of all of the peoples under the rule of the rule of the TPLF-led government. For a discussion of the relationship of *Oromummaa* to liberation of all oppressed nationalities in the Ethiopian Empire see Asafa Jalata, "Theorizing *Oromummaa*," *Journal of Oromo Studies* 22 (1), 2015, 1–35.

2. For detailed discussion, see Asafa Jalata, *Fighting against the Injustice of the State and Globalization: Comparing the African American and Oromo Movements* (New York: Palgrave, 2001).

FOUR

The Oromo National Movement and Gross Human Rights Violations

Despite the fact that the Oromo resistance to Ethiopian colonialism started with the process of colonization and subjugation, organized efforts by Oromo nationalists to liberate the Oromo people started in the 1960s. The emergence of the Macha-Tulama Self-Help Association (MTSA) in the early 1960s and the birth of the Oromo Liberation Front (OLF) in the early 1970s marked the development of Oromo nationalism or national *Oromummaa* and its national organizational structures. Currently, the Oromo people and their national struggle are at a crossroads because of four interrelated reasons: First, to suppress the Oromo people's struggle for national self-determination and multinational democracy, Ethiopian government with the help of global powers is systematically and clandestinely attacking, killing or imprisoning, torturing, and terrorizing Oromo nationalists and other Oromo. Second, the Oromo are suffering from absolute poverty characterized by recurrent famines, diseases, and malnutrition because the state elites and transnational capitalists are looting their economic resources. Third, at the same time, the Oromo elites who are supposed to provide guidance and leadership for the Oromo national movement are fragmented and have failed to understand the lethal danger the Oromo people are facing from the alliance of Ethiopian colonialism and global imperialism. Finally, the necessity of understanding the complexity of the Oromo national movement in order to take immediate tasks for consolidating the Oromo national struggle. Before I engage in my main discussion, let me briefly introduce my analytical and theoretical frameworks.

ANALYTICAL AND THEORETICAL INSIGHTS

By drawing from an analytical framework that emerges from theories of the world system, globalization, nationalism, and social/national movements, this chapter frames the Oromo national struggle in the global context. This work combines a structural approach to global social change with a social constructionist model of human agency of social/national movements. Hence, the Oromo national struggle is considered as an integral part of the global political project that has been attempting to humanize and democratize the racialized capitalist world system from below by establishing a single standard for humanity through eliminating all forms of exploitation and dispossession of economic resources and rights. Through examining the dynamic interplay of sociopolitical structures and human agencies that have facilitated the development of the Oromo national movement, this work employs interdisciplinary, multidimensional, historical, and critical approaches. The struggle for social emancipation, national self-determination, democracy, and popular sovereignty emerged in opposition to political absolutism, colonialism, racism, continued subjugation, and dispossession in the capitalist world system.

The critical understanding of the essence of global capitalism and its political structures and injustices are necessary to clearly recognize the principles for which the national struggle of the Oromo has developed. The Oromo have been denied basic aspects of their humanity since they were forced to enter into the global capitalist world system via slavery and colonialism that were facilitated by the alliance of Abyssinian/Ethiopian dependent colonialism and global imperialism (Holcomb and Ibssa 1990; Jalata 2005 [1993]). The capitalist colonial powers and their regional or local collaborators used superior military forces to enslave and colonize directly or indirectly pre-capitalist societies to exploit their labor power and/or to dispossess their economic resources through coercion, terrorism, looting, piracy, genocide, annexation, and continued subjugation (Jalata 2011). Consequently, the original accumulation of wealth and capital occurred; this capital accumulation gradually facilitated the transformation of mercantilism into industrial capitalism and the development and expansion of the industrial revolution in the West in the eighteenth and nineteenth centuries and increased the demand for more raw materials, free or cheap labor (mainly slaves), markets, and the intensification of global colonial expansion (Marx 1967 [1932]; Rodney 1972).

The development of global capitalism, the accumulation and concentration of capital or economic resources through the separation of the actual producers from their means of production, such as land, led to the racialization/ethnicization and socialization of labor. As Karl Marx (1967 [1932], 17) notes, "The expropriation of the agricultural producers, of the peasant, from the soil, is the basis of the whole process. The history of expropriation, in different countries, assumes different aspects, and runs through its various phases in different orders of succession, and different periods." The processes of expropriation, racial slavery, and colonialism resulted in hierarchical organization of world populations through the creation of an elaborate discourse of race or racism. As the meaning of race is illusive and complex, so is that of racism. Racism can be defined as a discourse and a practice in which a racial/ethnonational project is politically, socially, culturally, and "scientifically" constructed by elites in the capitalist world system to naturalize and justify racial/ethnonational inequality in which those at the top of the hierarchy oppress and exploit those below them by claiming biological and/or cultural superiority. "A racial project is simultaneously an interpretation, representation or explanation of racial dynamics," Howard Winant (1994, 24) writes, "and *an effort to organize and distribute resources along particular racial lines*" (author's emphasis). Simply put, racism is an expression of institutionalized patterns of colonizing structural power and social control in order to transfer labor and economic resources from the powerless to the powerful group.

By inventing nonexistent races, the racist ideology institutionalizes "the hierarchies involved in the worldwide division of labor" (Balibar & Wallerstein 1991, 6). Race and racism are socio-political constructs since all human groups are biologically and genetically more alike than different (Malik 1996). To justify racial slavery and colonialism, colonial terrorism, genocide, and the ideology of racism was developed in scientific and religious clothing and matured during the last decades of the 19th and the beginning of the twentieth centuries.[1] Since the 1970s, with the intensification of the crisis of the process of capital accumulation and the declining of US hegemony in the capitalist world system, the West under the leadership of the United States has started to promote a policy known as neoliberalism to revitalize global capital accumulation (Harvey 2005). As David Harvey (2005, 7) demonstrates, through the policy of neoliberalism the neoliberal state has intensified the process of capital accumulation by dispossession of economic resources and rights; the "fundamental mission [of the neoliberal state] was to facilitate conditions for profitable capital accumulation on the part of both domestic and foreign capital." Accumulation of capital by dispossession involves state terrorism and genocide as the case of the Oromo illustrates (Jalata 2011).

Bruce Hoffman (2006 [1998], 40) "defines terrorism as the deliberate creation and exploitation of fear through violence or the threat of violence in the pursuit of political change. . . . Terrorism is specifically designed to have far-reaching psychological effects beyond the immediate victim(s) or object of the terrorist attack." Although the struggle of the Oromo and other peoples forced the Ethiopian colonial state to "nationalize" the land and make it "collective property" between 1975 and 1991, the United States supported the emergence of the Tigryan-led Ethiopian government that has intensified state terrorism, genocide, and capital accumulation by dispossessing the land of Oromo farmers and that of other ethnonational groups in the Ethiopian Empire (Jalata 2005). Both the Ethiopian colonial state and the big powers of the capitalist world system as well as China have allied in maintaining capitalism through intensifying capital accumulation by any means necessary. "The process of integration of neocolonial states into the global economy, seeking the protection of the imperial state," Berch Berberoglu (2003, 108) writes, " has been to a large degree a reaction to a perceived threat to the survival of capitalism in the Third World—one that is becoming a grave concern for both imperialism and the local repressive capitalist states."

Although the struggle of the impoverished peoples like that of the Oromo cannot threaten global imperialism, powerful countries like the United States have sided with the Tigrayan-led minority regime of Ethiopia because of their racist and modernist political and economic models (Wolfe 1998) that ignore the principles of social justice, fairness, democracy, and national self-determination. As the Oromo national movement has continued to resist the criminal policies of the Ethiopian government, the regime has increased its terrorist activities and dispossession of lands and other resources with the support of Western powers, emerging powers of China, India, and some Arab countries, as well as international institutions, such as the World Bank and the International Monetary Fund.[2] With the support of powerful countries, terrorist regimes in Third World countries have used various forms of terror such as rape, physical and psychological torture, violent arrest, secret or open imprisonment and usually death, disappearances (euphemism for secret killings), assassinations, castration, etc. We should "regard life and liberty as something like absolute values and then try to understand the moral and political processes through which these values are challenged and defended" (Waltzer 1977, xvi). Since the international system, particularly the United Nations, lacks a single standard for humanity in a practical sense, some states get away with the crimes they commit against their own citizens and other peoples (Jalata 2011). The lack of demanding responsibility from certain states such as that of Ethiopia in the international system leaves room for engaging in state terrorism and committing genocide.

Despite the fact that the United Nations has theoretically recognized the problems of state terrorism and genocide, it did not yet develop effective policies and mechanisms of preventing them because powerful countries and their client states that commit such crimes against humanity have dominated the United Nations. Article II of the United Nations Convention defines genocide as "acts committed with intent to destroy, in whole or in part, a national, ethnical, racial or religious group." Kurt Jonassohn (1998, 9) also defines genocide as the planned destruction of any economic, political or social group." According to Frank Chalk and

Kurt Jonassohn (1990, 23), "GENOCIDE is a form of one-sided mass killing in which a state or other authority intends to destroy a group, as that and membership in it are defined by the perpetrator." Chalk and Jonassohn (1990, 23) identify two major types of genocide: the first type is used to colonize and maintain an empire by terrorizing the people perceived to be real or potential enemies. In this case, the main purpose of practicing genocide is to acquire land and other valuable resources. Then the maintenance of colonial domination by state elites requires the establishment of a cultural and ideological hegemony that can be practiced through repression and genocidal massacres. By destroying elements of a population that resists colonial domination, hegemony can be established on the surviving population. This is the second type of genocide; this form of genocide is called ideological genocide. Jonassohn (1998, 23) notes that ideological genocide develops "in nation-states where ethnonational groups develop chauvinistic [and racist] ideas about their superiority and exclusiveness." As it can be demonstrated below, since their incorporation into the racialized capitalist world system through the dependent colonialism of Abyssinia/Ethiopia, the Oromo have been facing state terrorism, genocidal massacres, and dispossession of economic and cultural resources that they have been fighting against in various forms.

THE PAST AND CURRENT STATUS OF THE OROMO PEOPLE

The Ethiopian colonial terrorism and genocide that started during the last decades of the nineteenth century still continue in the twenty-first century. The Abyssinian/Ethiopian or Amhara and Tigrayan warlords terrorized and committed genocide on the Oromo people during the Scramble for Africa with the help of European imperial powers such as Britain, France, and Italy, and the modern weapons they received from them (Holcomb and Ibssa 1990; Jalata 2005 [1993]). During Ethiopian (Amhara-Tigray) colonial expansion, Oromia, "the charming Oromo land, [would] be ploughed by the iron and the fire; flooded with blood and the orgy of pillage" (de Salviac 2005 [1901], 349). Calling this event as "the theatre of a great massacre," Martial de Salviac (2005 [1901], 349) states,

> The conduct of Abyssinian armies invading a land is simply barbaric. They contrive a sudden irruption, more often at night. At daybreak, the fire begins; surprised men in the huts or in the fields are three quarter massacred and horribly mutilated; the women and the children and many men are reduced to captivity; the soldiers lead the frightened herds toward the camp, take away the grain and the flour which they load on the shoulders of their prisoners spurred on by blows of the whip, destroy the harvest, then, glutted with booty and intoxicated with blood, go to walk a bit further from the devastation. That is what they call "civilizing a land."

The Oromo oral story also testifies that the Abyssinian armies looted the resources of Oromia (the Oromo country), and committed genocide on the Oromo people through terrorism, massacre, slavery, depopulation, cutting hands or breasts, series of famines, and diseases during and after the colonization. Recognizing this tragedy, "the Oromo said: 'It is *Waaqa* [God] . . . who has subjected us to the Amhara' [and Tigray]" (de Salviac 2005 [1901], 350). According to Martial de Salviac (2005 [1901], 8), "With equal arms, the Abyssinia [would] never [conquer] an inch of land. With the power of firearms imported from Europe, Menelik [Abyssinian warlord] began a murderous revenge."

The colonization of Oromia involved human tragedy and destruction: "The Abyssinian, in bloody raids, operated by surprise, mowed down without pity, in the country of the Oromo population, a mournful harvest of slaves for which the Muslims were thirsty and whom they bought at very high price. An Oromo child [boy] would cost up to 800 francs in Cairo; an Oromo girl would well be worth two thousand francs in Constantinople" (de Salvic 2005 [1901], 28). The Abyssinian/Ethiopian government massacred half of the Oromo population (five million out of ten million) and their leadership during its colonial expansion (Bulatovich 2000, 68). According to Alexander Bulatovich (2000, 68–69), "The dreadful annihilation of more than half of the population during the conquest took away from the [Oromo] all possibilities of thinking about any sort of uprising . . . Without a doubt, the [Oromo], with their least five million population, occupying the best land, all speaking one language, could represent a tremendous force if united." The destruction of Oromo lives, institutions, and Oromian natural beauty were aspects of Ethiopian colonial terrorism. The surviving Oromo who used to enjoy an egalitarian democracy known as the *gadaa* system (Legesse 1973, 2000) were forced to face state terrorism, genocide, political repression, and an impoverished life. Bulatovich (2000, 68) explains about the *gadaa* administration as follows: "the peaceful free way of life, which could have become the ideal for philosophers and writers of the eighteenth century, if they had known it, was completely changed. Their peaceful way of life is broken; freedom is lost; and the independent, freedom loving [Oromo] find themselves under the severe authority of the Abyssinian conquerors."

The Ethiopian colonialists also destroyed Oromo natural resources and the beauty of Oromia. Oromia was "an oasis luxuriant with large trees" and known for its "opulent and dark greenery used to shoot up from the soil" (de Salviac 2005 [1901], 21–22). De Salviac (2005 [1901], 20–21) also notes, "the greenery and the shade delight the eyes all over and give the landscape richness and a variety which make it like *a garden without boundary*. Healthful climate, uniform and temperate, fertility of the soil, beauty of the inhabitants, the security in which their houses seem to be situated, makes one dream of remaining in such a beautiful country." The Abyssinian colonialists devastated "the forests by pulling from it the laths for their houses and [made] campfires or firewood for their dwellings. . . . [T]he great destructors of trees, others [accused] them of exercising their barbarity against the forests for the sole pleasure of ravaging" (de Salviac 2005 [1901], 20). Bulatovich (2000, 21) applied to Oromia the phrase "flowing in milk and honey" to indicate its abundance of wealth in cattle and honey. The Ethiopian colonial state gradually established settler colonialism in Oromia and developed five major types of colonial institutions, namely, slavery, the colonial landholding system, the *nafxanya-gabbar* system (semi-slavery), the Oromo collaborator class, and garrison and non-garrison cities (Jalata 2005). It introduced the process of forced recruitment of labor via slavery and the *nafxanya-gabbar* (semi-slavery) system (Holcomb and Ibssa 1990, 135). The colonial state expropriated almost all Oromo lands and divided up the Oromo among colonial officials and soldiers and their collaborators to force them to produce agricultural commodities and food for local consumption and an international market.

The Oromo farmers were reduced to serfs or slaves or semi-slaves and coerced to work without remuneration for the settlers, intermediaries, and the colonial state for certain days every week. Whenever they failed to provide free labor or pay taxes or tributes, the settlers enslaved their children or wives (Jalata 2005; Holcomb and Ibssa 1990). The colonial policies that started during the reign of Menelik have continued under successive Ethiopian governments. The Haile Selassie government continued the policies of Menelik until it was overthrown by the popular revolt of 1974. The Selassie government terrorized the Oromo of Raya-Azabo, Wallo, Hararghe, Bale and other regions because of their political and cultural resistance to the Amhara-Tigray colonial domination. It also imprisoned, tortured, or hanged prominent Oromo leaders such as Mamo Mazamir and Haile Mariam Gamada who organized and led the Macha-Tulama Self-Help Association in the 1960s. The military regime that emerged in 1974 under the leadership Colonel Mengistu Haile Mariam continued state terrorism, dictatorship, and the subjugation of the Oromo. When Oromo activists and the people started to resist the military regime, it intensified state terrorism and genocide.

The military regime also known as the *derg* had committed massive human rights violations in the 1970s and 1980s in the name of the so-called Revolution and "socialism" with the assistance of the so-called socialist countries such as the former Soviet Union and its satellite countries.[3] In the 1980s, thousands of Oromo nationalists were murdered or imprisoned; the regime also terrorized other elements of Oromo society. According to Gunnar Hasselblatt (1992, 17–19), the military government

> repeatedly held mass shooting among the Oromo population, hoping to break the free, independent Oromo spirit. Sometimes a hundred,

sometimes two hundred men were shot on this raised dry field . . . and were buried with bulldozers. Over years this procedure was repeated several times. When the method did not work and the Oromo population could not be forced into submission, other methods were used. The victims were made to lie down with their heads on stone, and their skulls were smashed with another stone. The . . . government . . . tried everything to consolidate its reign of terror and exploitation of Oromia . . . When the Oromo movement could not be quenched by shooting or by the smashing of skulls, [the government] came up with a new idea. Men's testicles were smashed between a hammer and an anvil. Three men tortured and maimed in this way are still living.

Ethiopia has maintained its oppressive and repressive structures on the Oromo by the assistance of successive global powers, namely, Great Britain, the United States, the former Soviet Union, as well as China (Jalata 2012). Replacing Great Britain, the United States supported the Haile Selassie government between the 1950s and the early 1970s, when the former Soviet Union started to assist the new military regime that claimed to promote socialism. As the former Soviet Union supported the Mengistu regime, the United States, powerful European countries, and China support the Tigrayan-led Ethiopian government. The Tigrayan-led regime continues similar colonial policies and practices in Oromia and other places. The only difference was that the Tigrayan state elites were the ones that dominated and led the Ethiopian colonial state instead of the Amhara colonialists that led the Ethiopian state from the last decades of the nineteenth century until 1991.

Starting from 1992, the Tigrayan authoritarian-terrorist regime (Jalata 2010b) controlled the Oromo and denied them the freedom of expression, association, organization, the media, and all forms of communication and information networks. This government had been focusing on brutally attacking the Oromo national movement led by the Oromo Liberation Front (OLF) and on robbing the economic resources of Oromia in order to enrich the Tigrayan elites and their collaborators and to specifically develop the Tigrayan region. To achieve its political and economic objectives, the regime primarily used its puppet organization known as the Oromo People's Democratic Organization (OPDO), which was created and was controlled by the Tigrayan People's Liberation Front (TPLF); the OPDO had been staffed by Tigrayan cadres, elements of Oromo-speaking colonial settlers, and opportunistic Oromo who would do anything in exchange for luxurious lifestyles. The minority Tigrayan-led Ethiopian government attempted to give a final solution for a large political problem that has existed for several centuries—the relationship between the Oromo and their Amhara-Tigrayan colonizers. As we know from history, the policy of targeting and exterminating indigenous peoples has existed in different parts of the world, and it has been an integral practice of the racialized capitalist world system since the sixteenth century.[4] This regime was completing the forced removal of Oromo from the areas surrounding Finfinnee (Addis Ababa) (Worku 2008, 97–131).

The Tigrayan regime tried to implement the so-called Addis Ababa Master Plan that the Oromo called "the Master Genocide" in 2014. The Oromo in general and the Oromo students in particular peacefully resisted this genocidal policy that was intended to totally uproot Oromo farmers around the capital city and transfer their lands to Tigrayans and their supporters. The regime killed or imprisoned Oromo students and others who opposed the so-called Addis Ababa Master Plan. Almost all Oromo students opposed this plan and peacefully demonstrated all over Oromia. Furthermore, by evicting the Oromo farmers from their homelands with nominal or without compensation, the regime leased several millions hectares of Oromo lands to so-called investors from Ethiopia, China, Djibouti, Saudi Arabia, India, Malaysia, Nigeria, UK, Israel, as well as from Europe (Rahmato 2011; Giorgis 2009). The local and transnational capitalists intensified the process of capital accumulation by dispossessing of the Oromo lands under the leadership of the Tigrayn-led Ethiopian government. If the policy of land grabbing is allowed to continue, Tigrayans, Amharas, Chinese, Djiboutians, Indians, Malaysians, Nigerians, Arabs, English, Jews, Asians, Europeans and others will soon replace the Oromo people in Oromia and beyond.

The Tigrayan state elites never sold or leased Tigrayan lands, but have expanded modern agricultural development in their homeland, Tigray. Tamrat G. Giorgis (2009, 1), Addis Fortune staff writer, explains as follows: "A new global trend is rising whereby companies from emerging economies grab vast land in poor host nations to grow and export cereals and grains to their home countries. It has happened here in Bako [Oromia], where people from India have been granted tens of thousands of hectares of land for commercial farming. The locals, however, are unhappy." The Tigrayan regime also sold Oromo minerals and other natural resources while evicting and impoverishing the Oromo people. Whenever the Oromo resisted, the regime mercilessly brutalized or killed them. In this era of globalization, the Tigrayan regime was advised, financed, and legitimized by the transnational capitalist class. Global powers such as the United States, the European Union, and countries of emerging economies had collaborated with the Tigrayan-led regime to suppress the OLF in order to expropriate the economic resources of the Oromo people.[5] Millions of Oromo who had lost their economic resources and those who were targeted for their political views had immigrated to the Middle East, Australia, Europe, and North America and to different countries in Africa. They have been mistreated in some African countries and the Middle East, and they have been denied the right to be refugees. The majority of the Oromo who lived under the control of the Tigrayan-led regime were facing serious social and political problems in their own country.

The United States, the European Union, and China had built and consolidated the Tigrayan-led Ethiopian regime to perform the following important services: "(1) adopt fiscal and monetary policies that ensure macroeconomic stability; (2) provide the basic infrastructure necessary for global economic activity (airports and seaports, communication networks, educational systems, etc.); and (3) provide social order, that is, stability, which requires sustaining instruments of social control, coercive and ideological apparatus" (Robinson 2008, 33). The Tigrayan-led regime was an organ of capital accumulation for Tigrayan and transnational elites, and it used terrorism and massive human rights violations to separate the indigenous communities such as the Oromo and others from their lands and other resources (Jalata 2005). Furthermore, the World Bank, IMF, UN, EU, African Union, and most NGOs as structures of global capitalism are the facilitators of regional and global capital accumulators, and they are not interested in promoting human rights and democracy in peripheral countries like Ethiopia (Jalata 2005). The political and military leaders of the Ethiopian government are literally gangsters and robbers; they use state power to expropriate lands and other resources in the name of privatization—all with the blessing of the World Bank and the International Monetary Fund. In achieving its political and economic objectives, the Ethiopian government has been engaging in political repression, state terrorism, genocidal massacres, and gross human rights violations in Oromia and other regional states.

Since the Oromo people have been resisting Ethiopian colonial policies, they have been targeted by the regime; they have been attacked and terrorized because of their economic resources, their acceptance of the OLF as their national leadership, and their refusal to submit to the orders of colonial authorities and their collaborators. The Ethiopian government has also banned independent Oromo organizations including the OLF and declared war on those organizations and the Oromo people. It even outlawed Oromo journalists and other writers and closed down Oromo newspapers. As Mohammed Hassen (2002, 31) asserts, "The attack on the free press has literally killed the few publications in the Oromo language in the Latin alphabet. The death of Oromo publications . . . has been a fatal blow to the flowering of Oromo literature and the standardization of the Oromo language itself. The Oromo magazines that have disappeared include *Gada, Biftu, Madda Walaabuu, Odaa,* and the *Urjii* magazine. . . . Since 2002, there has not been a single newspaper or magazine that has expressed the legitimate political opinions of the Oromo in Ethiopia." Almost all Oromo journalists are either in prison, killed, or in exile. The regime also banned Oromo musical groups and all professional associations. Expanding their political repression, government authorities formed quasi-government institutions known as *gott* and *garee* to maintain tighter political control over Oromia; they "imposed these new structures on . . . [rural] communities. . . . More disturbing, regional authorities are using the *gott* and *garee* to monitor the speech and personal lives of the rural population, to restrict and control the movements of residents, and to enforce farmers' attendance at 'meetings' that are thinly disguised OPDO political rallies" (Human Rights Watch 2005b, 2).

Generally speaking, the Ethiopian government has continued to eliminate or imprison politically conscious and self-respecting Oromo. Today, thousands of Oromo are in official and secret prisons or concentration camps simply because of their nationality and their resistance to injustice. After jailed and released from prison after six years, Seye Abraha, the former Defense Minister of the regime who had previously participated in the massacring and imprisoning thousands of Oromo, testified on January 5, 2008, to his audience in the state of Virginia in the United States that "esir betu Oromigna yinager," ("the prison speaks Oromiffa [the Oromo language])" and also noted that "about 99 percent of the prisoners in Qaliti are Oromos." The Tigrayan state bureaucrats believed that Oromo intellectuals, businessmen and women, conscious Oromo farmers, students, and community and religious leaders are their enemies, and, hence, should be destroyed through political repression and state terrorism (Hizbawi Adera 1996, 1997). State terrorism is their main tool in repressing and destroying Oromo nationalists. It is associated with issues of control over territory and resources and the construction of political and ideological domination (Oliverio 1997). It has manifested itself as lethal violence in the form of war, assassination, murder, castration, burying alive, throwing off cliffs, hanging, torture, rape, poisoning, forcing people to submission by intimidation, beating, and disarmament of citizens (Pollock 1997; Trueman 2007).

The methods of killings have also included burning, bombing, and the cutting of throats or arteries in the neck, strangulation, shooting, and the burying of people up to their necks in the ground. The agents and militia of the regime have burned houses and entire villages, exterminating millions of Oromo men, women, and children. The regime has also practiced different forms of torture on imprisoned Oromo and others; former prisoners have testified that their arms and legs were tied tightly together on their backs and their naked bodies were whipped; large containers or bottles filled with water were fixed to their testicles, or if they were women, bottles or poles were pushed into their vaginas (Trueman 2001; *Survival International* 1995). There were prisoners who were locked up in empty steel barrels and tormented with heat in the tropical sun during the day and with cold at night; there were also prisoners who were forced into pits so that fire could be made on top of them (Trueman 2001). The cadres, soldiers, and officials of the regime have frequently raped Oromo girls and women to demoralize them and their communities and to show how Tigrayan rulers and their collaborators wielded limitless power. As Bruna Fossati, Lydia Namarra, and Peter Niggli (1996, 10) report, "in prison women are often humiliated and mistreated in the most brutal fashion. Torturers ram poles or bottles into their vaginas, connect electrodes to the lips of their vulva, or the victims are dragged into the forest and gang-raped by interrogation officers."

Ethiopian soldiers have collected young Oromo girls and women into concentration camps and gang raped them in front of their relatives, fathers, brothers, and husbands to humiliate them and the Oromo people. State-sanctioned rape is a form of terrorism. The use of sexual violence is also a tactic of genocide that a dominant ethnonational group practices in order to destroy a subordinate ethnonational group. What Catherine MacKinnon (1994, 11–12) says about ethnic cleansing in Croatia and Bosnia-Herzegovina applies to the sexual abuse of Oromo girls and women by the Tigrayan-led regime: "It is also rape unto death, rape as massacre, rape to kill and to make the victims wish they were dead. It is rape as an instrument of forced exile, rape to make you leave your home and never want to go back. It is rape to be seen and heard and watched and told to others: rape as spectacle. It is rape to drive a wedge through a community, to shatter a society, to destroy a people. It is rape as genocide." The Tigrayan-led regime used various mechanisms in repressing, controlling, and destroying the Oromo people. It has imprisoned or killed thousands of Oromo women and men. Its agents murdered prominent community leaders and left their corpses for hyenas by denying them burial to impose terror on the Oromo people.

Furthermore, relatives of the murdered Oromo were not allowed to cry publicly to express their grievances, a once cultural practice. For example, the wife of Ahmed Mohamed Kuree, a seventy-year-old elderly farmer, expressed on February 21, 2007, on the Voice of America, *Afaan Oromo* Program the following: "We found his prayer beads, his clothes and a single bone of his which the hyenas had left behind after devouring the rest of his body, and we took those items home. What is more, after we got home, they [government agents] condemned us for going to Gaara Suufii and for mourning. For fear of repercussions, we have not offered the customary prayer for my husband by reading from the Qur'an. Justice has not been served. That is where we are today." Another Oromo, Ayisha Ali, a fourteen-year-old teenager, was also killed and eaten by hyenas. Her mother said on the Voice of America, *Afaan Oromoo* Program, the following: "After we heard the rumor about the old man [Ahmed Mohamed Kuree] I followed his family to Gaara Suufii [in search of my daughter]. There we found her skirt, sweater, underwear and her hair, braided . . . That was all we found of my daughter's remains." Ayisha was probably raped before she was killed. According to *Human Rights Watch* (2005b, 1–2), "Since 1992, security forces have imprisoned thousands of Oromo on charges of plotting armed insurrection on behalf of the OLF. Such accusations have regularly been used as a transparent pretext to imprison individuals who publicly question government policies or actions. Security forces have tortured many detainees and subjected them to continuing harassment and abuse for years after their release. That harassment in turn has often destroyed victims' ability to earn a livelihood and isolated them from their communities." The regime even targeted Oromia's environment and its animals. According to Mohammed Hassen (2002, 37–38),

> Oromo men, women, children, animals, and even the Oromo environment are all targets of the [Tigrayan] tyranny. In cases where Oromo pastoralists were suspected of harboring OLF guerrilla fighters, [Tigrayan] soldiers punished them by destroying or confiscating their cattle or by poisoning the wells from which the cattle drank. On many occasions Oromo farmers, suspected of feeding OLF fighters, saw their farms burned to the ground and the defenseless members of their households brutally murdered. In 2000, when the [Tigrayan] government suspected OLF guerrillas of hiding in the forests of Oromia, its agents set fires that caused catastrophic environmental destruction in Oromia and other states in southern Ethiopia.

In addition to such environmental destruction and the murdering and raping of Oromo girls and women, the regime engaged in the genocidal massacres of Oromo. It engaged in such crimes with little or no opposition from Western powers, particularly the United States. All these crimes against humanity are committed in the name of democracy, federalism, and development. The Tigrayan-led government saw Oromia as part of its empire, controlled all of Oromia's resources, and attacked the Oromo since it perceived them as its potential or real enemies. It engaged in genocide with the intention of destroying sectors of the Oromo nation composed of nationalists and leaders. Tigrayan state leaders claimed to promote political ideologies such as "revolutionary democracy" and "federalism," while at gunpoint attempting to legitimize Tigrayan ethnocracy and state power.

These state elites denied that they engaged in human rights violations by claiming that they were democrats and revolutionaries; they were destroying the records of their political crimes. Jonassohn's description of a conspiracy of "collective denial" of genocide is applicable to the denial of the occurrence of genocide in the Ethiopian Empire. According to Jonassohn (1981, 11), "There are many reasons for this: (a) in many societies such materials are not written down, or are destroyed rather than preserved in archives; (b) many perpetrators have recourse to elaborate means of hiding the truth, controlling access to information, and spreading carefully contrived disinformation; and (c) historically, most genocides were not reported because ... there appears to have existed a sort of conspiracy of 'collective denial' whereby the disappearance of a people did not seem to require comment or even mention." While the Tigrayan regime had been eliminating Oromo leaders through genocide in order to deny the Oromo their own political leadership, it had been preparing

Tigrayan children for positions of leadership by providing them access to a better education. This regime also limited the educational opportunities of Oromo children to maintain racial/ethnic division of labor.

Although it is impossible to know exactly at this time how many Oromo have been murdered by the Tigrayan-led government, Mohammed Hassen (2001) estimates that between 1992 and 2001, about 50,000 killings and 16,000 disappearances (euphemism for secret killings) took place in Oromia; he also notes that 90 percent of the killings were not reported. The government hides its criminal activities and "does not keep written records of its extrajudicial executions and prolonged detention of political prisoners" (Hassen 2001, 30). Furthermore, the massive killings and genocide committed on the Sheko, Mezhenger, Sidama, Annuak, and Ogaden Somali peoples shocked some sections of the international community. For instance, in 2002, when the Sheko and Mezhenger peoples demanded their rights, the regime killed between 128 and 1,000 people. Nobody knows exactly how many people were killed since the government and the victims gave different numbers. Similarly, on June 21, 2002, between 39 and 100 Sidamas were killed when government soldiers fired at 7,000 peaceful demonstrators in Hawasa. Again government forces and colonial settlers committed genocidal massacres on the Annuak people of Gambella in December 2003 and beginning 2004; they killed 424 people and displaced about 50, 000 people. The regime engaged in genocidal massacres, imprisonment, and massive human rights violations in Ogadenia and Oromia. Because of these reasons Meles Zenawi and his followers were possible targets of the International Criminal Court (ICC) as were many leaders of African countries (Associated Press 2009, 1).

The president of Genocide Watch, Gregory Stanton (2009, 1), wrote on March 23, 2009, an open letter to the United Nations High Commission for Human Rights admiring the action that the ICC took in issuing a warrant for the arrest of President Omar al-Bashir of the Sudan and calling upon them to investigate the crimes Meles and his government had been committing against humanity in the Horn of Africa:

> The action that the International Criminal Court has taken in this situation has restored hope to peace and justice loving people, affirming that international human rights law not only exists on paper, but in reality. It also sends an important message to perpetrators throughout the world that impunity for their crimes is not assured forever; which may be a primary reason that one of the first leaders to defend Omar al-Bashir and condemn the warrant was Prime Minister Meles Zenawi of Ethiopia, whose government has also been implicated in a pattern of widespread perpetration of serious human rights atrocities in Ethiopia and in Somalia. He and those within his government may be keenly aware of their own vulnerability to similar actions by the ICC in the future that could upend a deeply entrenched system of government-

supported impunity that has protected perpetrators from any accountability.

Stanton demonstrates in this letter how the Meles government committed heinous crimes by being involved "in the inciting, the empowerment or the perpetration of crimes against humanity, war crimes and even genocide, often justified by them as 'counter-insurgency.'" He also stated that the Meles government organized Ethiopian National Defense Forces and civilian militia groups to ruthlessly massacre 424 persons from the Annuak people in Gambella on December 2003 in order to suppress opposition and to "exclude them from any involvement in the drilling for oil on their indigenous land." According to Stanton, as militia groups chanted "Today is the day for killing Annuak," both the military and militias used machetes, axes and guns to kill the unarmed victims, frequently raping the women while chanting, "Now there will be no more Annuak children."

Reports from Amnesty International, the U.S. State Department, and the Human Rights Watch had been continuing to list Zenawi's government extensive record of chilling crimes against the politically and economically oppressed peoples such as the Oromo. The Meles regime passed the so-called anti-terrorism law to legalize its crimes against humanity and to legally intensify its own repressive and terrorist activities. Ethiopia's anti-terrorism "law could provide the Ethiopian government with a potent instrument to crack down on political dissent, including peaceful political demonstrations and public criticisms of government policy that are deemed supportive of armed opposition activity" (Human Rights Watch 2009b, 1). Generally speaking, the policies and practices of the Ethiopian regime have forced millions of Oromo to become political refugees in Asia, Europe, Australia, and North America. The alliance of the West with this regime has frightened neighboring countries such as Djibouti, Kenya, Sudan, and Yemen, and turned them against the Oromo struggle and Oromo refugees. Using the leverage of Western countries, the regime pressured neighboring governments to return or expel Oromo refugees from their countries. The United Nations High Commission for Refugees (UNHCR) has even failed to provide reasonable protection for thousands of Oromo refugees in Djibouti, Kenya, Sudan, Somalia, and Yemen. For example, on December 21 and 22, 2000, while five thousand Oromo refugees were subject to refoulment to Ethiopia, the UNHCR office in Djibouti denied any violation of its mandate had occurred (The Oromia Support Group 2002, 17, 37).

Between 2000 and 2004, hundreds of Oromo refugees were forced to return to Ethiopia from Djibouti to face imprisonment or death (The Oromia Support Group 2003, 16–18). "The continuing refoulement of refugees from Djibouti," notes the Oromia Support Group (2002, 18–19), "especially the large scale refoulement of December 2000 and the 28 associated deaths by asphyxiation and shooting, should be publicly acknowledged by UNHCR and the Djibouti government." The security agents of Ethiopia and neighboring countries captured thousands of Oromo refugees and return them to Ethiopia. By crossing borders and entering Somalia and Kenya, agents of the Ethiopian regime assassinated prominent Oromo leaders. In 2007 and 2008, Ethiopian security forces assassinated Oromos in Somalia and Kenya. One human rights organization notes that on February 5, 2008, the combined security forces of Ethiopia and Puntland, Somalia, bombed two hotels and consequently murdered 65 Oromo refugees and seriously injured more than 100 people. In 2009, the regime killed four Oromo by poisoning their food in Puntland (The Human Right League of the Horn of Africa 2009).

When it comes to the Oromo, international organizations do not pay attention even if terrorist attacks occur and international laws are broken. The Oromo are being denied sanctuary in neighboring countries and are also even being denied the right to be refugees to some degree. Since some Oromo refugees are not welcomed by neighboring countries and international organizations, there are thousands of "internal" Oromo refugees in Oromia and Ethiopia. Fleeing from Ethiopian state terrorism, these internal refugees hide in the bushes and remote villages. Suspecting that these internal refugees support the Oromo national struggle, the Ethiopian government has attempted to control their movements and the movement of other Oromo. When the government has been mobilizing the West and the global system by using their resources to terrorize and control the Oromo, the revolutionary nationalist Oromo elites have failed to consolidate the Oromo national struggle because of their ideological confusion and political fragmentation.

As we shall see below, due to the lack of coherent, pragmatic, and strong political leadership, the Oromo national movement faces challenges from the unstable authoritarian-terrorist Ethiopian government. Moreover, the Oromo national struggle created political and economic opportunities for those reactionary and opportunist Oromo who promoted their personal and group interests by allying with and working for the Tigrayan-led Ethiopian government at the cost of the Oromo nation. The sad thing is that this government dispossessed Oromian economic and natural resources to pay for the Oromo collaborators it organized and led as the OPDO to do its dirty job in Oromia. Had the Oromo national struggle built itself as a more unified, structured, and strong movement, the umbilical cord that links Oromo society to its enemy could have been cut. Today the Oromo collaborators that are in the OPDO mainly maintain such links. Until these "social cancers" exist in Oromo society, it cannot be imagined to liberate Oromia from Ethiopian settler colonialism. These dangerous social elements survive in Oromo society because of the failure of the revolutionary nationalist Oromo elites in establishing a more unified and structured organization and leadership that can mobilize most of the Oromo people to defend their interests. At the same time, the fire of national *Oromummaa* (Oromo nationalism) survives and expands because of the few selfless and determined Oromo nationalists. However, such nationalist leaders need to expand their mental horizons to re-map and reinvent the Oromo national movement by providing a centralized, structured organization and leadership by mobilizing all organizational, cultural, and material resources of the Oromo for national survival and self-defense. Furthermore, the Oromo nationalist elites must maintain their strengths and overcome their weaknesses to mobilize the Oromo for social emancipation, national liberation, self-determination, social justice, and multinational democracy. Without achieving all these objectives, the human rights of the Oromo and other peoples cannot be protected.

THE MAJOR OPPORTUNITIES AND CONSTRAINTS FOR THE OROMO STRUGGLE

The Oromo national movement that emerged in the 1960s and 1970s by a few determined nationalists reached the Oromo populace in the early 1990s. It took many decades and heavy sacrifices in the lives and sufferings of these few nationalists to resurrect the Oromo name, language, nationhood, and the name of Oromia from the dustbin of history. In this process, national *Oromummma* has been resurrected. Ethiopian colonialism had disconnected the Oromo from one another and from the international community for more than a century. However, with the resurrection of the Oromo national identity, culture, and nationalism, the Oromo people have started to be represented in the world by its political refugees. For the first time in Oromo history, the Oromo people started to have its diaspora communities that have a great potential to link Oromia to the global community. The imposition of Ethiopian state terrorism on the Oromo to suppress Oromo nationalism and identity has created and expanded the Oromo Diaspora communities in the world (Jalata 2002). Consequently, a few serious Oromo intellectuals and friends of the Oromo emerged on the global level and started to dig the graveyards of history to uncover Oromo history and culture and to publish books and academic articles that are being stored in world libraries.

Furthermore, in Oromia, starting in 1991, when the OLF joined the Transitional Government of Ethiopia for almost a year, millions of the *qubee* generation (Oromo youth educated in the Oromo language) emerged as demonstrated by the recent Oromo student protest movement. The national projects that were designed by the OLF produced fundamental results that have become the cornerstones of the Oromo national struggle. These achievements are great political opportunities for the Oromo nation. Unfortunately, since the Oromo national struggle did not yet achieve its main objectives of reestablishing a democratic Oromia state by itself or in a multinational context, the enemies of the Oromo people have created political constraints to abort the struggle. Currently, the Ethiopian government that claims that it has allowed cultural autonomy for the Oromo and others opposes particularly the manifestation of basic and other forms of *Oromummaa*. According to the November 2014 report of Amnesty International entitled "Because I am Oromo," "Expression of Oromo culture and heritage have been interpreted as manifestations of dissent, and the government has also shown signs of fearing cultural expression as a potential catalyst for opposition to the government. Oromo singers, writers and poets have been arrested for allegedly criticizing the government and/or inciting people through their work. People wearing traditional Oromo clothing have been arrested at Oromo traditional festivals."[6]

There are also millions of Oromo who have betrayed their nation to satisfy their personal and economic interests. By creating and building the OPDO and recruiting such Oromo to this subservient organization, the Tigrayan-led Ethiopian regime used them to attack the Macha-Tulama Self-Help Association and the OLF and to suppress and control the Oromo people with the assistance from global powers. The regime had also mobilized several ethnonations against the Oromo people and their movement. There are also anti-Oromo forces such as Amhara colonial organizations and others who use any opportunity to undermine the interest of the Oromo nation. The constraints of the Oromo struggle are not limited to these problems. The Oromo national movement did not yet secure adequate sympathy and support for the Oromo national cause from the international community. It is very clear that the Tigrayan-led government with the support of global powers and its agents terrorized and ruled the Oromo not because of its strengths but because of the weaknesses of the Oromo movement, political leadership, and Oromo society. If some elements of Oromo society are well organized under one structured organization and leadership, they can rebel and dismantle the Ethiopian government within a short period. The Ethiopian soldiers, cadres, and their agents can be easily dismantled in Oromia if substantial numbers of Oromo engage in self-defense and coordinated uprisings. If the Oromo people intensify their national struggle, the international community will recognize the political problem of the Oromo nation. The Oromo people will achieve their national self-determination by intensifying their national struggle and by receiving international recognition.

Starting on November 12, 2015, the condition of the Oromo struggle has been transformed by the Oromia-wide peaceful protest movement. The current Oromo protest movement, that is led by Oromo school children and supported by their parents and relatives, demonstrates the maturation of national *Oromummaa* by overcoming the ideological problem of the Oromo movement. Triggered by the so-called Addis Ababa Master

Plan, peaceful protesters all over Oromia are facing the military and the police of the Ethiopian government, which had killed more than five thousand students. The Ethiopian forces have captured and sent thousands of people to prisons and hidden concentrations camps where they are tortured and girls and women are raped. Despite all these dangers and problems, this protest movement has created a new chapter in the Oromo national movement. Because of this ongoing protest movement, the Oromo national unity has been cemented in Oromia and on a global level and the international community has started to recognize the struggle of the Oromo people. Young Oromo, without fear of death, are articulating that we will liberate ourselves from Ethiopian colonialism and dictatorship.

CONCLUSION

The crisis of the Ethiopian Empire that started in the early 1970s still continues. The popular uprisings of ethnonations, classes, and social groups have challenged the collapsing Ethiopian state for several decades and introduced some changes. These uprisings have resulted in the overthrowing of the Haile Selassie government in 1974 and Mengistu regime in 1991 and facilitated the emergence of the Tigrayan-led Ethiopian government and Tigrayan ethnocracy. But these changes failed to transform the nature and essence of the Ethiopian colonial state. Ethiopia is still ruled by an authoritarian-terrorist government that practices colonial terrorism and clandestine genocide on the colonized peoples such as the Oromo, Somali, Sidama, Annuak, and others. The Tigrayan-led regime had intensified the crisis of the Ethiopian state.

We know that the Oromo nation lost its political opportunities in the 1970s and again in the 1990s and remained a politically insignificant force despite its numerical significance. Are the Oromo going to miss the current political opportunity? The sudden death of Meles Zenawi who led Ethiopia for twenty-one years with an iron fist on August 20, 2012, has opened a big crack in the Tigrayn-led Ethiopian government. The Tigrayan-led regime was rotten from inside, and it only survived because of the weaknesses of different political forces in the empire and the financial, military, and diplomatic support it received from powerful countries. Are the OLF and other Oromo political organizations ready to use the emerging political crisis? Oromo nationalists, liberation fronts, political organizations, community organizations and associations should start a serious national political dialogue to overcome their political naiveté and immaturity in order to build a national political consensus that will enable them to capture state power in Oromia and to build a multinational democracy with other nations that accept the principles of self-determination and democracy. While preparing themselves to use any available political opportunity, the Oromo national movement and society must start to fashion a national *Gumii Gayyo* (multitudes of legislative national assembly) to produce designed political results.

These designed political results can be produced through determination, hard work, sacrifice, and a collective effort of all Oromo liberation fronts, political organizations, and civic associations. History demonstrates that determined peoples can determine their political destinies by liberating themselves. In developing leadership and organizational capacity, emphasize should be given to build organizations and institutions rather than promoting the egos and leadership of individuals to avoid the pitfalls of other liberation movements that won liberation wars, but failed to build healthy and effective democratic societies. The disaster of the Tigrayan liberation movement is a living example. This movement only won the war against the Ethiopian state and eventually became its photocopy after capturing state power. The Tirayan-led regime excelled its predecessor by committing more crimes against humanity. All colonized subjects must ally with the Oromo protest movement based on the principles of national self- and mutual-interest, self-determination, and multinational democracy to dismantle this terrorist Ethiopian government.

Developing a united, skillful, knowledgeable, and determined leadership that believes truly in democratic principles and hard work is very crucial for the advancement and success of the Oromo and other movements in Ethiopia today. For Oromo society, building the kind of leadership and organization that reflect the Oromo democratic and consultative traditions is absolutely necessary to fully develop the Oromo organizational capacity. The same is true for the other societies. Those Oromo leaders, who created the Macha-Tulama Self-Help Association and the Oromo Liberation Front, reflected some Oromo democratic and consultative traditions, although such traditions were gradually undermined with external pressures and internal crises in the Oromo movement. If the colonized societies, such as the Oromo, cannot develop skills, knowledge, and capabilities to promote and exercise freedom and egalitarian democracy while engaging in protest and liberation struggles, they may inadvertently replace colonial dictatorships by national or other forms of dictatorships. Therefore, the Oromo liberation movement and other movements must start to practice freedom and egalitarian democracy while struggling to overthrow Ethiopian colonial dictatorship.

NOTES

1. Hannah Arendt explored the dynamic relationships among capitalist imperialism, colonialism, racism, fascism, and genocide (King and Stone 2007). According to Tony Barta (2007, 100), "Arendt brought us closer to historical understanding of the murderous progress of modernity, by relating—brilliantly but too briefly—genocide in the colonies to developments far away."

2. Edward S. Herman (1982, 3) recognizes the central roles of these entities in Third World counties like Ethiopia, and notes the following: "There is huge tacit conspiracy between the U.S. government, its agencies and its multinational corporations, on the one hand, and local business and military cliques in the Third World, on the other, to assume complete control of these countries and 'develop' them on a joint venture basis. The U.S. security establishment to serve as the 'enforcers' of this joint venture partnership carefully nurtured the military leaders of the Third World, and they have been duly supplied with machine guns and the latest data on methods of interrogation of subversives. . . . The 'side effects' in the form of widespread hunger, malnutrition, diseases, poverty and social neglect, millions of stunted children, and a huge reserve army of structurally unemployed and uncared for people are the regrettable but necessary costs of 'growth' and 'development.' These side effects have not been heavily featured in the Western media."

3. According to Norman J. Singer (1978, 672–673), "Those killed in the first three months of the campaign of the 'Red Revolutionary Terror' . . . numbered around 4000–5000 [in Finfinnee (Addis Ababa) alone], the killings continued in March 1978, spreading to the rest of the country . . . Those detained for political instruction numbered from 30,000 upwards . . . Torture methods emphasized in the Red Terror . . . included severe beating on the head, soles of the feet . . . and shoulders, with the victim hung by the wrists or suspended by wrists and feet from a horizontal bar . . . ; sexual torture of boys and girls, including pushing bottles or red-hot iron bars into girls' vaginas and other cruel methods." In 1980, one Oromo source said, "the Oromo constitutes the majority of the more than two million prisoners that glut Ethiopia's jails today" (The Oromo Relief Association 1980, 30).

4. While claiming to promote Christian civilization, modernity, and commerce, European colonialists exterminated indigenous peoples in the Americas, Australia, Asia, and Africa over a period of several centuries in order to transfer their resources to European colonial settlers and their descendants. Specifically, the plans and actions that King Leopold of Belgium had for the Congo or Andrew Jackson of the United States for the Cherokees or colonial Germany for the Herero and Nama peoples in South West Africa (Nambia) (Hochschild 1998; Kiernan 2007; Sturgis 2007; Herbert 2003) are very similar to the grand plan and action the Tigrayan-led Ethiopian government has for the Oromo nation.

5. In this process, some Oromo have been uprooted from their communal ancestral lands, alienated, and impoverished. As William I. Robinson (2008, 23) notes, "There is . . . the rise of a new global "underclass" of supernumeraries or "redundants" who are alienated and not absorbed into the global capitalist class economy and who are structurally under- and unemployed. Hundreds of millions of supernumeraries swell the ranks of a global army of reserve labor at the same time as they hold down the wages and leverage ability among those absorbed into the global economy. The supernumeraries are subject to new forms of repressive and authoritarian social control and to an oppressive cultural and ideological dehumanization. . . . This culture of global capitalism glorifies policing and militarization, constructs all those who resist, or even question the logic of the dominant order as incomprehensible, even crazed, *Other*."

6. Amnesty International, "Because I am Oromo: Sweeping Repression in the Oromia Region of Ethiopia," November 2014, p. 8.

FIVE
Theorizing *Oromummaa*

The main purpose of this chapter is to theorize *Oromummaa* by conceptualizing it on different levels and offering theoretical insights and critical analysis of the Oromo national movement in relations to the struggles of other colonized and oppressed peoples.[1] Theorizing and conceptualizing *Oromummaa* specifically in relation to the ideological problem[2] of the Oromo nation movement and that of the others require recognizing the need to transform thinking and scholarship in Oromo politics and studies in order to critically and thoroughly assess the prospects for Oromo politico-cultural transformation and liberation. Theoretically, critically, and practically comprehending *Oromummaa* as Oromo nationalism, national culture and identity is essential because the Oromo nation is the fulcrum for bringing about a fundamental transformation in the Ethiopian Empire and the Horn of Africa in order to establish sustainable peace, development, security, and an egalitarian multinational confederal or federal democracy.

The main reason for this assertion is that the Oromo are the largest national group in the empire and the region; Finfinnee, which the colonialists call Addis Ababa, is the heart of Oromia and the seat of the Ethiopian colonial state, the African Union, and many international organizations. In addition, Oromia is located in the heart of the empire state of Ethiopia, and the Oromo people have already created a cultural corridor with different peoples of the region. The foundation of this corridor is the *gadaa* system (Oromo democracy), which with other indigenous democratic traditions can be a starting point for building a genuine multinational democracy based on the principles of national self-determination. Although the starting point of this analysis is *Oromummaa*, the issues of other colonized and oppressed peoples are addressed. As we shall see below, the theory and ideology of *Oromummaa* embrace the principles of

75

human freedom and social justice, equality and equity, and national self-determination and egalitarian multinational democracy.

First, based on these theoretical insights and the principles of national self-determination and egalitarian multinational democracy, which emerges from the *gadaa/siqqee*[3] heritage and which also borrows from other democratic traditions that expand freedoms, this chapter theorizes *Oromummaa* as an Oromo movement theory. Second, the chapter specifically brings forth ideas about the need to develop Oromo liberation knowledge for advancing a greater understanding of Oromo liberation theory and practice. Third, it explains how the theory and practice of national *Oromummaa* facilitates the development of strategies and tactics for advancing the Oromo national struggle and that of other colonized and dominated peoples to their final destinies. Finally, the chapter notes that the development of national *Oromummaa*, the intensification of the Oromo national movement, overcoming of the deficits of leadership and organizational capability and achieving liberty and the removal unfreedoms in the Oromo society are dialectically interrelated. Finally, the chapter demonstrates that the theory and practice of *Oromummaa* cannot be fully understood and developed without liberation knowledge that emerges from critical Oromo studies and other subaltern knowledge and wisdom.

OROMUMMAA AS AN OROMO MOVEMENT THEORY

Beginning in the early 1960s, a few Oromo nationalists transformed, to a certain degree, the consciousness of the Oromo people who had been reduced to a collection of so-called tribes and raw material by the Ethiopian colonial state and its global supporters. In other words, these colonial and imperial forces intentionally separated the Oromo people from their history and culture and made them a collection of the so-called tribes and raw material from which they could form other nations. With the help of the European colonial powers, Abyssinia/Ethiopia defeated the Oromo nation eliminating its sovereignty, and separating its people from the democratic traditions they enjoyed under the *gadaa/siqqee* institution. Being conquered and colonized, the Oromo could no longer practice the free social and economic arrangements and institutions they had as an independent people. Previously, they had political and civil rights including the freedoms of organization, expression, and participation in public discussion they could use to remove major sources of unfreedoms.[4] Ethiopian colonialism has brought unfreedoms to Oromo society in abundance. Amartya Sen (1999) identifies such unfreedoms as poverty, social deprivation, dictatorship, repression, social control, terror, ignorance, and disease. The Ethiopian colonial institutional arrangements have prevented the Oromo nation from exercising its own agency, denying it economic opportunity, political freedom, and social and political power. The colonial power has also refused to allow the Oromo to develop a health and education infrastructure, build cultural capital, and make their motivation and creativity visible.

Consequently, *Oromummaa,* as Oromo nationalism, developed to remove these unfreedoms from Oromo society. The regimes of Haile Selassie and Mengistu Hailu Mariam tried their best to brutally suppress this flowering of Oromo nationalism by imprisoning and killing Oromo nationalists. Despite the fact that the Macha-Tulama Self-Association, the Afran Qallo Cultural movement, and the Bale Oromo armed struggle were suppressed, Oromo nationalism survived in the form of the Oromo Liberation Front (OLF). Beginning in the early 1990s, Oromo political awareness and consciousness began to expand; this was one of the victories of the Oromo national movement led by the OLF. As the consequence of the Oromo national struggle, *Oromummaa,* as a national identity, culture, and ideology, has been reshaped as the result of the heavy price paid by the lives of thousands of Oromo heroines and heroes at the hand of the Ethiopian state. In addition, *Afaan Oromoo* has become an official language in the Oromia Regional State, which is still a colony of Ethiopia; it has been written in *Qubee,* an adapted Latin alphabet rather than *Ge'ez,* the Amharic-Tigre alphabet. The Oromo national movement has forced the current Ethiopian regime to allow Oromo elementary and high school children to learn in their language although the content of the literature they learn is controlled and manipulated by the neo-*nafxanya* Tigrayans who distort Oromo history, culture, and politics. Although the colonial aggressors from the Tigrayan minority nation control and exploit Oromia, and some of its territories were given to other nations, it has been recognized as the regional state of the Oromo people.

Despite the fact that a few scholars have begun to study the recent changes taking place in Oromo society, adequate studies are not available. Oromo intellectuals in Oromia still lack the political freedom to scientifically study and publish scholarly articles and books on the changes taking place in Oromo society. In addition, Oromo intellectuals in the diaspora do not have unfettered access to their society because of the restrictions on political freedom in Oromia and its surroundings. For almost three decades, the Oromo Studies Association (OSA) has functioned in the diaspora and is unable to hold its annual conferences in Oromia because of the lack of political freedom. Oromo intellectuals and activists do not have the political space in Oromia to collectively debate and decide the future of Oromo studies. Despite all of these problems, the Ethiopian colonial state has been unable to stop the development of national *Oromummaa* in the form of language, national culture, and ideology and identity in Oromia and beyond. Although there are a lot of internal and external forces that are trying to abort the development of *Oromummaa,* it is slowly and surely becoming a reality. In this context, providing some theoretical insights on the issues of *Oromummaa* and the Oromo national movement is ncessary.

The theory of *Oromummaa* as a backward- and forward-looking phenomenon combines all the processes for the purpose of facilitating the development of cognitive liberation for building Oromo national leadership and organizational capacity. Without cognitive liberation in Oromo political consciousness and behavior, it is impossible to fully develop national *Oromummaa*, which is the ideological foundation of the Oromo national movement.

Ideology plays many roles in a society; its essential function is to define and promote the political, material, and cultural interests of a group, nation, social class, state, or other entity. It also "offers an explanation and an evaluation of political, economic, and social condition; provides its holders a compass that helps orient them and develop a sense of identity; and tenders a prescription for political, economic, or social action" (Hybel 2010, 1). Therefore, it is a priority of the Oromo national movement to have clarity in its ideology, which *Oromummaa* provides. Theorizing *Oromummaa* in general and its different levels in particular is essential for increasing cognitive liberation and building consensus and the unity of purpose in the diverse leadership of the Oromo movement in order to consolidate its organizational capacity. Furthermore, the theory and practice of *Oromummaa* help in exposing the ideological fallacy of Ethiopianism (Jalata 2009), universalism, progress, modernity, development, civilization, and humanity that mainstream theories and knowledge use as a legitimating discourse in order to hide the massive human rights violations of indigenous peoples such as the Oromo and other subaltern groups by contributing to the perpetuation of unfreedoms such as underdevelopment, poverty, and suffering. By refuting the false claims of Ethiopians, which supports and promotes colonialism, national *Oromummaa* advocates freedom, social justice, national self-determination, and egalitarian multinational democracy for all peoples who are suffering in the Ethiopian Empire and beyond.

The theorization of *Oromummaa* requires at least five levels of conceptualization: at the first level, having a basic form of *Oromummaa* means to manifest Oromoness by practicing some aspects of Oromo culture, language, belief systems, values, norms, customs, and traditions. Whether an Oromo is politically conscious or not, she or he automatically develops this form of *Oromummaa* because of the influence of Oromo family and community institutions. Hence, every Oromo, if not totally assimilated to another culture, has the basic form of *Oromummaa*. At this historical moment, most Oromo have this kind of *Oromummaa*, and their national political consciousness is limited. On the basic level, most Oromo, except the totally assimilated ones, speak the same language called *Afaan Oromoo*, claim a common historical and cultural background, and face similar challenges of Ethiopian colonial terrorism, repression, cultural domination, exploitation, and humiliation. To a greater or lesser extent, most Oromo manifest basic *Oromummaa* in their cultural values, norms, and belief systems that have been encoded in and expressed by *Afaan Oromoo*, which unites all Oromo branches as one people/one nation. Therefore, the Oromo language is the main carrier of the essence and features of Oromo culture, tradition, history, and peoplehood. Since the Ethiopian colonizers have failed to destroy *Afaan Oromoo* and replace it by their own language, Amharic or Tigre, they have been unable to successfully suppress this most basic form of *Oromummaa*.

As a result, *Oromummaa* has survived in scattered forms for more than a century since the conquest of Menelik. According to Bonnie K. Holcomb (2002, 1), "The essence of colonization was the replacement of the values of *Oromummaa* as the overarching, integrating mechanism of the Oromo superstructure and replacing it with the ideology and the resulting institutions of Greater Ethiopia." *Oromummaa* as the total expression of Oromo peoplehood has developed from the historical, cultural, religious, and philosophical experiences of Oromo society. As a self and collective schema, *Oromummaa* encapsulates a set of fundamental beliefs, values, moral codes, and guiding principles that shape the Oromo national identity and make Oromo society different from other societies (Holcomb 2002, 1). Consequently, basic *Oromummaa* is built on personal, interpersonal, and collective connections. It is "a historically shaped form of knowledge that emerged out of the Oromo experience of several centuries of life and living (*jiruf jireenya*). . . [It has] served as a mechanism that built Oromo society in the past and left its unique mark upon the people, and their environment" (Holcomb 2002, 1). Similarly, other colonized and dominated peoples have basic essence and features that are the foundations of their cultures, histories, and identities. Every national group in the Ethiopian Empire must have its rights to national self-determination and to develop its identity and self-esteem without being subordinated to another national group or groups. The politics of liberation and democracy involves these fundamental rights that *Oromummaa* as both theory and practice promotes.

The Tigrayan-led Ethiopian minority government that claimed that it had allowed cultural autonomy for the Oromo and others actually opposed the manifestation of basic and other forms of *Oromummaa*. The Ethiopian colonialists have been attacking the individual psyche and biography of the Oromo, as well as their collective culture and history. These attacks have been carried out through various forms of violence, including colonial terrorism (Jalata 2011). In order to make the Oromo people submissive and control and exploit their labor and economic resources, successive Ethiopian governments have used different forms of violence that have resulted in genocidal massacres and societal and cultural destruction. Until national *Oromummaa* (the second level) emerged, basic *Oromummaa* primarily remained at the personal and interpersonal levels because the Oromo were denied the opportunity to form and maintain national institutions. They have been also denied a formal education and free institutional spaces by successive Ethiopian governments, which have not tolerated the existence of independent Oromo leadership, institutions, and organizations.

The Ethiopian colonialists have also expropriated Oromo economic resources and destroyed Oromo institutions, cultural experts, and leaders. Oppressors don't only want to control the oppressed economically, culturally, and politically; they want also to control their minds, thus ensuring the effectiveness of domination. The mental control of the oppressed causes personal and collective damage. The passivity of the majority of the Oromo and the mental enslavement of most Oromo collaborator elites are the major reasons why the Oromo people who comprise almost the half of the population in the Ethiopian Empire are brutalized, murdered, and terrorized by the minority Tigrayan elites. Most Oromo collaborators have lost their Oromo norms and values through the process of Amharization/Ethiopianization and suffer from an inferiority complex. Without the emancipation of Oromo individuals and groups from this inferiority complex and without overcoming the ignorance and the worldviews that the enemies of the Oromo have imposed on them, the Oromo collaborative class and the Oromo masses lack the self-confidence necessary to facilitate individual liberation and Oromo emancipation.

The Oromo collaborative elites who are opportunists or lack a sense of Oromo nationalism have become raw material in the hands of successive Ethiopian regimes and have participated in the implementation of their terrorist and genocidal policies. Ethiopian Colonialism was and is maintained by engaging in mental genocide, cultural destruction, and the assimilation of a sector of the Oromo population that has lost its basic sense of *Oromummaa*. The Ethiopian colonialists have denied the Oromo opportunities to develop the Oromo system of knowledge by preventing the transmission of Oromo cultural experiences from generation to generation. All these have been designed to uproot basic *Oromummaa* in order to produce individuals and groups who lack self-respect and are submissive and ready to serve the colonialists at the cost of their own people. Under these conditions, the Oromo basic needs and self-actualizing powers have not been fulfilled.

The Ethiopian colonialists have caused the physical death of millions, and further attempted to introduce social and cultural death to the Oromo by suppressing their basic *Oromummaa* and by preventing them from developing Oromo nationalism. Those who were born from Oromo families and lost their basic *Oromummaa* developed inferiority complex and self-hatred that Ethiopian colonialism had introduced to them, and they have becomes the tools of the Ethiopian state. Since the colonization of the Oromo, one of the goals of the Ethiopian state has been the destruction of an independent Oromo leadership; the Amhara-Tigrayan state has used both violent and institutional mechanisms to ensure that the Oromo remain leaderless. In addition, to ensure its colonial domination, the Ethiopian state has destroyed or suppressed Oromo institutions while glorifying, establishing, and expanding the Amhara-Tigrayan institutions such as government and Orthodox Christianity in Oromia and beyond.[5] This state has also sought to suppress Oromo history, culture, and language while promoting that of the Abyssinians. The main reason for suppressing or destroying the major Oromo institutions was to prevent the transmission of the Oromo system of knowledge and wisdom, the Oromo belief systems and cultural norms from generation to generation.

Because of Ethiopian colonialism, Oromo relational identities have been localized and not strongly connected to the collective identity of national *Oromummaa*. Consequently, the Oromo have been separated from one another and prevented from exchanging goods and information on a national level for more than a century, and their identities have been localized into clan families and colonial regions. They have been exposed to different cultures and religions and have adopted some elements of these cultures and religions because of the inferiority complex that Ethiopian colonialism introduced to them. The Oromo national struggle has tried to solve the internal problems of Oromo society by developing national *Oromummaa* before it can fully confront and defeat its joined external enemies. Ethiopian colonial history demonstrates that most Oromo collaborator individuals and groups have been king makers and have protected the Ethiopian Empire without seeking authority for themselves and their people. These collaborators have acted more Ethiopian than their colonial masters.

Since they have been cut from their individual biographies and the collective Oromo history, most members of the Oromo collaborative class have only known what the Amhara or Tigrayan elites have taught them and, as a result, they have constantly wore "Ethiopian masks" that have damaged their psyches. The colonizers have never been content with occupying the land of indigenous peoples and expropriating their labor and other resources; they have also declared war on the psyches of the oppressed (Fanon 1965, 65). As the European colonialists did, the Amhara-Tigrayan colonizers have manufactured the Oromo collaborator elites to use them in their colonial projects. The so-called Oromo People's Democratic Organization that was manufactured in Tigray and Eritrean jungles by the Eritrean and Tigrayan liberation fronts from Ethiopian war prisoners in the 1980s, just on the verge of the collapse of the Mengistu regime. This organization was owned, controlled, and used by the Tigrayan-led regime to brutalize, kill, and imprison as well as evict Oromo farmers through land dispossession. The Tigrayan and Eritrean elites probably learned form the Siad Baree regime of Somalia that created the so-called Somali Abo Liberation Front in the 1970s from Oromo refugees and Oromo-speaking Somalis wishing to colonize some Oromo regions. Since some Oromo elites who have passed through Ethiopian colonial institutions including schools and military have not yet achieved psychological and cognitive liberation, they consciously or unconsciously prefer to work for their Ethiopian colonial masters rather than working as a team on the Oromo liberation project.[6] Some Oromo intermediaries who have passed through the Ethiopian colonial education system have been de-Oromized and Ethiopianized, and have opposed the Oromo struggle for national liberation. Colonial education mainly creates some submissive leaders that facilitate underdevelopment through subordination and exploitation in Africa (Rodney 1972, 241).

Oromummaa as a conceptual and theoretical framework is elastic and expands to a political arena. Therefore, an Oromo, who has an *Oromummaa* as a national ideology, is somewhat different on the level of political knowledge and consciousness from other Oromo who did not yet develop this ideology or Oromo nationalism. The combined process of developing the Oromo nationalist ideology and engaging in the struggle for national self-determination is the second level of *Oromummaa*. Between the first and the second levels of *Oromummaa*, however, there is a stage of having political awareness. Most Oromo started to develop national political awareness in 1991, when the OLF joined the Transition government of Ethiopia dominated by the Tigrayan Liberation Front that was then supported by its Godfather, the Eritrean People's Liberation Front, the governments of Sudan and the United States. The West had been supporting the Tigray Liberation Front financially, militarily, and diplomatically.

At the second level, *Oromummaa* is seen as a nationalist ideology that attempts to mobilize the entire Oromo people to restore their national culture, history, identity, language, human dignity, and freedoms that Ethiopian colonialism has destroyed or suppressed for more than a century. At this level of *Oromummaa*, Oromo political awareness is transformed into Oromo nationalism and enables Oromo individuals, families, groups, and communities to comprehend the illegitimacy, evilness, and criminality of Ethiopian colonialism and to struggle for their national liberation. In other words, *Oromummaa* as the nationalist ideology empowers Oromo to build and strengthen their ideological determination, solidarity, and capabilities to define, defend, and struggle for the Oromo national cause. More or less, the ideology of national *Oromummaa* increases the determination of Oromo individuals, groups, and communities to be ready for paying a sacrifice of different forms and levels including sacrificing lives for the Oromo national cause. Basic sacrifices include joining Oromo associations, investing in Oromo material and intellectual products, and spending time, energy, and money to promote the Oromo national cause. Levels of sacrifices depend on the level of national *Oromummaa* consciousness as well as commitment.

There have been Oromo nationalists who have been killed or tortured and imprisoned while struggling to liberate their people and their country. We can list thousands of them from very young to very old and from women to men who have given their precious lives to further build national *Oromummaa*. Furthermore, there have also been thousands of Oromo who have been suffering in Ethiopian concentration and military camps and secret prison cells because they have manifested national *Oromummaa* or sympathized with or struggled for the Oromo cause. There are also thousands of Oromo who have escaped from the brutality of the Ethiopian government and who are suffering in refugee camps in different countries or settled in foreign countries. But, there are millions of Oromo who have not yet developed the national *Oromummaa* ideology and who are not involved in the Oromo national struggle even at the basic level. As already explained, there are also Oromo who have joined the enemy camps because of their political opportunism or lack of political consciousness or ignorance. The main reason for not involving in the Oromo national struggle or joining the enemy camps is the deficit of Oromo leadership and organizational capacity, which is necessary to raise Oromo political consciousness, develop national *Oromummaa*, and to stop those who are joining the enemy camps through different mechanisms.

Without developing the national *Orommummaa* ideology, it is impossible to raise Oromo political consciousness in order to organize and build a formidable leadership and organizational capacity that can challenge and defeat the Ethiopian colonial state that is supported by global powers and the imperial interstate system. *Oromummaa* as the Oromo nationalist ideology defines and promotes the Oromo political, material, and cultural interests in order to develop an Oromo political community and transform it into a state through destroying all powers and ideologies, mainly Ethiopianism, which have been keeping Oromo society under political slavery by all possible ways. According to Antonio Gramsci (1971), political domination is practiced through ideological hegemony. Ethiopianism as an ideological hegemony has been imposed on the Oromo via physical coercion including terrorism and mental genocide and other political and cultural mechanisms. All forms of domination, including colonial domination, cannot be practiced without imposing "a structure of meaning that [reflects] its leading beliefs, values, and ideas"(Hybel 2010, 8); the process through which the dominated internalizes the ideology, worldview, culture, and mentality of the rulers as natural order is called ideological hegemony.

In order to consolidate the Oromo national movement, it is necessary to recognize its current ideological inadequacies and overcome them. The triple ideological problems of the Oromo national movement are Ethiopianism and the failed ideologies of the East and the West that have victimized the Oromo.[7] *Oromummaa* as a theory of liberation refutes false or biased knowledge and challenges reactionary narratives that naturalizes and justifies colonialism and all forms of social hierarchies, injustices, and exploitation because it is mainly informed by the principles of egalitarian Oromo democracy of the *gadaa/siqqee* system. Furthermore, as a theoretical foundation of the Oromo national movement, *Oromummaa* with other critical theories enables the Oromo to engage in producing knowledge for critical thinking and liberation to promote egalitarian democracy. Despite the fact that the development of this theory is mainly based on the Oromo cultural foundation, it recognizes the importance of multicultural and critical knowledge and theories. Therefore, in developing the theory of *Oromummaa*, it is essential to use the critical aspects of the theories of resource mobilization, political process, and framing and social construction.

These theories recognize that social movements such as the Oromo national movement are caused by collective grievances, the availability of political opportunities, political consciousness, cognitive liberation, common interests, and social or group solidarity. Resource mobilization theory, despite its weaknesses, informs the Oromo national movement that economic, political, ideological, and cultural resources are essential for developing leadership and organization capacity in Oromo society. Particularly, the theory of political process recognizes factors such as the availability of material, intellectual, and cultural resources; the necessity of leadership and organizational capacity to mobilize resources for collective political action; the existence of pre-existing networks and institutions; and the rationality to participate in the collective action of social movements by weighing costs and benefits. The savagery of Ethiopian colonialism by brutally repressing and exploiting the largest national group, the Oromo, and other nations by limiting their educational opportunities has undermined the material, intellectual, and cultural resources that are a prerequisite for building strong and capable leadership and organizational capacity. In addition, by killing or imprisoning or forcing to live in exile, the Ethiopian colonial state has separated a few revolutionary educated Oromo intellectuals and activists from their society so that they cannot build their leadership and organizational capacity in their own society. The theory of *Oromummaa* attempts to make these criminal policies to be clearly understood by Oromo society and others who are truly interested in promoting human rights and democracy.

Depending on the theory of framing and social construction, the *Oromummaa* theory focuses also on micro-level analysis of Oromo cultural studies that help in understanding Oromo social psychology to know how to increase micro-mobilization through developing skills and knowledge. At this moment, our understanding of Oromo psychology is limited, and we need psychologists and other social scientists to study and explain what the majority of Oromo think about their national struggle on individual, group, or community levels in Oromia and beyond. By recognizing that collective actions are socially constructed and not naturally given, the theory of *Oromummaa* assists in studying and suggesting ways of constructing meaning and understanding the essence of collective and individual grievances, motivation, identity formation, and recruitment. The theory also helps in critically analyzing and understanding social structures and subjective factors such as cognitive liberation by clearly recognizing the role of ideas and political consciousness in minimizing political ignorance and fatalism for shaping collective action. It is only by cultivating Oromo political consciousness and building strong Oromo leadership and organizational capacity that the Oromo nation can survive the genocidal attacks it faces from its enemies and it can also liberate itself from colonial and imperial savagery of the twenty-first century.

Scholars who are engaging in Oromo studies from all social science disciplines need to mobilize their intellectual resources to assist in building national *Oromummaa* both in theory and practice to enable the Oromo national movement to fully develop its leadership and organizational capacity through acquiring required skills and knowledge and overcoming the deficit of capabilities. As we have mentioned above, unfreedms that the Ethiopian colonial state has imposed on Oromo society have underdeveloped Oromo human capabilities that are required to build an effective and free democratic society. In 2014, when the racist and murderous regime brutalized, tortured, and killed Oromo students and others who were resisting the colonial policies of the regime such as the so-called Addis Ababa Master Plan that the Oromo students called Master Genocide, the majority of Oromo were kept quiet in Oromia by the barrel of gun. This student protest movement, however, galvanized and united most of the Oromo in diaspora on a global level for the first time by overcoming their divisions and political passivity to demonstrate and support the Oromo protest struggle at home. This clearly shows that national *Oromummaa* is developing in the Oromo Diaspora although it is not yet translated into building leadership and organizational capacities on global level. As many times suggested by a few activist Oromo scholars, there is a need for forming a global Oromo activist network that may be called a global *Gumii* Oromia, which will coordinate Oromo political, cultural, and social activities in different continents, countries, regions, and communities to advance the Oromo national struggle.[8]

Of course, the Oromo nationalist ideology develops through political agitation and building leadership and organizational capacity. As we shall see below, attacking and dismantling the political ignorance, fatalism, and inferiority complex that have chained the minds of the majority of Oromo is the first step toward freedom because the Habasha state has no power to control the Oromo nation if substantial numbers of the nation develop cognitive liberation by developing the nationalist ideology of *Oromummaa* that is replacing the false claim of Ethiopianism. On the third level, *Oromummaa* encapsulates a repertoire of knowledge and values that are prerequisites for building Oromo national leadership and organizational capacity for mobilizing and organizing the nation to liberate itself from all forces of unfreedoms. The *Oromummaa*-based knowledge that can be called Oromo cultural capital reveals the importance of getting access to an Oromo knowledge bank, which has been accumulated for centuries in Oromo culture and traditions in order to facilitate the development of knowledge for liberation and cognitive liberation among Oromo society. Without having the knowledge for liberation that develops cognitive liberation, Oromo society cannot effectively struggle against the forces of unfreedoms. Also, national *Oromummaa* as a revolutionary ideology promotes the Oromo struggle to build horizontal organizations through dismantling gender and class hierarchies instead of vertical organizations that buttress injustices and exploitation. This cannot happen without creating and building the third level of *Oromummaa* that promotes a revolutionary liberation knowledge and cognitive liberation.

On the fourth level, *Oromummaa* as a national project mobilizes the nation to build its national culture, history, political economy, sovereignty, and ethos that are the markers and emblem of the Oromo nation. Developing this kind of project requires the knowledge of Oromo history and culture for many centuries, critically and thoroughly understanding Oromo and global politics, and predicting and assessing possible scenarios for the future of the Oromo nation. *Oromummaa* as the national project empowers the Oromo people to plan about the future of their society. Oromo nationalists not only need to know about the Oromo past and the current condition, but they also need to develop policies that will help them in developing Oromo national culture, ideology, and action. Based on the accumulated past traditions, knowledge, and wisdom, *Oromummaa* introduces an ideological and theoretical innovation and facilitates the emergence and development of new cultural elements. As Antonio Gramsci (1985, 325) explains, "Creating a new culture does not only mean one's own individual 'original' discoveries. It also . . . means the diffusion in a critical form of truths already discovered . . . and even making them the basis of vital action, an element of coordination and intellectual and moral order." In reviving the best Oromo cultural elements, "a critical form of truths already discovered," Oromo nationalist intellectuals have a central role to play; such scholars must unearth the Oromo past and provide a critical theoretical guidance for the future of Oromo society. Again, Gramsci (1985, 330) asserts that "one could only have cultural stability and an organic quality of thought if there had existed the same unity between the intellectuals and the simple as there should be between theory and practice. That is, if the intellectuals had been organically the intellectuals of those masses, and if they had worked out and made coherent the principles and the problems raised by the masses in their practical activity, thus constituting a cultural and social bloc."

Without being limited by disciplinary boundaries, Oromo intellectuals and others in the Oromo Studies Association (OSA) and beyond need to form research working groups, study circles, policy advocacy groups and other bodies to critically and thoroughly study Oromo national problems and produce various white papers that can be disseminated among Oromo communities in Oromia and the diaspora through various outlets. The Oromo people have been chained mentally and psychologically by Ethiopian ignorance, evilness, and darkness that must be smashed by the liberation knowledge of critical Oromo studies, which are based on Oromo indigenous knowledge and human-centric critical knowledge of the world. Oromo organic intellectuals need to develop white papers based on a series of research projects that can be presented to Oromo communities on various subjects such as cultural and social capital, *Oromummaa* and its various aspects, knowledge for liberation and cognitive liberation, sexism and gender equality, democracy and equity, regional and global politics, Habasha culture and politics, Oromo networks and national conventions, leadership and capacity building, Oromo national institutions such as *gadaa/siqqee, irrecha* or *ireessa*, religion and religious diversity, and state building and sustainable development. Mechanisms should be developed to encourage particularly the Oromo youth and women to participate on forums, workshops, discussion groups, and study circles.

A nation that excludes or oppresses its youth and women cannot achieve total liberation. In addition, programs of developing the talents of revolutionary Oromo artists must be developed because Oromo artists can contribute immensely in developing national *Oromummaa*. Buying their art products and attending their concerts to build their financial muscles are necessary. If we do not support them, our enemies can buy a few of these artists and demoralize those committed nationalist ones. Furthermore, Oromo literature in *Afaan Oromoo* and English should be supported so that Oromo-centric knowledge and knowledge for liberation can flourish and bring about cultural and intellectual renaissance to Oromo society. Similarly, there is an urgent need to support Oromo radio and TV stations and encourage them to spend more time in educating the Oromo people through developing their national *Oromummaa*, which will empower them mentally and culturally. All Oromo, particularly nationalist ones, have historical and national obligations to encourage and support all activities that will build Oromo national identity, culture and liberation ideology. The fifth level of *Oromummaa*, which can be called global *Oromummaa*, expands the principles of freedom, justice for all, national self-determination, and egalitarian multinational democracy beyond the Oromo nation.

Using the philosophy *safuu* (moral and ethical order), global *Oromummaa* promotes horizontal and democratic relations among various peoples who have been colonized and brutalized by the Ethiopian colonial state. Furthermore, since this *Oromummaa* is about uprooting unfreedoms and establishing a just, democratic, and peaceful society, the Oromo national movement is totally against revenge and hate of any peoples including the colonizing nations of Ahmara and Tigray. Therefore, the Oromo national movement also struggles to demonstrate to these oppressing nations the importance of organizing societies horizontally and democratically rather than hierarchically and dictatorially in order to establish durable peace and justice. This movement recognizes the significance of restoring the best cultural and democratic elements similar to *gadaa/siqqee* (Oromo democracy) in the colonized peoples in the Ethiopian Empire because they are the foundations of building an egalitarian democracy. Overall, the theory of *Oromummaa* focuses on building strategies and tactics for overcoming unfreedoms and the deficits of leadership and organizational capability.

OVERCOMING UNFREEDOMS AND DEFICITS OF CAPABILITIES

Unfreedoms are obstacles for the development of human capabilities (Sen 1999). Starting during the last decades of the nineteenth century, when the Oromo nation and others were colonized and incorporated into the Ethiopian Empire, the Oromo and other peoples have been prevented from sufficiently developing their human capabilities. These peoples have been almost denied free social arrangements and institutions that are necessary for creating and building institutions such as education by successive Ethiopian colonial regimes. The denial of a formal education to these societies has underdeveloped their leadership and organizational capacities, which are the main instruments to tackle the problem of unfreedoms such as ignorance, underdevelopment, and poverty. Underdevelopment involves lack of independence/autonomy to determine one's destiny; it is characterized by poverty, illiteracy, powerlessness, lack of democracy, social crises, and disasters such as famines and wars (Rodney 1972, 241). Most of members of these societies have been lacking freedom of choice, skills and capacity, freedom of knowledge production and dissemination, and creativity, etc.

In addition to the lack of freedoms, the Oromo and other colonized peoples are still denied improved material well-being because they are prevented from having free social arrangements and institutions that help in developing their free cultural capital that is necessary for enjoying equality of opportunity and quality of life. As underdeveloped and impoverished societies, they still do not have the power to freely determine their national destinies because they lack adequate leadership and organizational capacities and military technology to fight against their enemies. Colonial unfreedoms have denied the Oromo and others educational and technological capacity. The Habasha tormentors and their collaborators have expropriated the economic resources of the colonized peoples and their economies including land and other natural resources, and labor has been owned or controlled by the Ethiopian colonial state. Ethiopian colonialism and its unfreedoms have introduced to the Oromo and others not only exploitation, but have also destroyed their cultural capital and social capital. Pierre Bourdieu expanded Karl Marx's use of capital from a narrowly conceived economic category of monetary exchange for profit to cultural capital[9] and social capital to demonstrate how these categories can be forms of money capital that can be invested in offspring to secure benefits and upward generational and intergeneration mobility (Bourdieu 1986, 1–2).

Bourdieu (1986, 2) established the relationship among three forms of capital: "capital can present itself in three fundamental guises; as *economic capital*, which is immediately and directly convertible into money and may be institutionalized in the forms of private property rights; as *cultural capital*, which is convertible, on certain conditions, into economic capital and may be institutionalized in the forms of [position of power] and educational qualifications; and as *social capital*, made of social obligations ('connections'), which is convertible, in certain conditions, into economic capital and may be institutionalized in the form of a title of nobility." He notes that as unequal access to money capital perpetuates social inequalities, unequal access to cultural capital and social capital in their continual transmission or conversion into accumulation from generation to generation reproduce social inequalities. As they have lost all their freedoms by Ethiopian colonialism, the Oromo and other colonized peoples have also lost all these forms of capital by the same system. In most cases, the successes of individuals, groups, and nations do not necessarily depend on respective talent or intelligence, but mainly depend on having access to all forms of capital; individuals' achievements depend on cultural capital and social capital that are inherited from institutions such as families, schools, and others. Capital in the form of cultural and social are relational and they exist with other forms of capital since one form of capital can be converted into another form of capital.

All forms of capital are generated and transmitted through social processes from family to children and through other institutions and the larger society. Bourdieu explains that one of form capital can be converted into another form; economical capital can be converted into cultural capital and cultural capital can be transformed into economic capital or social capital as social capital can be converted into both. Bourdieu's theories of cultural capital and social reproduction primarily focus on the roles of family and educational institutions in reproducing class inequalities. However, here the concept of cultural capital is broadly used to include all mental products, including informal education, of Oromo and other societies that have been accumulated from generation to generation to improve its way of life. As already demonstrated, Ethiopian colonialism has been stagnating the cultural capital of the colonized societies to make them weak, ignorant, and passive in order to easily dominate and control them to exploit their labor and other economic resources. The Oromo national movement with other similar movements in the empire must realize this difficult problem and start to unlock and solve it through new ideas and critical scientific thinking that are based on critical studies. Ethiopian colonialism has kept Oromo and other societies in the sea of ignorance and deep poverty by denying them all these forms of capital for more than a century.

Ideology as an element of cultural capital plays a central role in convincing the dominant classes and groups and the dominated ones in a given social system by explaining social inequalities as naturally given that survives from generation to generation. According to Hussein Abdilahi Bulhan (1985, 123), "The oppressed is made a prisoner within a narrow circle of tamed ideas, a wrecked ecology, and a social network strewn with prohibitions. His family and community life is infiltrated in order to limit his capacity for bonding and trust. His past is obliterated and his history falsified to render him without an origin or a future. A system of reward and punishment based on loyalty to the oppressor is instituted to foster competition and conflict among the oppressed." Based on their hierarchical positions in societies, the dominant groups and classes establish the rules of engagement with the dominated groups and classes economically, culturally, and socially. Consequently, the Habasha elites, depending on their colonial ideology of Ethiopianism, have used different forms of capital to keep the Oromo nation and others in their prison empire of Ethiopia.

Ethiopian colonialism has perpetuated economic expropriation, and also has stagnated the cultural capital and social capital of the colonized peoples in order to perpetuate unfreedoms. The destruction of cultural and political institutions of these peoples and the denial of formal education to the majority members of these societies have undermined the cultural capital of these societies. In addition, the attack on their identities and the partitioning of these societies into colonial regions by giving them names that have no relevance to them have underdeveloped their social capital. Developing these societies politically and economically require political freedoms, which involve critical thinking and improved organizational skills. These political freedoms include the philosophy of struggling for social equality in the form of gender and class equality among Oromo society and other similar societies. There is no longer any doubt that if Oromo nationalists fully develop national *Oromummaa* as their revolutionary ideology, build their united leadership and organizational capacity, and effectively organize the Oromo masses and ally with the other colonized peoples, they can defeat and eject Ethiopian colonial forces and their collaborators from Oromia and other colonized regions within a short time.

The Oromo national movement not only needs to build its leadership and organizational capacity, but also needs to develop strategic visions and political plans for working with other colonized nations who are interested in implementing the principles of national self-determination and egalitarian multinational democracy. While Oromo nationalists engage in debates and dialogues for formulating policies that reflect their indigenous democracy, they must also develop political plans that they can share with other peoples who have similar interests for discussion, debate, and consensus building. As mentioned above, the Oromo nation can play a central role in implementing the principles of national self-determination and multinational democracy provided that it will effectively mobilize its abundant human and economic resources and ally with others to build their human capabilities. In developing leadership and organizational capacity, emphasis should be given to build organizations and institutions rather than promoting the egos and leadership of individuals to avoid the pitfalls of liberation fronts that won liberation wars but failed to build healthy and effective democratic societies. The disasters of the Eritrean and Tigrayan liberation fronts are living examples. They only won the wars against the Ethiopian state and eventually became its photocopy.

Developing a united, skillful, knowledgeable, and determined leadership that believes truly in democratic principles and hard work is very crucial for the advancement and success of the Oromo and other national movements in the empire. For Oromo society, without building the kind of leadership and organization that reflect the Oromo democratic and consultative traditions, it is impossible to effectively and fully develop national *Oromummaa* and mobilize and organize the Oromo to liberate themselves. The same is true for the other colonized societies. Those Oromo leaders who created the Macha-Tulama Self-Help Association and the OLF reflected some Oromo democratic and consultative traditions, although such traditions were gradually undermined with external pressures and internal crises in the Oromo national movement. If the colonized societies such as the Oromo cannot develop skills, knowledge, and capabilities to promote and exercise freedom and democracy while engaging in liberation struggles, they may not liberate themselves or they may inadvertently replace colonial dictatorships by national ones. Therefore, the Oromo liberation movement and other movements must start to practice freedom and democracy while struggling to overthrow Ethiopian colonial dictatorship. For example, in order to totally mobilize Oromo girls and women to actively participate in the Oromo struggle, the Oromo national movement must start dismantling the ideology of sexism and values of patriarchy.

Furthermore, the theory and practice of *Oromummaa* must enable all Oromo nationalists to engage in a politico-economic paradigm shift prior to liberation in order to build a free and democratic society. Similarly, the movements of the other colonized societies need to promote and implement similar strategies and tactics in order to establish an egalitarian multinational democracy. Amartya Sen (1999) identifies five factors for developing capabilities and freedoms in a given society; they are (1) *political freedoms*, (2) *economic facilities*, (3) *social opportunities*, (4) *transparency guarantees* and (5) *protective security*. All of these factors are combined to develop the general capacity of a person and a society. As Sen (1999, 10) notes, "Public policy to foster human capabilities and substantive freedoms in general can work through the promotion of these distinct but interrelated instrumental freedoms." *Political freedoms* involves political and civil rights, such as the right to determine who should govern and on what principles, the right to scrutinize and criticize authorities, the right of political expression and an uncensored press, and the freedom to choose between political leaders and organizations.

If the Oromo and other national movements cannot start these political freedoms now, it is impossible to practice them after liberation. The experiences of liberation movements in the world, including the Horn of Africa and their failure to build democratic societies, demonstrate this reality. The principles of economic freedoms also should be articulated while engaging in liberation movements. The principles of *economic facilities* oppose the control of market through state dictatorship and unregulated capitalism because they are undemocratic and corrupt. The Oromo people and others should struggle to form a state that should balance public and private ownership of the means of production in order to protect the respective national economic resources from the robbery of private forces in the name of the so-called free markets. The Oromo and other peoples should own their lands and natural resources. Balanced public and private economic agendas should involve the policies of freely participating in markets and generating wealth and public resources, the availability and access to finance, and utilizing economic resources for the purpose of consumption, production, or exchange, and allowing all citizens to have access to basic economic security and entitlement (Sen 1999, 10).

The principles of *social opportunities* deal with social arrangements such as education, employment, and health care; equal access to these services influences the individual's substantive freedom to live better and longer and increases more effective participation in socio-economic and political activities. The Oromo and other national movements must openly declare such policies to encourage their respective people to liberate themselves from the robbery of the Ethiopian colonial state and its regional and global supporters. In a truly democratic society there must be also *transparency guarantees* that allow individuals to have the freedom to openly and freely deal with one another, and the right to disclose and prevent corruption, financial irresponsibility, and underhand dealings. Furthermore, having *protective security* enables a society to enjoy access to a social safety net that protects people from abject misery, starvation, disasters, death, and disease. Theoretically speaking, the founders and members of the Macha-Tulama Association and the OLF envisioned to a certain degree the notion of developing national *Oromummaa* as a vision of Oromo liberation and sustainable development to enable the Oromo to have political freedoms and to achieve economic facilities, social opportunities, transparence guarantees, and protective security.

Based on these and other factors, the Oromo and other national movements should start to expand and develop such policies. Whenever they can, these movements must demonstrate that they are struggling to enable their respective people to regain all their freedoms and overcome their deficits in human capabilities. The struggle for empowering of the people is an endless process that goes beyond decolonization; these processes require constantly building institutional and instrumental freedom. Oromo nationalists and others must be sure that their country will be liberated if they are determined and work hard; they also need to develop policies that must be translated into actions based on the five factors that Sen has identified above to convince the people that their future will be free, better, and democratic. Particularly organic intellectuals in the Oromo Studies Association (OSA) and others should continue to theorize and develop national *Oromummaa* through formulating policies that will bring about a paradigm shift in Oromo studies in particular and the Oromo national movement in general. These intellectuals should also study other colonized societies in order to establish the commonality and differences of their interests with that of the Oromo.

CRITICAL OROMO STUDIES AND KNOWLEDGE FOR LIBERATION

One of the great successes of the Oromo national movement in the diaspora is the creation and development of OSA and its publications. Annual proceedings of OSA and the *Journal of Oromo Studies* are two important publications, which demonstrate the intellectual productivity of this organization. Furthermore, a few Oromo and other scholars who are members of this association have published many books and refereed articles in regional and international journals and refuted false or biased knowledge on the Oromo on regional and international levels. In this age of globalization, when knowledge and relevant information are becoming prerequisites for the successes of social and national movements such as the Oromo movement, do Oromo publications reach to the Oromo people to bring about cognitive liberation and social transformation? Does OSA facilitate among the Oromo the culture of reading, debating, thinking, and formulating serious policy issues?

Anybody who wants to advance the Oromo national cause must confront these difficult questions and seek correct answers. A society that does not have organic intellectuals that produce and disseminate knowledge for cognitive liberation cannot defend itself from savagery of colonialism and imperialism. When the previous generations of informally educated Oromo leaders between the sixteenth and nineteenth centuries built Oromo democracy and the *gadaa/siqqee* government and defended Oromo society from their enemies, the current generation of formally educated Oromo nationalists have not yet fully built the knowledge base for cognitive liberation for building Oromo leadership and organizational capacity to mobilize and organize the Oromo masses to liberate themselves. This reality shows that there is still a huge gap between Oromo nationalists and the majority of Oromo who are not participating in the Oromo national movement. Those few Oromo leaders who understood the complex problem of Oromo leadership have been easily eliminated because of their small number by the Ethiopian colonial state and surrounding states that have wanted to keep Oromo society in permanent servitude in order to control them and use their resources. Despite the fact that numbers of Oromo intellectuals live in exile, some of them are not actively participating in the Oromo national movement because of their low level of political development.

OSA did not yet develop mechanisms of increasing its membership and ways of packaging and disseminating the knowledge and information that it has been producing for almost three decades. It is the responsibility of OSA members and its leadership to find practical solutions through discussion, debate, and consensus building in Oromo society. Despite the fact that OSA was the product of the Oromo national struggle and has laid the intellectual foundation of the Oromo national movement, it did not yet build its capacity to disseminate liberation knowledge for developing cognitive liberation among Oromo society. Therefore, OSA needs to listen to Oromo society and make itself more relevant by developing critical Oromo studies that will look forward for solving the current problem of Oromo society. Despite the fact that the Oromo recognize the values of competence, intelligence, hard work, moral authority, patriotism, bravery, self-sacrifice, respect for the rule of law, and achievements because of their *gadaa/siqqee* tradition, in the contemporary Oromo society these qualities are dwindling. History demonstrates that all *gadaa* members and leaders emerged based on these values and other criteria, and these values and other criteria are also very important for now and the future.

It is very clear that Oromo intellectuals and political leaders have been pulled away from their people by the colonization of their minds, and they lack knowledge, experience, wisdom, and expertize of organizing their people. OSA must be a main platform to address and solve these complex problems of Oromo society. In order to further develop their national *Oromummaa* and develop their knowledge and skills for establishing organic unity with their society, Oromo intellectuals and political leaders and other activists should overcome their internalization of victimization, alienation, arrogance, individualism, and appreciate and promote the spirit of team or collective work by replacing the knowledge for domination and self-aggrandizement by the knowledge for liberation and emancipation, which is congruent with *gadaa/siqqee* values and principles. The restoration of such values and principles for liberation and emancipation in the Oromo movement is the product of "heroic courage and contributions of thousands of largely unsung heroes and heroines."[10] Organic intellectuals in OSA and beyond can play a central role in developing national *Oromummaa* as a national project to intensify the Oromo national struggle by increasing the participation of the Oromo people in their national struggle.

DISCUSSION AND CONCLUSION

Theorizing and conceptualizing *Oromummaa* on five levels help in knowing the differences among social, cultural, political, and ideological aspects of the Oromo national movement and in advancing the ideological and political clarity of the Oromo national struggle. Some Oromo confuse being Oromo and Oromo nationalists and claim that they have *Oromummaa* by birth. This is partially true because such Oromo have basic *Oromummaa*. But having this kind of *Oromummaa* cannot automatically make one a nationalist. As the national ideology of the Oromo national movement, national *Oromummaa* develops through knowledge for liberation, which facilitates cognitive liberation and political consciousness. *Oromummaa* as both theory and practice looks backward at Oromo history and culture for many centuries and also aims forward for suggesting mechanisms of building Oromo leadership and organizational capacity that emerges from the repertoire of liberation knowledge, skills, and wisdoms. The purpose of doing this is to consolidate the struggles for national self-determination and egalitarian multinational democracy with other colonized peoples who have similar objectives. There are collaborator Oromo and non-Oromo who claim wrongly that *Oromummaa* is necessarily an exclusive ideology. In contrary, the opposite is true.

These processes are not naturally given, but they are products of constant efforts and hard work. That is why the Oromo national struggle requires various levels of sacrifices including the ultimate sacrifice of dying for the Oromo national cause as other colonized peoples have been doing for their national causes. Consequently, the Oromo national movement has produced thousands of heroes and heroines who have sacrificed their lives to liberate their people and country despite the fact that there are millions of Oromo who are passive and neutral observers. Similar conditions exist in other colonized societies. The theory of *Oromummaa* informs us that although the Oromo national movement has achieved a lot, it will go a long way until the majority of the Oromo develop Oromo nationalism by recognizing the illegitimacy of the Ethiopian colonial state and its Oromo collaborators and join their national struggle. This theory also explains that the main reason why the minority Tigrayan-government ruled the numerical majority Oromo nation and others by its iron fist, despite its weaknesses and ideological bankruptcy, was the deficit of Oromo leadership and organizational capacity. Other colonized societies also lack these important elements at this historical moment. Successive Ethiopian states have denied a formal education to the majority of Oromo and other societies as well as butchered thousands of real and potential leaders to create leadership crises in these societies and to make them leaderless.

Of course, killing real and potential leaders did not stop the Oromo and others from struggling for their national liberation. Although the leadership and organizational deficits in these societies was initially caused by the savagery of Ethiopian colonialism and global imperialism that killed leaders and educationally and economically impoverished these societies, these problems currently continue to exist mainly because the elites of the Oromo and others did not yet form a united and consultative democratic leadership that reflects the democratic traditions of these societies. Another main reason is that these elites did not yet recognize the centrality of acquiring liberation knowledge that is essential in developing cognitive liberation. As a result, their efforts have been mainly based on trial and error and common sense that rarely lead to victory in the age of scientific revolutions and information technology. The theory of *Oromummaa* indicates that the Oromo nation and others can liberate themselves by uniting and mobilizing their human, cultural, intellectual and material resources through democratic and consultative leadership and by building the organizational capacity of the Oromo and other national movements. It also suggests that while solving its internal political problems and struggling for the Oromo liberation, the Oromo movement should develop and forward political proposals for other colonized nations and others in the Ethiopian Empire that are interested in implementing the principles of national self-determination and egalitarian multinational democracy in order to bring about permanent peace, sustainable development, and security in the Horn region.

OSA's division of labor is to engage in social scientific research to expand knowledge for liberation that is the foundation of the Oromo national struggle and liberation. In addition, the role of OSA is emphasized in developing and disseminating critical or liberation knowledge that is necessary for developing cognitive liberation in Oromo and other societies. This scholarly organization can produce variety of white papers that can help in formulating profound policies. Finally, the theory of

Oromummaa informs that the liberation of the Oromo nation and that of others are an inevitable fact that the Oromo people and others and their enemies should recognize. Young Oromo nationalists in Oromia have manifested their determination that has emerged from the development of national *Oromummaa*. Particularly, Oromo students who are dubbed as a *qubee* generation are leading the Oromo national protest struggle without any fear to take the Oromo national struggle to its final destiny through transforming national *Oromummaa* into a material force that unites all Oromo in their national movement.

The students of other colonized nations must join the Oromo students protest movements rather than passively watching the crimes that are perpetuated by the Ethiopian government and its collaborators. While the Oromo Liberation Army as lifeblood of the Oromo national struggle is mainly working in rural Oromia, the Oromo student movement is intensifying its protest struggles in urban areas. Overall, the theory of *Oromummaa* has articulated the necessity for building leadership and organizational capacity to unite all Oromo forces for the Oromo liberation struggle and to build alliances with the movement of other colonized societies in the Ethiopian Empire. While the four levels of *Oromummaa* described above deal with the internal issues of Oromo society, the fifth level of *Oromummaa* illustrated how the Oromo national movement builds the unity of purpose and alliance with other colonized societies who are struggling for national self-determination and egalitarian multinational democracy.

NOTES

1. These colonized and oppressed nations include the Sidama, Annuaks, Ogaden-Somali, Hadiya, Nuer, and others. The oppressed Amharas and Tigrayans who are not part of the Ethiopian colonizing structures can be part of the egalitarian multicultural democratic project by rejecting the colonial ideology of Ethiopianism, which has perpetuated colonial terror, underdevelopment, poverty, and famine in the Ethiopian Empire and beyond for more than a century.

2. For the better understanding the ideological problem of the Oromo national movement, see Asafa Jalata and Harwood Schaffer, "*Gadaa/Siqqee* as the Fountain of *Oromummaaa* and the Theoretical Base of Oromo Liberation," *Journal of Oromo Studies* 21(1), 2014.

3. For further understanding, see Asafa Jalata and Harwood Schaffer, "The Oromo, *Gadaa/Siqqee* and the Liberation of Ethiopian Colonial Subjects," with Harwood Schaffer, *AlterNative: An International Journal of Indigenous Peoples*, 9(4), 2013, 277–295.

4. Through imposing unfreedoms at gun point, Ethiopian colonialism tried to erase *Oromummaa* (Oromoness) from the minds of the Oromo by giving the Oromo derogatory names such as Galla, which they hated and tried to run away from it by taking the religious name of Christianity or Muslim or clan names or taking the identities of others like that of Amharas, Tigres, Adares, Somalis, or Gurages. In these processes, several millions of Oromo had lost their culture and identity and took that of others.

5. Ethiopian settler colonialism established five institutional arrangements in Oromia in order to tightly control Oromo society and intensify its exploitation: (1) garrison

cities and towns, (2) slavery, (3) the colonial landholding system, (4) the *nafxanya-gabbar* system (semi-slavery), and (5) the Oromo collaborative class. The colonialists were concentrated in garrison cities and towns and formulated political, economic, and ideological programs that they used to oppress their colonial subjects. The settlers expropriated almost all Oromo lands, and forced most Oromos to work on these lands without payment. The Oromo intermediaries were used in subordinating the Oromo people to the colonial society. Many people were enslaved and forced to provide free labor to the colonial ruling class, and others were reduced to the status of semi-slaves to provide agricultural and commercial products and free labor for their colonizers.

6. What Walter Rodney says about the consequences of the colonial educational system in Africa also applies to the situation of Oromo intermediaries: "The colonial school system educated far too many fools and clowns, fascinated by the ideas and way of life of the European capitalist class. . . . Some reached a point of total estrangement from African conditions and the African way of life . . . 'Colonial education corrupted the thinking and sensibilities of the African and filled him with abnormal complexes.'" Walter Rodney, *How Europe Underdeveloped Africa* (Washington, DC: Howard University Press, 1972), pp. 248–249.

7. The Oromo national struggle is taking place when the modern world system is at a crossroads, and when the modernization perspective of the West and the so-called socialist/communist model of the East have drastically failed in the peripheral part of the world such as Oromia, Ethiopia, and the Horn of Africa. On one hand, the modernization theory that has claimed that all societies would gradually develop by becoming "modern" under the leadership of powerful capitalist countries is proved to be false and a self-serving ideology of Western countries and their client states in the rest of the world. On the other hand, the socialist perspective that has asserted that since the capitalist world system has been reactionary and exploitative and it should be overthrown by a revolutionary means under the leadership of the working class dictatorship has become a version of the modernization model and ended up in failure in the peripheral part of the world.

As the policies of the West, particularly that of the United States, have promoted colonialism, neocolonialism, and dictatorship and contributed to underdevelopment and gross human rights violations in peripheral areas of the world such as Oromia and Ethiopia, the policies of the former Soviet Union and currently that of China have contributed to the same problems in the Ethiopian Empire. For the Oromo both the capitalist and the socialist ideological and theoretical models have contributed to their colonization, terrorization, and impoverishment.

8. For example, listen to the interview made by Abdujalil Abdalla on Voice of Oromia-KFAI Radio, Minneapolis, Minnesota, on 06/08/2014. The interviewee was Asafa Jalata on his paper titled "The Need for Forming of Oromo Global Activist Networks Known as Gumii Oromia."

9. Pierre Bourdieu (1986, 2) identifies three forms of cultural capital: "in the *embodied* state, i.e., in the form of long-lasting dispositions of the mind and body; in the *objectified* state, in the form of cultural goods . . . and in the in the *institutionalized* state, a form of objectification which must be set apart because . . . in the case of educational qualifications, it confers entirely original properties on the cultural capital which is presumed to guarantee."

10. Quoted in Richard A. Couto, "Narrative, Free Space, Political Leadership in Social Movements," in *The Journal of Politics*, 55(1), 1993, 58.

SIX

Gadaa/Siqqee as the Fountain of *Oromummaa* and the Theoretical Base of Oromo Liberation

With Harwood Schaffer

Every society has its unique central organizing and ruling ideology[1] and theoretical models in a given historical epoch that it uses as its lenses to look at and interpret the world and to survive freely and advance its civilization or ways of life without disruption from within and without. Ideology plays many roles in a society, and its essential function is to define and promote the political, material, and cultural interests of a group, a nation, a social class, a state or other entities (Hybel 2010, 1). Before the Oromo were colonized, they had also their central organizing and ruling ideology and theoretical models that were embedded in the *gadaa/siqqee* civilization that organized and guided them as a society socially, culturally, religiously, politically, militarily, and economically. We advance the idea that without retrieving and developing the best elements of this civilization, the Oromo cannot fully develop *Oromummaa* (national culture, identity, and ideology) as their organizing and central ideology and their theoretical models of liberation to empower themselves as a nation in the twenty-first century by recognizing and overcoming the devastating ideologies, behaviors, and theoretical models of their oppressors that have confused and disempowered them.

Oromo nationalists that are proud of the Oromo democratic tradition of the *gadaa/siqqee* and their egalitarian principles need to critically and adequately study and ideologically and theoretically incorporate the best elements of this tradition to their nationalist narratives and practices. Oromo intellectuals have uncritically adapted the knowledge, theories, and ideologies that they have learned from colonial education that include mainstream theories such as modernization and oppositional theories such as Marxism that do not neatly fit to the Oromo condition need to critically learn about their democratic tradition. We argue that the major reason why the national movement has not yet developed a coherent ideology and organization emerges from the contradictions between the ideologies and theories that the movement has uncritically borrowed and the *gadaa/siqqee* ideology and theory that the Oromo masses manifest in their daily lives. Without developing an *Orommummaa* ideology and *gadaa/siqqee* theoretical models that will appeal to the ordinary Oromo, it is very difficult to raise their political consciousness, organize them, and build a formidable institutional and organizational capacity that can challenge the Ethiopian colonial state that is supported by global imperialism and the imperial interstate system.

Oromo foremothers and fathers who resisted foreign domination and exploitation and who preserved the reservoir of Oromo cultural and historical knowledge had translated their experiences into collective action by building a national movement that started to manifest itself in the Bale armed struggle, the birth and growth of the Macha-Tulama Self-Help Association, the cultural and artistic renaissance of the Affran Qallo Oromo, and the galvanization of these cumulative experiences into the birth and survival of the Oromo Liberation Front (OLF). Prominent Oromo nationalist leaders such Waqo Gutu, Elemu Qilxu, Haile Mariam Gamada, Alemu Qixeesa, Mamo Mazamir, Baro Tumsa, and others had played key roles in building institutions and organizations and the Oromo national movement and in writing Oromo history with their suffering and blood. Tens of thousands of Oromo heroines and heroes who have followed these giants have built the Oromo national movement by sacrificing their precious lives for the liberation of the Oromo. The current generations of Oromo nationalists are still killing and dying in the forests of Oromia and cities and others are suffering in prisons and concentration camps to defend the national rights of their people. Imagining the liberation of the Oromo nation and fearing its potential, the Ethiopian colonial state and the new and old colonial settlers are attacking Oromo nationalists to destroy Oromo nationalism and to continue their terrorist and colonial practices in Oromia.

The Oromo national movement is engaged in the politics of liberation that is rooted on Oromo values, beliefs, ideas or ideologies, and culture that reflect the Oromo national identity and political interests. All these cultural and ideological aspects are encapsulated and manifested in *Oromummaa*. *Oromummaa* as the Oromo national ideology defines and promotes the Oromo political, material, and cultural interests to develop an Oromo political community and transform it into a state through destroying all powers and ideologies, mainly Ethiopianism (Jalata 2009), that have been keeping the Oromo society under colonialism and political slavery by all possible ways. Ethiopianism has been imposed on the Oromo via physical coercion including terrorism and mental genocide. All forms of domination, including colonial domination, cannot be practiced without imposing "a structure of meaning that [reflects] its leading beliefs, values, and ideas" (Hybel 2010, 8); the process through which the dominated internalizes the ideology, worldview, culture, and mentality of the rulers as natural order is called ideological hegemony by Gramsci. The triple ideological problems of the Oromo national movement are Ethiopianism and the failed ideologies and theories of the East and the West in the Horn of Africa that have victimized the Oromo people and other peoples.

THE INADEQUACY OF BORROWED IDEOLOGIES AND THEORIES

The Oromo national struggle is taking place when the modern world system is at a crossroads, and when the modernization perspective of the West and the so-called socialist/communist model of the East have drastically failed in the peripheral part of the world such as Oromia, Ethiopia, and the Horn of Africa. On one hand, the modernization theory that has claimed that all societies would gradually develop by becoming "modern" under the leadership of powerful capitalist countries (So 1990) is proved to be false and a self-serving ideology of Western countries and their client states in the rest of the world. On the other hand, the socialist perspective that has asserted that since the capitalist world system has been reactionary and exploitative and it should be overthrown by a revolutionary means under the leadership of the working class dictatorship has become a version of the modernization model and ended up in failure in the peripheral part of the world (Frank 1966).

As the policies of the West, particularly that of the United States, have promoted colonialism, neocolonialism, and dictatorship and contributed to underdevelopment and gross human rights violations, the policies of the former Soviet Union and currently that of China have contributed to the same problems in the Ethiopian Empire (Jalata 2011). For the Oromo, both the capitalist and the socialist ideological and theoretical models have contributed to their colonization, terrorization, and impoverishment. Western countries, particularly England, France, Italy, and later the United States, and the so-called socialist countries, mainly the former Soviet Union and China, have supported the successive colonial governments of Ethiopia and immensely contributed to the dehumanization and the suffering of the Oromo and other colonized and oppressed peoples. So the question is: what has happened to the West's proclaimed liberal democracy and the protection of human rights and the East's socialist rhetoric that have claimed to eliminate injustices and exploitation under the dictatorship of the working class?

The Oromo case demonstrates that the idea that the West would advance capitalist development, liberal democracy, and human freedoms and rights in the rest of the world is intended to hide the crimes committed against humanity in different corners of the world by states and transnational corporations. In the capitalist civilization, dominant ethnonations, classes, corporations, institutions, and powerful individuals who have controlled state power for the last five hundred years have created and maintained two sides of the same world: One of version this world is "heavenly" or paradise, and the other one is "hellish" or torturous. The process in the capitalist world system that has created and maintained the wealthier and healthier societies is metaphorically called above heavenly has also produced the impoverished and suffering societies both in the West and the rest through various forms of violence and continued subjugation. The conditions of indigenous Americans, Australians, Oromos, Palestinians, and others demonstrate this reality (Jalata 2013).

Out of about a 7 billion world population, more than "three billion people live on less than two dollars a day. . . . Eight hundred and forty million people in the world don't have enough to eat. Ten million children die every year from easily preventable diseases. AIDS is killing three million people a year and is still spreading. One billion people in the world lack access to clean water; two billion lack access to sanitation. One billion adults are illiterate. About a quarter of the children in the poor countries do not finish primary school" (Easterly 2006, 8). Most of these impoverished and suffering peoples are the descendants of colonial subjects. Those rich and powerful classes and well-to-do ethnonations ignore the devastating consequences of absolute poverty and associated violence on the indigenous and stateless people in the world. The Oromo as one of the colonized and stateless peoples are one of the most impoverished, uneducated, and suffering colonial subjects (Jalata 2010a). They are also denied basic political, social, and civil rights that are essential to expand their human capabilities and freedom and democracy; achieving these capabilities assist them to define their social and economic needs by actively increasing their agency and their human creativity and potential to collectively solve their problems by overcoming their ignorance, fatalism, and powerlessness by critically understanding the roles of social and political systems.[2]

In the capitalist world system, the processes of societal destruction and construction have occurred and been maintained through various forms of violence and other mechanisms (Jalata 2016). The ways of the colonial state formations and the destruction of indigenous peoples have simultaneously occurred. Despite the fact that those who have created and maintained this kind of unjust world have claimed to promote justice, democracy, security, fairness, the rule of law, equality, fraternity, and human rights, the processes that we have mentioned above have continued. Religious ideologies such as Christianity and Islam and the political ideologies of democracy and socialism could not help in overcoming human greediness and ethnonational/racial, class, and gender hierarchies and oppression that have been established and maintained through various forms of violence including terrorism and genocide. In fact, these ideologies are sometimes used to hide terrorism, genocide, and gross human rights violations. Most people, including the Oromo, still cling to these failed ideologies and theories because "every individual is . . . in a two-fold sense predetermined by the fact of growing up in a society: on the one hand he [or she] finds a ready-made situation and on the other he [or she] in that situation performed patterns of thought and of conduct" (Mannheim 1936, 3). By using the ideologies and theories of the oppressors, however, human groups cannot bring about a fundamental social transformation to change their deplorable conditions.

What is disappointing about humanity is that one time the so-called revolutionaries and progressive forces that engaged in promoting the ideology of revolution as an emancipatory project had changed their minds after they captured state power in the former Soviet Union, China, and other the so-called socialist countries and started to develop state capitalism to accumulate more capital/wealth at any cost. These countries implemented their ideological and economic policies through all forms of violence including terror, torture, and genocide as imperialist countries have done. Alexander Dallin and George W. Breslauer (1970, 111–112) note that "political terror is one of the essential instrumentalities at the service of" the so-called socialist system, and the system has "a monopoly of ideology and organization by the ruling elite, as well as its control of all relevant assets—organized force, economy, communications, arts, and science."

As the system of the West, the so-called socialist system has combined dictatorship, all forms of violence and repression, and gross human rights violations[3] and has drastically failed to implement what it promised. As powerful capitalist countries and their collaborators have practically opposed liberal democracy in poor countries, the so-called socialist countries have worked against democracy, equality, and social justice. Without an egalitarian democracy and popular participation of ordinary people, a society cannot build a better society. Knowingly or unknowingly, most Oromo nationalists are influenced either by the failed ideologies of liberal democracy or by the aborted ideology of socialism. Above all, the Oromo national movement is going on when the capitalist world system is facing deep crises because of its ideological and cultural crises, when the models or perspectives of capitalism and socialism have failed in the peripheral part of the world, when religious fundamentalism in the form of Christianity or Islam is flourishing, and when the future of this world system is not clear. All these factors raise fundamental ideological and theoretical challenges to the Oromo national struggle. As Karl Mannheim (1936, 108) asserts, "Crises are not overcome by a few hasty and nervous attempts at suppressing the newly arising and troublesome problems, nor by flight into the security of a dead past. The way out is to be found only through the gradual extension and deepening of a newly won insights and through careful advances in the direction of control."

The engineers of the capitalist world system have used modernization theory, Christian absolutism, and the claim of Euro-American racial and/or cultural superiority to explain and justify the capitalist civilization that they have constructed and maintained on the destruction of world indigenous peoples (Jalata 2016). The liberation and development of indigenous peoples like the Oromo is impossible under these conditions because "development requires the removal of major sources of unfreedom: poverty as well as tyranny, poor economic opportunities as well as systematic social deprivation, neglect of public facilities as well as intolerance of or over activity of repressive states. Despite unprecedented increases in over all opulence, the contemporary world denies elementary freedom to vast numbers—perhaps even the majority—of people" (Sen 1999, 3–4). The Oromo who enjoyed an egalitarian democracy, although not perfect, prior to their colonization have been denied all forms of freedom by successive Ethiopian colonial governments and their global supporters. Unfortunately, the harsh socio-economic and political conditions are also making the Oromo the targets of Christian and Islamic fundamentalists. Consequently, currently there are Oromo who are abandoning their culture and nationalism and imitate Franjii (Westerners) or Arab fundamentalists by claiming religious commitment and focusing on the life-after-death. Explaining the significance of religious fundamentalism due to the failure of the modernist projects of capitalism and socialism, Tariq Ali (2003, 67) notes, "By the end of the twentieth century with the defeat of secular, modernist and socialist impulses on a global scale, a wave of religious fundamentalism swept the world."

Above all, the modern capitalist system is changing very fast and drastically; existing national and international institutions, such as states, international organizations, and transnational corporations are incapable of adequately dealing with the emerging cultural, political, ecological, economic, and technological challenges. Those who are immensely benefiting from the current system are trying to maintain status quo by using all forms of violence, including terrorism, and those who want reform or change are engaging in all forms of resistances and different forms of social movements that deal with issues of ethnonational/racial problems as well as environmental and human rights issues. At the same time, religious fundamentalists, mainly Christian and Islamic fundamentalists, try to pull back the wheel of history to return societies to what they call "golden eras." However, since most people know about such golden eras, some fanatics and true believers buy their narratives. "Antiquated and inapplicable norms, modes of thought, and theories are likely to degenerate into ideologies," Karl Mannheim (1936, 95) writes, "whose function it is to conceal the actual meaning of conduct rather than to reveal it."

The fast changes that are taking place currently include developments in communications and information technologies that collapse space and time, changes in military technology and the nature of warfare, changes in political and economic structures, processes of environmental degradation and the possible depletion of natural resources, unbalanced imperial interstate relations, and the declining of the legitimacy of national and supranational governance, the emergence of national and global forces as anti-systemic movements, and the failure or inadequacy of some peripheral states because of their lack of domestic legitimacy and external interventions (Robinson 1996; Hirst 2001). Similarly, the Oromo national movement is confronted with global ideological and religious crises, and, consequently, Oromo political and intellectual leaders and organizations lack an ideological roadmap and a coherent theoretical model. The attempts of Oromo nationalists and leaders to uncritically borrow certain ideologies and theoretical models from the West and other societies without knowing the social and cultural history, worldview, philosophy, and political thought of their people have created a very dangerous situation for the survival and liberation of the nation in the twenty-first century.

PRACTICING *GADAA/SIQQEE* AND DEVELOPING *OROMUMMAA* AND THE THEORY OF LIBERATION

In their history, the Oromo have lived under two forms of socio-political orders: The first one was sovereign, democratic, more or less peaceful and secure although not perfect. The Oromo liberation ideology and theoretical model must emerge from these socio-cultural and historical foundations. Before they were colonized during the last decades of the nineteenth century, the Oromo were governed by an egalitarian democratic order called the *gadaa/siqqee* system that encapsulated all aspects of Oromo cultural, political, military, social, and economic, religious, and philosophical perspectives. According to Mannheim (1936, 85–86), "Knowledge, as seen in the light of the total conception of ideology, is by no means an illusory experience, for ideology in its relational concept is not at all identical with illusion. Knowledge arising out of our experience in actual life situations, though not absolute, is knowledge nonetheless. The norms arising out of such actual life situations do not exist in a social vacuum, but are effective as real sanctions for conduct." The second one has been a colonial order characterized by terror, physical and mental genocide, political slavery, illiteracy, and impoverishment.

By committing "the genocide of the mind," (Moore 2003) the intellectual perspectives of the colonialists and imperialists have misled Oromo intellectuals and nationalists to ignore their indigenous socio-cultural foundations and borrow the theoretical and ideological models of the East or the West that do not have relevance for the Oromo situation. Since the Oromo people have not been adequately represented in academic, media, and government institutions, their voices have been muzzled and hidden and most people, including Oromo students, are still misinformed and know little about the Oromo and their institutions. Explaining the similar conditions of indigenous Americans, MariJo Moore (2003, xv) argues that the colonialists and their descendants have committed "genocide of the mind" on the surviving indigenous Americans "to destroy and/or misrepresent the histories, futures, languages, and traditional thoughts of Native peoples." Similarly, the Habasha colonialists not only occupied the Oromo country, but they have also controlled the Oromo mind and framed the way Oromo think, act, and behave. Consequently, some Oromo still identify themselves with Ethiopians knowingly or unknowingly and work against the Oromo national interest ideologically, politically, militarily, and culturally.

Oromo nationalists need to achieve total mental liberation by overcoming the devastating effects of the genocide of the mind that Ethiopian colonialism and global imperialism have imposed on them. After studying many forms of civilizations, we have reached the conclusion that *Oromummaa* that is based on the best elements of the *gadaa/siqqee* civilization, worldview, egalitarian democracy, and justice for all can help Oromo nationalists to overcome the ideological and theoretical confusions that attempt to hijack or abort the Oromo struggle for liberation, sovereignty, peace, and security. Since there are many external and internal forces that directly or indirectly stifle the development of *Orommummaa* through undermining the restoration of *gadaa/siqqee*, what should the genuine Oromo nationalists do? *Gadaa/siqqee* are the central sources of Oromo politics, philosophy, wisdom, worldview, moral values, ethics, laws, and customs from which *Oromummaa* flows and develops as the intellectual, ideological, and theoretical powerhouse of the Oromo nation. Since Oromo nationalism is not yet fully grounded in *gadaa/siqqee*, it is corrupted by alien ideologies and theories that contradict the Oromo fundamental values and democratic principles.

Because of such corruption and the lack of a clear ideological and theoretical approach, the Oromo national movement is currently stifled and misused by misguided Oromo and other forces that are against the Oromo national interest. However, those determined Oromo nationalists are engaging in the liberation struggle, defending Oromo civic institutions, and providing the values that have allowed a new generation of activists and leaders to challenge the Ethiopian colonial system. Consequently, the Ethiopian rulers commit wide scale level of human rights violations on the Oromo and others. These abuses are testament to the fear that is in the hearts of the Tigray and Abyssinian leadership. But, imprisonment, torture, death, and suffering did not prevent Oromo nationalists from fighting for the rights of their people. Therefore, we are more convinced that Oromo nationalists who are determined to advance the Oromo liberation and emancipation must return to the source of the *gadaa/siqqee* civilization that still survives in the minds and hearts of the ordinary Oromo. As Amilcar Cabral (1973, 61) notes, "the question of a 'return to the source' or of a 'cultural renaissance' does not arise and could not arise for the masses of these people, for it is they who are the repository of the culture and at the same time the only social sector who can preserve and build it up and *make history*."

Since the Oromo society has been the repository of *gadaa/siqqee* principles and practices, between 1991 and 1992, when the OLF appeared on the Ethiopian political platform by joining the Tigrayan-led Ethiopian Transitional Government, hearing about democracy and *gadaa* and seeing *odaa* (Sycamore) on the OLF flag, the majority of the Oromo supported this organization claiming *kayyoon deebitee* (our freedom returned). Unfortunately, the OLF had no adequate strategies and tactics and organizational capacity to use *gadaa/siqqee* principles and practices in organizing and empowering the Oromo people to struggle for their liberation and emancipation as a nation. Using these weaknesses as a political opportunity and realizing and fearing the Oromo political potential, with the support of Eritrea and the West, particularly the United States, the Tigrayan People's Liberation Front (TPLF) and its surrogate organizations attacked the OLF and diminished its capacity, humiliated the Oromo people, postponed the Oromo liberation and emancipation, and continued Ethiopian colonialism under the Tigrayan leadership.

Although a lot of progress has been made in developing *Oromummaa*, now the Oromo national movement must focus on the mental liberation of the Oromo people to fundamentally break the colonization of their minds and enable the entire society to own and engage in their own liberation and emancipation project rather than being passive observers and reluctant supporters. This is only possible by fully developing *Oromummaa* by restoring *gadaa/siqqee*, building civic organizations, and improving Oromo political culture. *Oromummaa* is above the individual, regional, and religious identities; it is the foundation of Oromo survival, and without it, the Oromo cannot practice their culture and religions freely and promote their national interests. Based on the accumulated past traditions, knowledge, and wisdom, *Oromummaa* also introduces an ideological and theoretical innovation and facilitates the emergence and development of new cultural elements.

In reviving the best Oromo cultural elements and diffusing "a critical form of truths already discovered" Oromo nationalist intellectuals have a central role; such committed scholars must unearth the Oromo past and provide a critical theoretical guidance for the development of *Oromummaa*. Antonio Gramsci (1985, 330) asserts that there should be "between the intellectuals and the simple [ordinary people] as there should be between theory and practice. That is, if the intellectuals had been organically the intellectuals of those masses, and if they had worked out and made coherent the principles and the problems raised by the masses in their practical activity, thus constituting a cultural and social bloc." Recognizing the role of committed intellectuals at this time of tribulation in the Oromo national struggle, some Oromo nationalists demand that the Oromo Studies Association should find a solution by participating in the struggle.

The Oromo recognize the values of competence, intelligence, hard work, moral authority, patriotism, bravery, self-sacrifice, respect for the rule of law, and achievements; these values emerge from their *gadaa/siqqee* traditions. However, they are decreasing in the contemporary Oromo society. History demonstrates that all *gadaa/siqqee* leaders emerged based on these values and other criteria, and these values and other criteria are also very important for now and the future. Unfortunately, some of these qualities are missing in most Oromo intellectual and political leaders today. These Oromo leaders are challenged to maintain organic unity with fellow Oromo to further flourish *Oromummaa* through developing political consciousness, coherent ideology and theory, and worldview. It is very clear that Oromo intellectuals and political leaders have been pulled away from their people by the colonization of their minds, and they lack knowledge, experience, wisdom, and expertize of organizing their people.

In order to develop their *Oromummaa* and develop their knowledge and skills for establishing organic unity with their society, Oromo intellectual and political leaders and other activists should overcome their internalization of victimization, alienation, arrogance, individualism, and appreciate and promote team or collective work by replacing the knowledge for domination and self-aggrandizement by the knowledge for liberation and emancipation, which is congruent with *gadaa/siqqee* values and principles. The restoration of such values and principles for liberation and emancipation in movements are the product of "heroic courage and contributions of thousands of largely unsung heroes and heroines."[4] We know a few names of those leaders who ignited the fire of *Oromummaa* by sacrificing their precious lives, but we do not know the names of thousands Oromo nationalists who have been killed or assassinated, tortured, punished by life imprisonments, crippled or blinded, and raped by the enemies of the Oromo people.

In Oromia, the main roadblock for restoring *gadaa/siqqee* and developing *Oromummaa* is the Ethiopian colonial government that has imposed political slavery on the Oromo by denying them the freedom of organization and association for more than a century. But, the Ethiopian government did not or does not have absolute power to prevent the Oromo people from organizing themselves because Oromo nationalists could create the Macha-Tulama Self-Association in the early 1960s openly and the Oromo Liberation Front in the early 1970s clandestinely. Hence, the Oromo have the power to organize civic and political organizations in Oromia clandestinely, despite the brutality of the Ethiopian political system, and in the diaspora openly and intensify the Oromo national struggle. So why don't the Oromo have effective civic institutions and political organizations both at home and in the diaspora today?

BUILDING MORE EFFECTIVE CIVIC INSTITUTIONS AND POLITICAL ORGANIZATIONS

Oromo nationalists need to address the following four major issues to build more effective institutions and organizations. First, Oromo nationalists need to recognize the importance of civic culture and institutions and avoid subordinating them to politics. Strong independent civic institutions can democratically challenge the Oromo political leadership and force them to make a transparent and accountable decision. Without a strong civic national association, Oromo nationalists do not have a platform for national debate and discussion to build national consensus. Second, building *Oromummaa* as a national culture, nationalism, and an ideology is absolutely necessary for consolidating more effective national institutions and organizations. Third, the Oromo need to develop a clear national self-image based *Afaan Oromoo* (the Oromo language) on *gadaa/ siqqee* democracy. Every society is organized and functions around its dominant preferred self-image, which is determined by its dominant forces; this self-image unites a people or a nation as an identifiable entity (Cormack 1992, 12). According to Mike Cormack (1992, 12), "A society undergoing crisis, particularly a crisis over which groups should dominant, will manifest competing self-images, but one must eventually become accepted as the dominant image or else the society will lose its coherence." The dominant self-image creates "the core of a framework of interlocking concepts (such as democracy, liberty, morality, justice. . . . These concepts take their place in linguistic and social practices, which provide the means by which any member of that society can produce meaning and thereby communicate with other members of the society" (Cormack 1992, 12).

The ideological self-image on which all Oromo agree is Oromo democracy know as *gadaa/siqqee* and *Afaan Oromoo* that must be recognized and celebrated in the national ideology of *Oromummaa*. Ideology mainly works in two ways: Social cement and social control. As social cement, ideology is the social force that binds society together by providing a framework in which social action can happen; as social control, ideology has a more direct and coercive effects on social actors by focusing on policing the social structure of a society. Consequently, the development of national *Oromummaa* facilitates the consolidation of the Oromo unity and stops those forces that undermine this unity from within and without. National ideology such as *Oromummaa* "is a process which links socio-economic reality to individual consciousness. It establishes a conceptual framework, which results in specific uses of mental concepts, and gives rise to our ideas of ourselves. In other words, the structure of our thinking about the social world, about ourselves and about our role within that world, is related by ideology ultimately to socio-economic conditions" (Cormack 1992, 13).

The Oromo nationalist ideology and national culture cannot be built on simple emotions without the restoration of the best elements of the Oromo traditions such as the *gadaa/siqqee* and their democratic principles and the rule of law. The borrowed ideologies of modernization and Marxism could not effectively help in organizing the Oromo society. If Oromo activists and politicians want to promote the Oromo national interest, they do not have choice except becoming organic intellectuals that know their own traditions and develop them intelligently and borrow other models that may help in facilitating the liberation and emancipation of the Oromo society. Fourth, existing Oromo institutions such as churches and mosques are not Oromo-centric and they focus on the life-after-death as well as on the culture, ideology, and values of the West and the Middle East respectively. The Reverend Dr. Martin Luther King criticized this position by combining the social and otherworldly gospel in leading the Civil Rights Movement in the United States and by expressing that the church has an obligation to deal with moral and ethical issues in society as "the voice of moral and spiritual authority on earth" and as "the guardian of the moral and spiritual life in the community" (King 1967, 96). He seriously criticized the white church for ignoring its social mission and supporting American apartheid, colonialism, the racial caste system, and the underdevelopment of Black America. Like Martin Luther King, Jr., the Reverend Gudina Tumsa without fear of death stood up against Ethiopian colonialism and dictatorship without hiding under the ideology of Christian fundamentalism. The Ethiopian military regime imprisoned and killed him. At this moment, the Oromo do not have other Gudina Tumsas from the Oromo Christian Church in Oromia.

As Martin Luther King did, Malcolm X developed revolutionary Black nationalism and challenged the white establishment in the United States by mobilizing the African American material, intellectual, and ideological resources and tried to develop a new direction for the African American struggle. His Islam religion did not prevent him from fighting for the liberation of his people. He insisted that African Americans should rethink their past experience by recognizing the importance of history and criticism and by overcoming "the confusion and inaction which resulted from the internalization of the racist ruling class's view of the world."[5] The Oromo also had revolutionary religious Muslim scholars such as Sheik Bakari Saphalo who died in a refugee camp in Somalia and Dr. Sheik Muhammad Rashad Abdulle who recently passed away. Such Oromo nationalist religious scholars are almost absent in the Oromo society today. Currently, both Christian and Islam fundamentalists misdirect young Oromo men and women by focusing on the otherworld or life-after-death at the cost of ignoring the Oromo national struggle. In reality, all European Christians and almost all Muslims have their own countries that they rarely share with co-religionist refugees. If Christian and Islamic fundamentalists believe in what they teach, they should have struggled against their own governments and their geopolitical boundaries to open them for other peoples. So, why do they teach and mislead innocent Oromo with something they do not believe in? How can Oromo nationalists mobilize their people to organize and enable them to take collective action to liberate themselves?

THE TRANSITION FROM PASSIVISM TO COLLECTIVE ACTION

We know that the Oromo were effectively organized in all aspects of life and maintained their sovereignty, security, and peace for many centuries until they were colonized. So, what factors have prevented them to repeat this history? The Oromo can repeat similar history by building national civic institutions and an effective political organization or organizations that can raise their political consciousness or *Oromummaa* and organize them to fight for their liberation and emancipation. Without effective civic institutions, political organizations, and an effective military establishment, a society cannot defend itself from those who are organized and ready to attack, terrorize, and kill them to expropriate their resources.

Almost all the Oromo love *gadaa/siqqee* because they empowered them to have political freedom and their country. In the early 1990s, most Oromo believed that the OLF would repeat this reality because it restored some *gadaa* symbols and declared about democracy, the sacred principle of the Oromo nation. After bringing hope to the Oromo people between 1991 and 1992, the OLF was attacked and weakened by the TPLF, Eritrean and Western powers because it could not build an organizational capacity both politically and militarily. Furthermore, because of the ideological and political immaturity of the Oromo political elites and the absence of strong national leadership that could build the OLF through dialogue and national consensus, the organization that the Oromo people thought as the rebirth of *gadaa/siqqee* was partitioned and owned by self-proclaimed leaders who started to see themselves as organizations. In addition, several elites started to create their mini-organizations to seek political power rather than empowering the Oromo people.

When millions of Oromo openly joined the Oromo People's Democrat Organization of the Tigrayan People's Liberation Front (TPLF) without any fear and shame, most of the Oromo have become passive and demobilized. Consequently, the TPLF had engaged in terrorism, genocide, and expropriation of Oromo lands and other resources. The TPLF was doing all these crimes against the Oromo not because of its strength, but because Oromo institutions and organization were weak and fragmented. One would expect that Oromo nationalists would recognize the dangers from the TPLF and work in collective to overcome their conflicts and divisions through national dialogue and consensus based on the Oromo democratic traditions and revolutionary commitment. So, what should the Oromo nationalists do now to overcome public passivism and institutional and organizational ineffectiveness in the Oromo society?

The raising of *Oromummaa* consciousness and formulating the theory of liberation to build on institutional and organizational capacity in order to empower the Oromo nation require some committed, determined, and hardworking nationalists who are ready to sacrifice their intellectual and material resources and when it is necessary even their lives. Such nationalists must engage in rebuilding Oromo national civic institutions and political organizations based on the rule of law and *gadaa/siqqee* principles to enable the Oromo people to acquire all forms of freedom. The Oromo national struggle is about social development and "expanding human freedoms" (Sen 1999). Identifying institutions and instrumental freedom that advance "the general capability of a person," Amartya Sen (1999, 10) notes five types of freedom, namely "(1) *political freedoms*, (2) *economic facilities*, (3) *social opportunities*, (4) *transparency guarantees* and (5) *protective security*."

Sen explains *political freedoms* as political and civil rights that include the right to determine who should govern and on what principles; the right to scrutinize and criticize leaders; the right to political expression and uncensored press; and the right to choose between political parties. He sees *economic facilities* as free participation in markets and generation of wealth and public resources, the open access to finance, the utilization of economic resources for the purpose of production, consumption, or exchange, and basic economic security and entitlement. *Social opportunities*, according to Sen, involve social arrangements such as education and health care and influence the individual's substantive freedom to live better and to increase more effective participation in socio-economic and political activities that are absolutely necessary to overcome unfreedoms. Furthermore, having *protective security* involves a social safety net that protects people from misery, starvation, death, and disease. What Sen calls *transparency guarantees* help in preventing corruption, financial irresponsibility, and underhand dealings by creating the freedom to be open and honest to deal with one another in civic institutions and political organizations. The Oromo national struggle attempts to enable the Oromo people to build civic and political institutions that will restore all forms of their freedom by expanding their human freedoms that the Ethiopian colonial state has successfully denied them.

Ethiopian colonialism and global imperialism have exposed the Oromo people to terrorism, gross human rights violations, famines, undernutrition, morbidity, premature mortality, and denied them access to health care, clean water or sanitary facilities, and education. To overcome all these unfreedoms, the Oromo national movement must build strong civic and political institutions and organizations to take a decisive collective political action. Explaining the necessity of institutions for societies, Sen (1999, 142) states the following: "Individuals live and operate in a world of institutions. Our opportunities and prospects depend crucially on what institutions exist and how they function. Not only institutions contribute to our freedoms, their roles can be sensibly evaluated in their contributions to our freedom. To see development as freedom provides a perspective in which institutional assessment can systematically occur."

We believe that Oromo nationalists must reinvent the Macha-Tulama Self-Help Association and the OLF based on *gadaa/siqqee* principles, and they cannot afford to be divided into different small institutions and political organizations that follow different political trajectories. Above all, all Oromo nationalists who left the OLF and formed other organizations should engage in an open national dialogue and consensus building to resolve existing political contradictions and try to reinvent the OLF based on the principles of *gadaa/siqqee* and *Oromummaa*. Furthermore, Oromo communities should build independent associations in the diaspora and in Oromia that will be linked to national institutions and organizations without being subordinated. The Oromo must avoid subordinating their associations to political organizations to avoid past mistakes. For example, the OLF misused the political goodwill of the Union of Oromo Students in North America in the 1990s because its members agreed to be its mass association. When the OLF opened its office in Washington, DC, it started to discredit and disorganize the union. Independent associations and civic institutions can stop political organizations from making serious strategic and tactical blunders. If the Oromo had strong associations and institutions, they could have prevented the Oromo national movement, particularly the OLF, from making tragic mistakes in the 1990s and later.

DISCUSSION AND CONCLUSION

History demonstrates that the survival of a people depends on their collective consciousness, organization, and the capacity to militarily defend themselves from their common enemies that would like to subjugate them or commit genocide on them to expropriate their homeland and other resources. Consequently, the survival and liberation of the Oromo mainly depend on the capacity to fully develop *Oromummaa* that is enshrined in *gadaa/siqqee* principles to restore their accumulated historical and cultural knowledge for developing strategies and tactics for liberating Oromia. In other words, the Oromo must fully develop *Oromummaa* as their national ideology and power in order to have economic, military, and organizational resources that are required for empowering the nation and restoring the Oromo state. According to Michael Mann (1993, 9), "The struggle to control ideological, economic, military, and political organizations provides the central drama of social development."

In order to defeat Ethiopianism and its colonial structures and determine their national destiny, the Oromo must first develop *Oromummaa* as their national ideological power. According to Mostafa Rejai (1984, 3–4), ideology covers five dimensions, namely the cognitive, the affective, the evaluative, the programmatic, and the social base. *Oromummaa* as the cognitive dimension helps in understanding the social and political conditions of the Oromo; as a national ideology "it appeals to sentiments and strives to elicit an emotional response from its followers . . . 'what gives ideology its force is its passion . . . in fact, the most important, latent, function of ideology is to tap emotion." Ideology justifies or denounces an existing social and political order; in its attempt to advance an alternative order, it "is designed to . . . transform an existing social and political order; it attempts to evoke a sense of rage, injustice, and moral protest against its counterparts" (Rejai 1984, 3–4).

Similarly, *Oromummaa* as the embodiment of the *gadaa/siqqee* democratic principles exposes the crimes of Ethiopianism and promotes freedom and justice. The programmatic dimension of ideology "focuses on how each ideology strives to translate values into active commitments. Each ideology sets forth . . . a hierarchy of values and objectives, and each sometimes includes statements of priorities identifying immediate, intermediate, and ultimate goals" (Rejai 1984, 3–4). In the same fashion, *Oromummaa* provides a plan of action in implementing Oromo democratic values and revolutionary commitments in the Oromo national movement. As every ideology has its social-base dimension to have mass appeal, *Oromummaa* has the Oromo national base that it mobilizes for action. The transformation of Oromo resistance struggles to form the Macha-Tulama Self-Help Association in the early 1960s and the OLF in the early 1970s and the objectives of the Oromo struggle for liberation and emancipation are still correct and have yielded some results for the Oromo nation. The central objective of the Oromo struggle has been the empowering of the Oromo people to determine their destiny by having their political power reflect and practice *gadaa/siqqee* principles.

The attempt to delegitimize the objectives of the Oromo liberation from without and within in the names of the pseudo-objectives of democracy, citizenship, and federation violate the vision of *Oromummaa* that is engrained in the *gadaa/siqqee* philosophy, values, and practices. The Oromo do not request democracy, self-determination, and sovereignty from the Ethiopian colonial state since they can only achieve them through fully developing *Oromummaa* and building the national organizational capacity based on the best elements of their traditions. Borrowing ideologies without clearly developing *Oromummaa* and formulating a theory of liberation based on the Oromo democratic tradition, the Oromo national movement cannot overcome its current ideological crises and political paralysis. *Oromummaa* celebrates the Oromo collective self-interest that is built on the foundation of Oromo social and political institutions. When Oromo nationalists do not understand that the individual and the collective self-interests of the Oromo are interconnected, they ignore to engage in civic engagement for public or greater good of the Oromo society assuming that they can achieve their individual interests. When an Oromo takes this position, he or she develops an essentially destructive ideology and develops a rapacious and predatory interest at the cost of other Oromo.

Civic engagement helps in going beyond a narrow circle and transcending the private by engaging with a wider Oromo public for the Oromo national interest. It refers to "people's connections with the life of their communities" (Putnam 1995, 665) through building trust among diverse individuals by overcoming their suspicions and isolations. "Trustworthiness lubricates social life. Frequent interaction among a diverse set of people tends to produce a norm of generalized reciprocity. Civic engagement and social capital entail mutual obligation and responsibility of action" (Putnam 2000, 21). Increased trust, social contact and interaction further develop and widen "our awareness of the many ways in which we are linked" and increase "tolerance and empathy" (Putnam 2000, 288). Just mere connections are not enough for building trust, but there must be the capacity for civic engagement through participation in giving speeches, running meetings, managing disagreements, and bearing administrative responsibilities (Putnam 2000, 66). The connections based in trust involve friendship, respect, truth, charity, humanity, liberty, patriotism, benevolence, brotherly and sisterly love, justice, and fairness (Skocpol 2003, 116).

Political activism and civic engagement play two essential roles in society: First, they help identify and overcome weaknesses of social institutions and social interaction. Second, they empower citizens by overcoming a failure of institutions (Levine 2011, 7). They must be practiced on a common denominator. Civic engagement and the development of *Oromummaa* are interconnected. *Oromummaa* must be built on a common ground since the Oromo people are a diverse and multi-religious society.

"The more enduring and the more basic the common ground, the more substantial the connection; the more we identify with what is, or is felt to be, essential in the other, the more meaningful we experience our connection to be. When this more essential identification develops, then we no longer relate as strangers. We feel secure in the connection with the other and less alone in a world of people who are essentially different from us" (Levine 2011, 169).

While the Oromo are fully developing *Oromummaa*, engaging in civic action, and building institutions, they can build alliance with other colonized and oppressed peoples who are struggling for national liberation. The Oromo nationalists should realize that in addition to developing their central ideology of *Oromummaa* and building organizational capacity recognize that "[v]ictory has often come to the side of the actor with the deepest commitment to a cause and the greatest capacity to withstand exceedingly high costs for lengthy periods" (Hybel 2010, 199). The Oromo national movement must struggle to establish popular power and self-government by going beyond official or elite democracy and by engaging in the process of "democratic imagination" to expand the knowledge of democracy.[6] Recognizing the failure of official or elite democracy in promoting equity and justice for all peoples in the West and the rest of the world, James Cairns and Alan Sears (2012, 1–23) see democracy as "an open question" and propose the struggle to promote "democracy from below" in order to empower people to achieve collective self-government, to fundamentally change society, and to promote the principle that real democracy emerges from genuine equity. Oromo democracy and democracy from below are synonymous since they include political, social, and economic equity and justice.

NOTES

1. For further discussion on ideology, see Karl Mannheim, *Ideology and Utopia: An Introduction to the Sociology of Knowledge*, translated from the German by Louis Wirth and Edward Shils (New York: A Harvest/HBJ Book, 1936); Mike Cormack, *Ideology* (Ann Arbor: The University of Michigan Press, 1992); Alex Roberto Hybel, *The Power of Ideology: From the Roman Empire to Al-Qaeda* (New York: Routledge, 2010).

2. For more discussion of the importance of freedom and democracy, see Amartya Sen, *Development as Freedom* (New York: Knopf, 1999), pp. 146–159.

3. Contrary what they promised, the policies of these countries resulted about 20 million deaths in the former USSR, 65 million in China, 1 million in Vietnam, 2 million in North Korea, 2 million in Cambodia, 1 million in Eastern Europe, 150,000 in Latin America, 1.7 million in Africa, 1.5 million in Afghanistan, and 10,000 deaths in other places—in total about 100 million deaths. This is historical tragedy that has dashed the hope of humanity. China is currently engaging in imperialism and the exploitation of as many poor countries as Western countries by extending its domestic policies. See Stéphane Coutois, N. Werth, Jean-Lous Panné, et al., *The Black Book of Communism: Crimes, Terror, Repression* (Cambridge: Harvard University Press, 1999), p. 4.

4. Quoted in Richard A. Couto, "Narrative, Free Space, Political Leadership in Social Movements," in *The Journal of Politics*, 55(1), 1993, 58.

5. "Preamble, Statement of the Basic Aims and Objectives of the OAAU," in George Breitman, *The Last Year of Malcolm X: The Evolution of a Revolutionary* (New York: Merit, 1967), p. 43.

6. For detailed discussion of "the democratic imagination," see James Cairns and Alan Sears, *The Democratic Imagination: Envisioning Popular Power in the Twenty-First Century* (Toronto: The University of Toronto Press, 2012).

SEVEN

The Oromo Movement

The Effects of State Terrorism and Globalization in Oromia and Ethiopia

The Oromo movement is engaging in a struggle to empower the Oromo people to restore control of their economic and cultural resources and to overcome the effects of Ethiopian state terrorism and globalization. The Oromo people were colonized and incorporated into Abyssinia/Ethiopia and the capitalist world system during the "scramble for Africa" by the alliance of Ethiopian colonialism and European imperialism (Jalata 2005, 2015). The Oromo resistance that started with the colonization of the Oromo developed into the anti-colonial movement of the 1960s and still continues in various forms. Successive colonial Ethiopian governments have been using various forms of violence to destroy the Oromo struggle for national self-determination. Starting in 1992, and with the assistance of big powers and international institutions, the Tigrayan-led Ethiopian government had been imposing state terrorism, genocide, and political repression on the Oromo, the largest ethnonational group, as well as other groups. The regime had tried its best to destroy the Oromo national movement, led by the Oromo Liberation Front (OLF), and to dominate the political economy of Oromia (the Oromo country) and Ethiopia in order to transfer economic resources, particularly land, to Tigrayan state elites and their supporters.

This chapter first provides some historical background. Second, it outlines theoretical and methodological approaches to this topic. Third, it explains the role of big powers in supporting the Ethiopian colonial state at the cost of democracy and human rights in order to promote "savage development" (Quan 2012) or "violent development" (Rajagopal 2003) in the age of neoliberal globalization. This section also explores how the Tigrayan-led Ethiopian government and its international supporters were using the discourses of democracy, human rights, and economic development at the same time as they terrorized the Oromo and other indigenous peoples and dispossessed them of their rights, ancestral lands, and natural resources. Fourth, the chapter explains how the ongoing peaceful mass protest movement emerged in Oromia, how and why the regime was violently cracking down on protestors, and why the West was facing a political dilemma regarding its support of a government that was openly massacring peaceful protestors to repress dissent. Finally, the chapter explores the larger political and economic consequences of the Oromo peaceful protest movement in bringing about a fundamental transformation to the political economy of Oromia and Ethiopia.

BACKGROUND

The Ethiopian colonial terrorism and genocide that started during the last decades of the nineteenth century with the assistance of England, France, and Italy still continue in the twenty-first century with the support of global powers (Jalata 2010a). Menelik terrorized and colonized the Oromo and others to obtain commodities such as gold, ivory, coffee, musk, hides and skins, and slaves and lands. He controlled the slave trade (an estimated 25,000 slaves per year in the 1880s), owned together with his wife 70,000 enslaved Africans, and became one of the richest capitalists of the country: "The Abyssinian ruler had extended the range of his financial operations to the United States, and [was] a heavy investor in American railroads . . . with his American securities and his French and Belgian mining investments, Menelik [had] a private fortune estimated at no less than twenty-five million dollars" (*New York Times*, November 7, 1909).

The Ethiopian colonizers massacred the Oromo people and their leadership (Bulatovich 2000, 68). The surviving Oromo were forced to face state terrorism, genocide, political repression, and an impoverished life. The Ethiopian colonial state introduced a process of forced recruitment of labor (Holcomb & Ibssa 1990, 135) and developed the *nafxanya-gabbar* (semi-slavery) system, whereby the *nafxanya* (gun holder) had absolute power over the *gabbars* (Oromo semi-slaves). The *nafxanya-gabbar* system was established to coerce Oromo farmers to provide the colonial settlers with food, labor, and tax revenues both in cash and in kind (Jalata 2005, 88). Between 1935 and 1941, Italian colonialism, the scarcity of *gabbars*, and the development of agro-capitalism gradually undermined this system. The Haile Selassie government consolidated colonial institutions and practices before and after Italian colonialism. Although the military regime that emerged in 1974 under the leadership of Colonel Mengistu

Haile Mariam uprooted the *nafxanya-gabbar* system by nationalizing the land, it continued state terrorism, dictatorship, and the violent repression of political resistance.

The military regime had committed massive human rights violations in the 1970s and 1980s in the name of the so-called revolution with the assistance of socialist countries such as the former Soviet Union and its satellite countries. As Norman J. Singer (1978, 672–73) notes, those who were killed during the initial three months of

> the campaign of the "Terror" . . . numbered around 4000–5000 in Addis Ababa alone; the killings continued in March 1978, spreading to the rest of the country. . . . Those detained for political instruction numbered from 30,000 upwards. . . . Torture methods . . . included severe beating on the head, soles of the feet . . . and shoulders, with the victim hung by the wrists or suspended by wrists and feet from a horizontal bar . . . sexual torture of boys and girls, including pushing bottles or red-hot iron bars into girls' vaginas and other cruel methods.

In 1980, as one Oromo source reported, "the Oromo constitute the majority of the more than two million prisoners that glut Ethiopia's jails today."[1] In the 1980s, thousands of Oromo activists or nationalists were murdered or imprisoned. The military government terrorized the Oromo population by holding mass shootings and burying them with bulldozers:

> Over years this procedure was repeated several times. When the method did not work and the Oromo population could not be forced into submission, other methods were used. The victims were made to lie down with their heads on stone, and their skulls were smashed with another stone. . . . When the Oromo movement could not be quenched by shooting or by the smashing of skulls, [the government] came up with a new idea. Men's testicles were smashed between a hammer and an anvil. (Hasselblatt 1992, 17–19)

As explained below, in the following years Ethiopia has continued its oppression of the Oromo people with the assistance of global powers such as Great Britain, the United States, the former Soviet Union, and China.

THEORETICAL AND METHODOLOGICAL CONSIDERATIONS

This work combines a structural approach to globalization, neoliberalism, and capital accumulation with a social constructionist model of human agency. In the era of neoliberal globalization, in the name of democracy, development, and human rights the Ethiopian state and its global supporters have been engaging in dispossessing lands and other resources of the Oromo and others while repressing social movements and terrorizing civil society. Some scholars have described capitalist/socialist development as a process of "violent development" or "savage development" (Quan 2012, Rajagopal 2003). Balakvi Shohen Rajagopal (2003, 3) explains "the realization among social movements and progressive intellectuals that it is not the lack of development that caused poverty, inflicted violence, and engaged in destruction of nature and livelihood; rather it is the very process of bringing development [to indigenous peoples] that has caused them in the first place." Claiming to be promoting development, the Ethiopian colonial state and global institutions such the World Bank and the International Monetary Fund (IMF) have joined in implementing policies that massively violated the human rights of indigenous peoples through the dispossession of lands, forced resettlements, and the destruction of livelihoods and cultures (Oakland Institute 2013, 2014, 2015).

Understanding the complex, dynamic interplay between repressive political structures and human agency requires a critical approach that combines a bottom-up perspective with an analysis of the long-term and large-scale global social changes identified by the world system theory. In particular, serious attention should be given to the role of the Oromo social movement in resisting the global and regional imposition of colonialism and neoliberalism and in promoting an alternative option of development, self-determination, and multinational democracy. The Oromo have been denied basic aspects of their humanity since they were forced to enter into the global capitalist world system via slavery and colonialism, which were facilitated by the alliance of Ethiopian dependent colonialism and global imperialism (Holcomb & Ibssa 1990). The capitalist world powers and their regional or local collaborators have used superior military forces to enslave and colonize pre-capitalist societies in order to exploit their labor power and/or dispossess their economic resources through coercion, terrorism, looting, piracy, genocide, annexation, and continued subjugation.

The development of global capitalism and the accumulation and concentration of capital or economic resources through the separation of the producers from their means of production such as lands led to the racialization/ethnicization and socialization of labor (Marx 1967 [1932], 17). The processes of expropriation of land, racial slavery, and settler colonialism resulted in the total or partial destruction of indigenous peoples such as indigenous Americans, Australians, and others (Jalata 2011), justified through the creation of an elaborate discourse of race or racism (Jalata 2012; Malik 1996). Since the 1970s, with the intensification of a crisis of capital accumulation and the declining of the US hegemony in the capitalist world system, the Western world under the leadership of the United States has started to promote a new economic formation known as neoliberalism, whose "fundamental mission was to facilitate conditions for profitable capital accumulation on the part of both domestic and foreign capital" (Harvey 2005, 7). In the name of development, neoliberal globalization has continued state terrorism and massive human rights violations that had started during direct colonialism: "Over the last fifty years, millions have been uprooted from their homelands, communities have been destroyed, and the environment has been desecrated in the process of transforming 'traditional' or 'peasant' economies into 'modern' economies. Many more millions have been the subject of state and private violence in the name of modernization and development" (Rajagopal 1999, 16).

Accumulation of capital by dispossession involves state terrorism and genocide, as the case of the Oromo illustrates (Jalata 2011). State terrorism can be defined as the systematic practice of violence against a given population group with the goal of eliminating any form of political struggle by destroying the group's leaders and culture of resistance. States that fail to establish ideological hegemony are unstable and insecure; hence, they engage in state terrorism (Oliverio 1997, 48–63). Bruce Hoffman (2006, 40) defines terrorism as "the deliberate creation and exploitation of fear through violence or the threat of violence in the pursuit of political change. . . . Terrorism is specifically designed to have far-reaching psychological effects beyond the immediate victim(s) or object of the terrorist attack." As the Oromo national movement has continued to resist the criminal policies of the Ethiopian government, the regime has intensified its acts of terrorism and dispossession with the support of Western powers, the emerging powers of China, India, and some Arab countries, as well as international institutions such as the World Bank and the IMF. Because the international system, particularly the United Nations, lacks a single standard for defining humanity in a practical sense, countries such as Ethiopia get away with the crimes they commit against their own citizens and other peoples (Jalata 2011).

Although the United Nations theoretically recognizes the problems of state terrorism and genocide, it has not yet developed effective policies and mechanisms to prevent them because powerful countries and their client states that commit crimes against humanity have dominated this international body. Article II of the United Nations Convention defines genocide as "acts committed with intent to destroy, in whole or in part, a national, ethnical, racial or religious group"; similarly, Frank Chalk and Kurt Jonassohn (1990, 23) define genocide as "a form of one-sided mass killing in which a state or other authority intends to destroy a group, as that and membership in it are defined by the perpetrator." These authors identify two major types of genocide. The first type is used to colonize and maintain an empire by terrorizing those perceived as real or potential enemies; in this case, the main purpose of genocide is to acquire land and other valuable resources. The second type of genocide, called ideological genocide, takes place because the maintenance of colonial domination by state elites requires the establishment of cultural and ideological hegemony; by destroying elements of a population that resist colonial domination, hegemony can be established on the surviving population. Kurt Jonassohn (1998, 23) notes that ideological genocide develops "in nation-states where ethnonational groups develop chauvinistic [and racist] ideas about their superiority and exclusiveness."

GLOBAL POWERS AND THE NEOCOLONIAL ETHIOPIAN STATE

Ethiopia maintained its neocolonial status in the global order with the help of British global hegemony until the United States inherited this role in the mid-twentieth century. As it replaced Great Britain as the global hegemonic power after World War II, the United States used the Horn of Africa for its strategic interest during and after the Cold War (Jackson 2018). Because of its interest in the region, the United States was receptive to Ethiopian requests for support and sent a technical mission in 1944 to help build the Ethiopian political economy. The Haile Selassie government and its officials effectively used the state bureaucracy and their US connections to accumulate wealth and capital just as the US government did use Ethiopia and its ruling class to its strategic and economic advantage.

The alliance between the Ethiopian colonialists and the US imperialists emerged strongly in the early 1950s. Between 1946 and 1973, the United States spent more than $62 billion worldwide on military assistance programs (U.S. Agency of International Development 1974, 6), building its hegemony in the less developed world through military assistance to the ruling classes and their governments (Magdoff 1970). The Ethiopian client state was among the beneficiaries of such assistance. The Ethiopian state was mainly interested in dependable security against internal and external forces, whereas the United States was interested in securing continuing base rights in Asmara and in developing a major military and monitoring station there. The United States also considered "its political investment in Ethiopia as an investment toward the future realization of its wider interests in Africa" (Agyeman-Duah 1984, 209). Therefore, the United States expanded its Asmara base and modernized the Ethiopian military by training and equipping it with modern weapons. A US military advisory group replaced the British Military Mission in Ethiopia. Fred Halliday and Maxine Molyneux (1981, 215) note that "between 1951 and 1976 Ethiopia received over $350 million economic aid from the U.S.A. and a further $279 million in military aid. In the years 1953–75, 3,552 Ethiopian military personnel were trained in the U.S.A. itself." When the British military mission withdrew in 1951, "the Ethiopian army was still only partially organized and poorly trained and equipped. It was under such conditions that Haile Selassie turned to the

U.S. for assistance" (Agyeman-Duah 1984, 110), and he was successful in obtaining military aid (Schwab 1979, 92).

In the 1960s, however, following a series of events—an attempted military coup, the emergence of various anti-colonial movements, and the appearance of a radical student movement—the modernization approach of the United States through state-building proved vulnerable. Consequently, a politics of order began to emerge. "The military, in conjunction with other security forces," Agyeman-Duah (1984, 179) writes, "became the instrument for social control and counterinsurgency during the turbulent years of the 1960s, and an active American support in all this was by no means limited." To help the Ethiopian colonial regime stay in power, "the United States sent in counterinsurgent teams, increased its military aid programs, and expanded its modernization and training program for the Ethiopian military. An extensive air force was also created with United States vintage jets" (Schwab 1979, 95). There is no doubt that the US military and economic assistance prolonged Haile Selassie's regime. In the 1960s, the decolonization of British and Italian Somaliland, the Soviet alliance with the newly emerged Somali state, the emergence of anti-colonial movements, and the internal rivalry within the Ethiopian ruling class had threatened the foundation of the Haile Selassie regime. Harold Marcus (1983, 114) points out that "by forcing Washington continuously to increase its commitments, Addis Ababa made the United States an actor in Ethiopia's internal politics."

The US alliance with Ethiopia was mainly for strategic and geopolitical reasons, not economic ones, and US business investment was insignificant (Mohammed 1969, 76). The US modernization programs of the 1960s and the 1970s were both economic and educational. The United States was mainly interested in consolidating the Ethiopian ruling class by providing technical and administrative expertise (Luther 1958, 132). For almost 26 years, the United States dispatched its diplomats and intellectuals to apply its modernization principles in building and maintaining the Ethiopian Empire in accord with US national and global interests. However, following the overthrow of the Haile Selassie government by the popular revolt of 1974, the military regime led by Mengistu Haile Mariam allied with the former Soviet Union. Consequently, between 1974 and 1991 the influence of the United States on Ethiopia declined.

NEOLIBERAL GLOBALIZATION, STATE TERRORISM, AND DISPOSSESSION

At the end of the 1980s, a structural crisis that manifested itself in national movements, famine, poverty, and internal contradictions within the ruling elite eventually weakened the Amhara-dominated military regime and led to its demise in 1991. The US government used this opportunity to reestablish its relations with the Ethiopian Empire by allying this time with the Tigrayan People's Liberation Front (TPLF). Opposing the Soviet influence in Ethiopia and recognizing that the Amhara-based Ethiopian government had lost credibility, the United States started to support the TPLF in the 1980s and prepared it financially, ideologically, diplomatically, and militarily to replace the Amhara-led military regime by creating the so-called Ethiopian People's Revolutionary Democratic Front (EPRDF) from three puppet organizations it created, known as the Oromo People's Democratic Organization (OPDO), the Amhara National Democratic Movement (ANDM), and the Southern Ethiopia People's Democratic Movement (SEPDM). With the use of Western relief aid and financial support, the TPLF leaders converted the famine-stricken Tigrayan peasants and the militias captured at war fronts into guerrilla fighters. The Eritrean People's Liberation Front also played a central role in building the TPLF/EPRDF army.

One of the major reasons why the US government chose to sustain the TPLF was that the Tigrayan elites were perceived as a legitimate successor to an Amhara-led government because of the ideological assumptions of the West. Another reason was that these elites were ready to be agents of global imperialism at any cost. In fact, the main rationale of the alliance of the United States and other big powers with the Tigrayan-led government was to maintain global capitalism through intensifying capital accumulation. As Berch Berberoglu (2003, 108) writes, "The process of integration of neocolonial states into the global economy, seeking the protection of the imperial state, has been to a large degree a reaction to a perceived threat to the survival of capitalism in the Third World—one that is becoming a grave concern for both imperialism and the local repressive capitalist states." The United States, the European Union, China, and others have built and consolidated the Tigrayan-led Ethiopian regime to perform the following important services: "(1) adopt fiscal and monetary policies that ensure macroeconomic stability; (2) provide the basic infrastructure necessary for global economic activity (airports and seaports, communication networks, educational systems, etc.); and (3) provide social order, that is, stability, which requires sustaining instruments of social control, coercive and ideological apparatus" (Robinson 2008, 33).

The Tigrayan-led regime had become an organ of capital accumulation for both Tigrayan and transnational elites, and it had been using terrorism, genocide, and massive human rights violations to separate the indigenous communities such as the Oromo from their lands and other resources (Jalata 2005). The World Bank, IMF, UN, EU, the African Union, and even some NGOs operate as facilitators of such regional and global capital accumulation, and they do not seem interested in promoting human rights and democracy in poor countries like Ethiopia. The political and military leaders of the Ethiopian government are literally gangsters and robbers; they use state power to expropriate lands and other resources in the name of privatization—all with the support and blessing of the World Bank and the IMF. The regime had been mainly targeting the Oromo for repression and destruction, banning independent Oromo organizations, including the Oromo Liberation Front (OLF), and declaring war on this organization and the Oromo people:

> Because the Oromo occupy Ethiopia's richest areas and comprise half of the population of Ethiopia, they are seen as the greatest threat to the present Tigrayan-led government. Subsequently, any indigenous Oromo organization, including the Oromo Relief Association, has been closed and suppressed by the government. The standard reason given for detaining Oromo people is that they are suspected of supporting the OLF.[2]

The regime even had outlawed Oromo journalists and other writers and closed down Oromo newspapers (Hassen 2002). Almost all Oromo journalists were in prison, have been killed, or are in exile. The regime had also banned Oromo musical groups and all professional associations. Expanding their political repression, regional authorities formed quasi-government institutions known as *tokko-shanee*, *garee*, and *gott*[3] and to maintain a tighter political control of Oromia.[4] Thousands of Oromo were in official and secret prisons simply because of their nationality and their resistance to injustice. As Seye Abraha noted, the Ethiopian prisons "speak Afaan Oromoo (Oromiffa) [the Oromo language])" under the Tigrayan-led regime.[5] The Tigrayan state officials treated Oromo intellectuals, businessmen and women, conscious Oromo farmers and students, and community and religious leaders as enemies to be eliminated (Hizbawi Adera 1996/1997). The cadres, soldiers, and officials of the regime had frequently raped Oromo girls and women to demoralize them and their communities and to show their limitless power. State-sanctioned rape is a form of terrorism as well as a tactic of genocide that a dominant ethnonational group practices to destroy a subordinate ethnonational group (MacKinnon 1994, 11–12). As Bruna Fossati et al. (1996, 10) report, "in prison women are often humiliated and mistreated in the most brutal fashion. Torturers ram poles or bottles into their vaginas, connect electrodes to the lips of their vulva, or the victims are dragged into the forest and gang-raped by interrogation officers."

The Tigrayan-led regime had used various mechanisms in repressing, controlling, and destroying the Oromo people. According to Human Rights Watch (2005b, 1–2),[6]

> Since 1992, security forces have imprisoned thousands of Oromo on charges of plotting armed insurrection on behalf of the OLF. Such accusations have regularly been used as a transparent pretext to imprison individuals who publicly question government policies or actions. Security forces have tortured many detainees and subjected them to continuing harassment and abuse for years after their release. That harass-

ment in turn has often destroyed victims' ability to earn a livelihood and isolated them from their communities.

It is impossible to know exactly how many Oromo had been murdered, as the government hid its criminal activities and did "not keep written records of its extrajudicial executions and prolonged detention of political prisoners" (Hassen 2001, 30).

The massive killings of Sheko, Mezhenger, Sidama, Annuak, and Ogaden Somali people had shocked some sections of the international community. For instance, the president of Genocide Watch, Gregory Stanton, wrote on March 23, 2009, an open letter to the United Nations High Commission for Human Rights praising the International Criminal Court for issuing a warrant for the arrest of President Omar al-Bashir of Sudan and calling upon them to investigate the crimes against humanity that Meles Zenawi, the Prime Minister of the TPLF, and his government had committed in the Horn of Africa (Stanton 2009). Stanton also claimed that in December 2003 the government organized Ethiopian National Defense Forces and civilian militia groups to ruthlessly massacre 424 persons from the Annuak people in Gambella in order to suppress opposition and to "exclude them from any involvement in the drilling for oil on their indigenous land." According to Stanton, as militia groups chanted "Today is the day for killing Annuak," both the military and the militias used machetes, axes, and guns to kill the unarmed victims, frequently raping the women while chanting, "Now there will be no more Annuak children." Reports from Amnesty International, the US State Department, and the Human Rights Watch had been listing Zenawi's extensive record of chilling crimes against the Ethiopian people. The regime passed a so-called anti-terrorism law to legitimize its crimes against humanity and to legally intensify its repressive and terrorist activities. Ethiopia's anti-terrorism "law could provide the Ethiopian government with a potent instrument to crack down on political dissent, including peaceful political demonstrations and public criticisms of government policy that are deemed supportive of armed opposition activity."[7]

The policies and practices of the regime had forced millions of Oromo and others to become political refugees in Asia, Europe, Australia, and North America. The alliance of the West with this regime had frightened neighboring countries such as Djibouti, Kenya, Sudan, and Yemen, turning them against the Oromo struggle and pressuring them to return or expel the Oromo refugees. The United Nations High Commission for Refugees (UNHCR) had failed to provide reasonable protection for those refugees. For example, in December 2000, while 5,000 Oromo refugees were subject to refoulment to Ethiopia, the UNHCR office in Djibouti denied any violation of its mandate.[8] Between 2000 and 2004, hundreds of Oromo refugees were forced to return to Ethiopia from Djibouti to face imprisonment or death.[9] "The continuing refoulement of refugees from

Djibouti, especially the large scale refoulement of December 2000 and the 28 associated deaths by asphyxiation and shooting, should be publicly acknowledged by UNHCR and the Djibouti government."[10] The security agents of Ethiopia and neighboring countries captured thousands of Oromo refugees and returned them to Ethiopia. Agents of the Ethiopian regime had also assassinated prominent Oromo leaders in Somalia, Sudan, and Kenya.[11]

Poor states such as that of Ethiopia "lack the capacity to meet the demands and rights of citizens and improve the standard of living for the majority of population" (Welsh 2002, 67–68). Consequently, they engage in state terrorism and genocidal massacres in order to suppress the population groups that struggle for political and economic rights and to dispossess their economic resources. State terrorism and genocide occur when a "dominant group, frightened by what its members perceive as an onslaught of . . . internal movements for democracy and socioeconomic change, harnesses the state apparatus to destroy the subordinate group altogether" (Sharlach 2002, 107). State terrorism, therefore, is associated with the control of territory and resources and the construction of political and ideological domination (Oliverio 1997, 52). Ethiopian state terrorism manifests itself in different forms such as war, assassination, murder (including burying people alive, throwing them off cliffs, and hanging them), castration, torture, and rape. The police and the army are forcing the Oromo people into submission by jailing, intimidating, beating, torturing, and killing them as well as by confiscating their properties (Jalata 2016). According to Trevor Trueman (2001),

> Torture . . . is commonplace . . . in unofficial places of detention. Female detainees estimate that several soldiers and policemen on several occasions rape 50 percent of women during detention, often. The Minnesota Center for Victims of Torture has surveyed more than 500 randomly selected Oromo refugees. The majority had been subjected to torture and nearly all of the rest had been subjected to some kind of government violence.

The Tigrayan-led Ethiopian regime was completing the forced removal of Oromo farmers from the areas surrounding Finfinnee (Addis Ababa) (Worku 2008). The government had been implementing the so-called Addis Ababa Master Plan, which in 2014 the Oromo dubbed "the Master Genocide." The Oromo in general and the Oromo students in particular had been peacefully resisting this genocidal policy intended to totally uproot Oromo farmers around the capital city and to transfer their lands to Tigrayan colonial elites and their supporters. However, their resistance had been met with a violent repression. In a paper entitled "Because I am Oromo," Amnesty International (2014, 8) notes that in relation to the Addis Ababa Master Plan, "between 2011 and 2014, at least 5,000 Oromo have been arrested as a result of their actual or suspected peaceful opposition to the government, based on their manifestation of dissenting opinions, exercise of freedom of expression or their imputed political opinion." In 2014, the regime also massacred over 78 university students in Ambo for peacefully protesting against the plan. Large-scale arrests, massive shootings, rapes, tortures, extra-judicial executions, and deaths due to torture or lack of medical treatments were common events in Oromia. Oromo students accused of organizing demonstrations were arrested and tortured; singers were detained and tortured for cultivating Oromo nationalism and for not praising the government; people were imprisoned and tortured for not providing false testimonies against others or for supporting the OLF (Amnesty International 2014, 7).

By evicting the Oromo farmers from their lands with nominal or no compensation, the regime had leased several millions hectares of Oromo lands to investors from Ethiopia, China, Djibouti, Saudi Arabia, India, Malaysia, Nigeria, the United Kingdom, Israel, and Europe (Giorgis 2009, Rahmato 2011). Under the leadership of the Tigrayan-led Ethiopian government, the local and transnational capitalist elites had intensified the process of capital accumulation by dispossession; if this land grabbing is allowed to continue, Tigrayans, Amharas, Chinese, Djiboutians, Indians, Malaysians, Nigerians, Arabs, English, Jews, Asians, Europeans, and others will soon replace the Oromo people in Oromia and beyond. The Tigrayan regime also sold Oromo minerals and other natural resources; however, the Tigrayan state elites had never sold or leased Tigrayan lands but had rather expanded modern agricultural and industrial developments in their homeland (Giorgis 2009, 1). Therefore, while the Oromo are facing abject poverty and hunger, some Tigrayans who in the 1980s depended on international food aid for their survival have amassed huge amounts of power and wealth.

This policy of violent development has also been devastating the peoples of the Lower Omo region and Gambella; several ethnonational minority groups, including the Kwegu, Bodi, Suri, Mursi, Nyangatom, Hamer, Karo, and Dassenach, have been targeted for destruction through land dispossession and forced resettlements (Oakland Institute 2013, 1–2; 2014; 2015). When the United States, the United Kingdom, and the World Bank have provided their so-called development aid, the Ethiopian government has used its military to violently dispossess these peoples of their lands and resources and to force them to settle in new areas that were hostile to their livelihoods and cultural traditions. Ethiopia received "$3.5 billion on average . . . in recent years, which represents 50 to 60 percent of its national budget" in development aid from the United States, the United Kingdom, and the World Bank; the development strategy developed in 2010 aimed at removing "1.5 million people from areas targeted for industrial plantations under the government's 'villagization' program" (Oakland Institute 2013, 1).

The European Union, Australia, Italy, Germany, Ireland, as well as the International Monetary Fund, and the World Bank Group have also financed such programs of land dispossession and forced resettlement. Overall, the Tigrayan-led Ethiopian government had dispossessed and leased about 2.5 million hectares of lands to Tgrayan elites and global investors by impoverishing millions of farmers and herders (Jeffrey 2016).

THE OROMO PEACEFUL PROTEST MOVEMENT AND ITS RAMIFICATIONS

The current Oromia-wide peaceful protest movement is a product of the political consciousness developed during the national struggle of the 1960s, 1970s, 1980s, and 1990s, of years of accumulated grievances, and of the recent intensification of land grabbing policies, particularly the Addis Ababa Master Plan. In 1992, the Tigrayan-led minority regime pushed the OLF out of the transitional government, and the activist networks of *qeerroo/qaree* (Oromo youth) gradually blossomed as a form of *Oromummaa*, or Oromo nationalism. The collective grievances have accelerated the Oromo struggle for self-determination, statehood, and democracy by involving the entire Oromo society in the protest movement. The *qeerroo/qaree* protest movement erupted in Ginchi, near Ambo, on November 12, 2015, and it quickly spread throughout Oromia like wildfire. The Oromo elementary and secondary students of this small town ignited the movement by protesting against the privatization and confiscation of a small soccer field and the selling of the nearby Chilimoo forest to be cleared (Jeffrey 2016).

Oromo individuals from all walks of life joined the peaceful protests by opposing the Addis Ababa Master Plan. For the first time the revolutionary flame of Oromo nationalism had brought the Oromo people together to take a coordinated action in defense of their national interest. The plan was intended to expand Addis Ababa (Finfinnee) to 1.5 million hectares of surrounding Oromo lands by evicting Oromo farmers, and it would have destroyed Oromo identity, culture, and history by replacing them with those of Tigrayans and their collaborators (Thomson & López 2015). The Oromo have interpreted this project as a replication of the policy of the Amhara-led government, which had uprooted and destroyed the Oromo in Finfinnee and replaced them with Amhara colonial settlers and their collaborators during the formation and development of Addis Ababa as the capital of the Ethiopian Empire.

Oromia has been under martial law since the protests began, even though the state of emergency was officially declared only on October 9, 2016. The government has used these exceptional measures to kill or detain thousands of Oromo, holding them in prisons and concentration camps. Security structures called *tokkoo-shane* (one-to-five), *garee*, and *gott* have also been implemented. Their responsibilities include spying, identifying, exposing, imprisoning, torturing, and killing Oromo who are not willing to serve the regime. Thousands of Oromo have also been maimed or blinded as a result of torture, beatings, or during the suppression of protests.[12] For example, during the Oromia-wide day of peaceful protest on July 6, 2016, the regime's army known as *Agazi* massacred nearly 100 Oromo.[13] According to Amnesty International, 400 Oromo were killed before July 6.[14]

The Tigrayan state elites and their Oromo collaborators, being used to thinking of the Oromo people as a collection of "tribes," could not understand the essence of the Oromo protest movement, and thought that by beating, torturing, raping, and murdering Oromo students, farmers, educators, and merchants they could stop the Oromo struggle for statehood, sovereignty, and democracy. By contrast, the Oromo activists and revolutionaries are inclusive and have been inviting all the suffering peoples to join the movement against colonialism, neoliberal globalism, and violent development. The ongoing Oromo protest movement has opened a new chapter in the history of Oromia and Ethiopia. This history is mainly written in Oromo blood, and the relationship between the Oromo and their colonizers has been changed forever. However, the final chapter of this history is not yet written, although many things have changed as the result of the Oromo protest movement. The movement forced the resignation of Haile Mariam Desalegn, the prime minister of the Tigrayan-led government, on February 15, 2018. The new Prime Minister, Abyi Ahmed, who also belongs to the same ruling party, replaced him and started to introduce some political reforms, such as releasing political prisoners, which is still short of democratic transition. The cost the Oromo have paid in lives and suffering is very high. Within five months from the beginning of the protest, more than 500 Oromo, including school children, pregnant women, and elderly people had been massacred, and tens of thousands of Oromo had been imprisoned, beaten, tortured, and decapitated.[15] In fact, at this time we do not have enough data on the killings, imprisonments, and other crimes committed against the Oromo. Journalists estimated that between five and ten thousand Oromo were killed until 2018.

Despite all these tragedies, however, the Oromo people have restored the national pride, patriotism, and bravery they had enjoyed between the sixteenth and the mid-nineteenth centuries, when they had successfully defended themselves from their internal and external enemies. *Biyya Oromoo*, what today we call Oromia, was sovereign and no enemies exercised political power over it. The ideology of national *Oromummaa* that the young Oromo protesters are equipped with has uprooted the existing divisions among different Oromo groups. Some Oromo individuals who had been suffering from the internalization of their victimization have been forced to start to rethink their national identity and their role in the Oromo national struggle. Particularly, members of the Oromo diaspora are learning about national *Oromummaa* and rallying behind the national struggle in Oromia. The Oromo diaspora all over the world has showed solidarity with Oromo protesters by demonstrating in their support and by financially and diplomatically supporting them. Oromo collaborators and opportunists who had been evicting Oromo farmers from their ancestral lands by joining the Tigrayan criminal elites have started to feel national shame. The protest movement is demonstrating that it can destroy Oromo intermediaries or mercenaries who work for the enemy, and that the Oromo people will not accept the submissive and subservient leaders the enemy created for them. Oromo protesters publicly honor the heroes and heroines who have sacrificed their lives as OLF leaders and fighters, and they proclaim that "the OLF is our leader" without any fear of the TPLF government and its OPDO collaborators.

Because the Oromo protesters have only targeted their enemy, other national groups in Ethiopia have somewhat changed their attitudes toward the Oromo people and their national struggle. Many Amhara elites who used to be suspicious or disapproving of the Oromo struggle have temporarily become neutral or sympathetic to the Oromo activists and protesters. Many of them have openly denounced Tigrayan state terrorism and invited their fellow citizens to join the movement. But, recently they have started to attack the Oromo and their national movement. Peoples like the Sidama, Konso, Hadiya, Benishangul, and Annuak have manifested political solidarity with the fight of the Oromo people to dismantle Tigrayan colonialism and the racist minority regime of the TPLF. These are great political, ideological, and psychological victories for the Oromo national movement.

Globally and diplomatically, the Oromo protest movement has won world attention because of its political maturity, determination, inclusiveness, and for totally disproving the ideology and political program of the Tigrayan-led minority government. For the first time in Oromo history, global media outlets such as the *Washington Post*, BBC, CNN, al Jazeera, *Newsweek*, AFP, the *Guardian*, and others have reported on the Oromo protest movement and its brutal crackdown by the Ethiopian government. On January 21, 2015, the European Parliament condemned the violent crackdown of Oromo protesters and called for the establishment of a credible, transparent, and independent body for investigating the murdering and imprisoning of thousands protesters in Oromia.[16] But, the Ethiopian government rejected the proposal. The US Department of State vaguely expressed concern about the violence associated with the protest movement. At the same time, however, manifesting its firm support for the regime, the United States signed a security partnership agreement with the Ethiopian government to exchange "logistics, services, supplies" and planned "for a future security cooperation activities designed to meet mutual defense priorities."[17]

CONCLUSION

The Oromo movement for self-determination, statehood, and democracy has gained momentum. As a result of it, the Oromo people have developed their national *Oromummaa*, determination, and the capacity to confront and defeat the policies of violent development and autonomously decide the Oromo national destiny. The Oromo movement has shaken the foundation of the Tigrayan terrorist regime and its surrogate organization, OPDO, in Oromia and beyond, and a new Oromo-based system is emerging and replacing the dying structures of Tigrayan colonialism. Looking forward, the Oromo activist networks and leadership must redouble their efforts to build their national organizational capacity, and they should work to develop specific principles of national self-determination and multinational democracy to open new chapters in Oromia, Ethiopia, and the Horn of Africa in collaboration with progressive communities and peoples of the region. As other social movements of the twenty-first century that are engaging in democratic movements and forms of globalization from below (Rajagopal 1999, 2003), the Oromo movement is challenging the strategies of violent development of capitalist modernity and seeking to advance the autonomy of the Oromo people, the formation of a democratic state, and an alternative form of development.

NOTES

1. The Oromo Relief Association, 1980; it is an Oromo humanitarian organization, which provided victims of war and famine with health and relief services. It has a bulletin titled the Oromo Relief Association.

2. The Oromia Support Group (1997, 1), an Oromo human rights bulletin organized by Trevor Trueman, a British medical doctor and a human rights activist.

3. *Tokko-shane, garee,* and *gott* are security structures and included 5 members, 10 households, and 90 to 150 households respectively to spy on one another and report to government officials about political behavior and activities of members. Interviewed Desalegn Nagari on 7/17/2018 by phone.

4. Human Rights Watch. 2005a. "Human Rights," www.genocidewatch.org, accessed on 7/17/2018.

5. Seye Abraha was the defense minister of Ethiopia; he was jailed in the Qaliti prison. See "The Prison speaks Oromiffa," *Ethiopian Review*, January 17, 2008.

6. Human Rights Watch, 2005b, 1–2. It is an international non-governmental organization that conducts research and advocacy on human rights.

7. https://www.hrw.org/world-report-2009, p 1, "An Analysis of Ethiopia's Draft Anti-Terrorism Law," accessed on 7/17/2018.

8. The Oromia Support Group, 2002, 17, an Oromo human rights bulletin.

9. *Ibid.*, 2003, 16–18.

10. *Ibid.*, 2002, 18–19.

11. In 2009, the regime killed four Oromo by poisoning their food in Puntland (Human Rights League of the Horn of Africa 2009).

12. See "Ethiopian Protests," https://www.hrw.org/tag/ethiopian-protests, accessed on 07/17?2018.

13. See http://www.bbc.com/news/world-africa-37015055, accessed on 06/09/2017.

14. See http://www.newsweek.com/ethiopia-hundreds-killed-excessive-force-oromo-protests-says-hrw-470800, accessed on 6/10/2017.

15. See https://vimeo.com/166427775?from=outro-embed, accessed on 05/13/2016.

16. See "European Parliament resolution on the situation in Ethiopia," http://www.europarl.europa.eu/sides/getDoc.do?pubRef=-//EP//TEXT+MOTION+P8-RC-2016-0082+0+DOC+XML+V0//EN, accessed on 04/14/2016.

17. See "US, Ethiopia sign new agreement, enhance security partnership," http://www.hiiraan.com/news4/2016/Apr/104913/us_ethiopia_sign_new_agreement_to_enhance_defense_and_security_partnership.aspx, accessed on /14/201.

EIGHT

Politico-Cultural Prerequisites for Protecting the Oromo National Interest

A nation that is prevented from freely developing its political and cultural institutions by colonialism, and forced to serve the interest of another society, suffers from political domination, exploitation, underdevelopment, and poverty (Rodney 1972; Jalata 2001). Similarly, the Oromo nation has been denied the right to develop its independent cultural, political, and economic institutions since its colonization and incorporation into the Ethiopian Empire. As explained elsewhere (Jalata 2005 [1993], 2010), there have been several internal and external problems that have contributed to the destruction of Oromo cultural and political institutions and the subordination of the Oromo national interest to that of the Ethiopian colonial state and its regional and global supporters. Ethiopian colonialism has partitioned the Oromo society mentally and geographically in order to divide and conquer and to undermine the Oromo identity and national unity.

Specifically, successive Ethiopian colonial elites have effectively destroyed/suppressed Oromo cultural foundations and political institutions, created subservient Oromo leaders, replaced *Oromummaa* (Oromo national culture, identity, and ideology) by Ethiopianism, partitioned and renamed Oromian territories, looted Oromo economic resources, and dehumanized the Oromo society (Jalata 2010a). The Oromo national movement emerged in the 1960s and 1970s to solve these complex problems and to protect the Oromo national interest (Jalata 2007). The chapter briefly provides background information on the Oromo cultural and institutional foundations; identifies and explains the major challenges of the Oromo national movement; and explores the current Oromo cultural and political strengths and challenges and the main ideological and political roadmaps of the Oromo national struggle in relation to Oromia's national interest.

LOOKING BACK AT OROMO CULTURAL FOUNDATIONS AND INSTITUTIONS

A clear understanding of the relationship between culture and politics is very important because of the influence of cultural capital on the development of democracy.[1] The histories of Oromia and Ethiopia demonstrate that ignoring the cultural capital of the indigenous democracy such as that of the Oromo called the *gadaa/siiqqee*[2] system and imposing an authoritarian/ethnocratic state on various national groups produce continuous economic and political crises. Without critically and thoroughly addressing and solving these complex problems, the Oromo national movement cannot adequately achieve its political objectives and protect the Oromo national interest. Before its colonization, *Biyyaa* Oromoo or Oromia (the Oromo country) was sovereign under the *gadaa republic* (Baisa 2014, 1971, 1993; Lepisa 1975). The Oromo people started to practice their democratic system more than 4000 years ago (Jaaraa and Saaddoo 2011, 61). The Oromo oral tradition indicates that the original center of *Abbaa Gadaa*, the president of the Oromo assembly known as *caffee*, and the center of *Abbaa Muda*, the leader of Oromo indigenous religion known as *Waaqeefannaa*, was Abbaya or Mormor (ancient name for the Blue Nile) until it moved to Odaa Nabee in the fifth century A. D. (Oromia Culture and Tourism Bureau (OCTB) 2006, 74). A few Oromo branches such as Galan and Yaya settled for many centuries on both sides of the Blue Nile, the northern part of the Shawa Plateau, before the Christian immigrants began to arrive between the eleventh and thirteenth centuries (Bulcha 2016; Hassen 2015).

The *gadaa* system evolved through the processes known as *cinna* (decentralization based on extended clan families) and *haroomisa* (renewal and reorganization of *gadaa* at national level) (OCTB 2006). The center of *gadaa* gradually moved to Odaa Nabee. Currently, there is not enough information on the renewal of *gadaa* at Odaa Mormor and its movement to Odaa Nabee, near Finfinnee (central Oromo country). According to the Oromo oral tradition, the central *gadaa* system, *caffee* (Oromo assembly) was practiced at Odaa Nabee from fifth century A. D. to 756 A. D. (OCTB 2006). The eighth century A. D. was characterized as the year of *cinna gadaa* (decentralization) and 1116 A. D. was called the year of *haroomsa gadaa* (renewal, centralization, and consolidation) (OCTB 2006, 52). The Oromo were facing both the Muslim and Christian empire builders who were competing with each other on the issues of religion, land and other economic resources. The Muslim empire builders, which started in the late tenth century, and the Christian empire builders, which consolidated after thirteenth century, engaged in religious and political wars and destabilized the Oromo society for many centuries in the Horn of Africa (OCTB 2006, 94–95). Between the thirteenth and fourteenth centuries, the Oromo people were attacked by Abyssinian Christians from the North and by Muslim Somalis from the South East (Jarraa and Saaddo 2011). Both groups wanted to dismantle the Oromo identity, culture, religion, and the *gadaa* system, and to take over the Oromo country. These external pressures created instability that negatively affected the efficient functioning of the *gadaa* system in the Tulama Oromo (Northern Shawa) and instigated the movement of the Oromo toward the south, and the decentralization of the *gadaa* system into clan-based autonomous administrations. These factors facilitated the transfer of the center of the *gadaa* system from Odaa Nabee (near Finfinnee) to Odaa Roba and then to Madda Walaabuu (the stream of liberty), located in Bale (Jarraa and Saaddo 2011).

From around 1316 to 1378, Odaa Roba started to function as the center of an Oromo politico-religious system by replacing Odaa Nabee, and then the center was transferred to Madda Walaabuu in 1450 (Jarraa and Saaddo 2011). In the same year, the *Abbaa Muda*, the main Oromo religious figure, moved to Madda Walaabuu (OCTB 2011). When the Abyssinian Christian kingdom attacked the Tulama Oromo, the Muslim Somali empire builders also attacked the Oromo branches who were living in the area that is currently called Somalia (OCTB 2011). After the decentralization of the *gadaa* system at Odaa Nabee because of the external pressure from the Christian kingdom, "the total *gadaa* revival was successfully completed at the Odaa Roba 'caffee' center in 1316. It should be noted here that . . . the movement of *gadaa* revival took place at Odaa Mormor, Odaa Nabee, Odaa Roba and Madda Walaabuu shows that two different institutions were working for a common goal. When *gadaa* revival was taking place at Odaa Nabee, it served as the center of both politics and religion for the Oromo clans living in the area" (OCTB 2011, 56). The renewal movement of the *gadaa* system occurred at Odaa Roba in Bale by replacing "Odaa Nabee, which had been a politico-religious center for several hundred years before the fourteenth century," and "Odaa Roba had become a new holy politico-religious center of the Oromo people at large that had been periodically visited by the various representatives of Oromo groups from all directions for such celebrations like *Jilaa Gada* and *Mudaa* [pilgrim]" (OCTB 2011, 90–91).

Gradually the politico-religious center of Odaa Roba moved to Madda Walaabuu for reasons that are not clear at present. The Bale Oromo living around Madda Walaabu also started to reorganize and reconsolidate their power starting from the eleventh century (Jarraa and Saaddo 2011, 104). The general assembly of the Oromo nation was held between 1518 and 1519 for six months at Madda Walaabuu to discuss and deliberate how to liberate the Oromo country from the Christian and Muslim invaders; delegates from different parts of the Oromo country participated on this assembly (Jarraa and Saaddo 2011). Particularly, the Tulama Oromo sent delegates of twelve people led by Dachaasa to Madda Walaabuu (Jarraa and Saaddo 2011). The main question Walaabuu Jiloo, *Abbaa Gadaa* of Madda Walaabuu, asked at the general assembly was "*Maal Taana?*" ("What are we going to be?") After thorough discussions and deliberations for six months, the general assembly defined the enemies of the Oromo people as those Christian and Muslim empire builders who were attacking the Oromo people in their own country to kill them, take their lands and other resources, and to force them to abandon their culture, religion, and identity. The assembly also passed major resolutions to mobilize the entire nation to liberate their country (Jarraa and Saaddoo 2011). The Oromo people still have in their memory pool the name Madda Walaabuu because they started the defensive and liberation wars there in the early sixteenth century.

The history of Madda Walaabuu demonstrates that the most significant revival and reorganization of the *gadaa* institution occurred there at the beginning of sixteenth century (Jarraa and Saaddoo 2011, 96). Since the sixteenth century, the renewal and reorganization of the *gadaa* system involved fundamental changes; these changes included rules, regulations and objectives. There were two main objectives: "Firstly, it was aimed [at] defending the *gadaa* system and the Oromo people from the pressure of Islam. Secondly, the change was sought to reinforce the military power of the people and enable them to regain their old area of settlement lost as the result of the incessant wars of the Christian and Muslim states. . . . The changes in . . . the formulation of new rules and regulations were, therefore actions of paramount importance in order to realize those objectives" (OCTB 2011, 96). Consequently, the Oromo decided "at least one *Butta* military campaign to be launched every eight years in all directions in order to regain the old settlement areas of the Oromo people who were forced to desert and unite them with their kinsmen that remained behind. [It] was [also] decided to strengthen *Muda* religious pilgrimage made to the seat of the *Qaallu* every eight years" (OCTB 2011, 96–97). In 1522, the Oromo started their resistance struggle to recover their lost homeland. This was before the Muslims seriously confronted Christian Abyssinia/Ethiopia in 1527.

The Muslims destroyed Christian rule and established their own under the leadership of one Ahmed Gragn for more than a decade in the Horn of Africa. The Oromo were caught in the wars of the Christian and Muslim empire-builders, and according to Darrel Bates (1979, 7), "The [Oromo] . . . had suffered in their time from both parties, and were waiting in the wings for opportunities . . . to recover lands which had been taken from them." The wars between Christians and Muslims endangered the Oromo's survival as a people. With the renewal and reorganization of *gadaa*, the Oromo carried out *butta* wars every eight years, when power transferred from one *gadaa* grade to the next. In the beginning of the sixteenth century, when they began to intensify their territorial recovery through the *butta* wars, all Oromo were under one *gadaa* government. The ability of the *gadaa* system to reconsolidate the people both militarily and organizationally enabled them to recover their lost territories and accommodate their increased population and stock (Legesse 1973). Their movement and recovery signaled their survivability (Ta'a 1986). The Oromo fought twelve *butta* wars between 1522 and 1618, recovering and reestablishing the Oromo country that is called Oromia today (Ta'a 1986). In the course of their continued movements and their liberation struggle, different Oromo groups gradually established autonomous *gadaa* governments. At the same time, various Oromo groups kept their relations through the office of *Abbaa Muuda* (the father of anointment) (Ta'a 1986) and formed alliances or confederations during times of difficulty (Etefa 2012).

However, the development of class differentiation within the Oromo society in northern, central, and western Oromia, external factors—such as Turko-Egyptian colonialism in eastern Oromia between 1875 and 1885 and European and Ethiopian colonialism—the emergence of an Oromo collaborator class, and the spread of Islam and Christianity undermined the political, military, and ritual/spiritual roles of the *gadaa* system. Both internal socio-economic transformations and external interactions with neighboring peoples slowly facilitated the emergence of class and the *moottii* system (kingdom) in some Oromo areas. As some Oromo clans moved to far-flung regions and interacted with Abyssinian and Omotic kingdoms and Nilo-Saharan societies and as they settled and engaged in farming and trade, they developed class differentiation that gradually led to the transformation of the *gadaa* system into the *moottii* system in northern, central, and western Oromia. With the development of class differentiation, the egalitarian democratic system was challenged and replaced by the *moottii* system in some areas. Constant wars led to the evolution of the *abba dulas* (military leaders) to hereditary *moottiis* (leaders). In the eighteenth century, the Wallo Oromo had replaced the *gadaa* administration with that of kingdoms. In the Gibe region, the *moottii* system developed through confiscation of land, collection of booty, tribute and market dues, and through the establishment of hereditary rights to ownership of property and political office in the nineteenth century. The emergence of powerful autocratic leaders and their private armies led to the control of marketplaces, trade routes and land, and the development of an agricultural economy that led to further class differentiation and the formation of the *mootti* system (Hassen 1990).

The egalitarian democratic *gadaa* system was incompatible with the new *moottii* system due to the fundamental changes in the landholding system. In other words, the emergence of class differentiation and the rise of the Oromo kingdoms suppressed the *gadaa* system in some parts of Oromia.

For example, in the Gibe region, five Oromo states—Limmu-Ennarya, Guma, Jimma, Gera, and Goma—emerged between the seventeenth and nineteenth centuries (Lewis 2001). Here in the seventeenth century, the differentiation of wealth went beyond the wealth of cattle when the *sorressa* (the wealthy merchant and landlord class) emerged. With the emergence of this wealthy class, the principle of adopting the conquered populations as "equal" through the *mogassa* process ended; the institutions of slavery and *qubisisa* (tenancy) emerged. The emergence of a hierarchical structure reduced the egalitarian aspects of the *gadaa* to religious rituals. The *moottii* (king) continuously accumulated wealth with incomes he extracted from tribute on the land and its products, and from commerce. This produce extraction enabled the *moottii* to create and maintain regulatory institutions like a military, bodyguards, and courts. Also, the emergence of *moottii* systems in Leqa-Naqamte and Leqa-Qellem, western Oromia, was actually based on the initiation of warfare and appropriation of rights to land and labor, control of trade and market places. Externally, the *gadaa* system was attacked and weakened in eastern Oromia by the Turko-Egyptian and Harari conspiracy. The interethnic alliance and interdependence between the Harari, residents of the walled city of Harar and the eastern Oromo was shattered when a faction of the former invited the Turko-Egyptian power to colonize the Hararge region in 1875. Between 1875 and 1885, the Harari retained their position and accumulated wealth at the cost of the majority Oromo under the Turko-Egyptian rule (Jalata 2005 [1993]).

Similarly, in the regions presently called Sidamo, Arssi, Bale, Illubabor, and Gamu Gofa and in some parts of Shawa, the *gadaa* system was suppressed by the alliance of global imperialism and Ethiopian colonialism. The capitalist penetration of the last decades of nineteenth century laid the economic foundation of the modern Horn states, followed by the occupation of strategic positions by European powers along the Red Sea littoral. Generally speaking, the partition of the Horn of Africa in the last decades of the nineteenth century, the alliance between European imperialists—namely France, England, and Italy—and Ethiopian warlords, and the colonization of Oromia ended Oromo statehood and sovereignty, which the Oromo national movement is currently struggling to restore. As an egalitarian system, *gadaa* did not compete well with hierarchical social systems that engaged in the extraction of economic surplus and political oppression by building a permanent professional bureaucracy, expanding formal education, and developing limited technological capabilities. The intervention of the Ethiopian and European powers through military, mercantile, colonial and neo-colonial forces in Oromo society demonstrated the challenge the Oromo political leadership was facing because of an externally imposed exploitative and oppressive social system. Because of the external influence and the internal weakness of the *gadaa* system after its decentralization, autocratic and hereditary chiefs emerged by overthrowing the democratically elected leadership in some parts of Oromia.

The historical legacy of Oromo political leadership is the sovereignty the Oromo experienced under the *gadaa* government and its egalitarian framework. Consequently, under the *gadaa* system, the Oromo society enjoyed relative peace, stability, sustainable development and political sovereignty although technologically and bureaucratically not well developed. The imposition of the Ethiopian colonial system and the emergence of the Oromo collaborator class had denied the Oromo the opportunity of rebuilding their national institutions and organizations. Consequently, the Oromo have been facing monumental external and internal challenges in rebuilding their national organizational capacity that could have helped them in reestablishing the rules of the game, and in building strong national organizations that could have effectively mobilized them to successfully carry out the national projects of liberation, egalitarian democracy, and development. The Ethiopian colonial state had partitioned the Oromo society physically and mentally, and the Oromo national movement did not yet totally destroy the foundations of these divisions. These divisions have undermined *safuu* (Oromo moral and ethical order) and the rules of the game that they used to have. Consequently, some Oromo individuals and groups have become the agents of the colonial system to benefit themselves and their colonial masters. The Ethiopian colonial state has used brute force and developed elaborated ideological mechanisms such as Ethiopianism to prevent the Oromo people from rebuilding their independent national institutions, organizations, and leadership.

The rebuilding of Oromo national organizations and institutions started with the emergence of the Macha Tulama Association and the Oromo Liberation Front (OLF) and currently consolidated by the *Qeerro/Qarree*-led Oromo national movement.[3] Currently the commercialization and fragmentation of Oromo ideologies and politics by different Oromo political organizations and the absence of strong national organizational capacity are the two major pitfalls of the Oromo national interest. At the same time, the availability of political opportunities such as politicized collective grievances; the existence of the OLF and other Oromo political organizations; the increase of political consciousness among students and others; the activities of legal Oromo political organizations; the cultural renaissance initiated by the MTA and students; the further development of national *Oromummaa*; and the introduction of technological innovations such as social media including mobile phones, Internet and tweets, satellite TVs, and radios have galvanized the Oromo people in general and the youth in particular to engage in the clandestinely organized and systematically networked peaceful protest movement that mobilized almost all sectors of the Oromo society.

As we shall see below, this movement has produced far-reaching consequences for the Oromo national struggle and politics. It has already demonstrated that the foundation of the Ethiopian colonial state has been built on a shaky foundation that cannot survive the determined and organized Oromo revolutionary force. For the first time since their colonization, the Oromo people under the leadership of *Qeerroo/Qarree* have demonstrated that they are capable of dismantling Ethiopian colonialism and its political structures. Particularly, the Oromo youth have changed the potential of the Oromo nation into collective action by uniting most sectors of the Oromo society. As a consequence of the recent Oromo protests, politically conscious Oromo and others have realized that it is only a matter of time before the Oromo nation achieves its political objective of national self-determination and democracy. Farsighted political activists and serious nationalists have realized that without building strong national institutions and organizations protests or revolts alone may not necessarily lead to a fundamental regime change in the Ethiopian Empire. Developing new political strategies, building broad-based alliances, and working on building strong national institutions and political organizations are absolutely necessary to bring the Oromo national struggle to fruition. The Oromo youth protest movement has created conducive conditions for these factors. The political agenda of combining the principles national self-determination and egalitarian multinational democracy has resulted in creating consensus among the Oromo and Amhara youths and others to remove the Tigrayan-led authoritarian-terrorist regime (Jalata 2016).

At the same time, the series of protests created a serious crisis in the Oromo People's Democratic Organization (OPDO) and led to the stepping down of the president of the Regional State of Oromia, Muktar Kedir (2014–2016), and his replacement by Lemma Megersa in October 2016. The election of Lemma Megersa was a special event because for the first time the OPDO elected its popular leader without asking for permission from the Tigrayan People's Liberation Front (TPLF), which dominated the Ethiopia government. So, we can say that the *Qeerroo/Qarree* movement has initiated the process of the liberation of OPDO from the yoke of their masters although the organization is still a member of the Ethiopian Peoples Revolutionary Democratic Front (EPRDF), which was dominated and led by the TPLF almost for twenty-seven years. As the *Qeerroo/Qarree* peaceful movement consolidated its political base in Oromia and extended its solidarity to other regional states, such as the Amhara youth movement[4] known as *Fanoo* and the Gurage movement known as Zarma, and the Sidama youth movement called Ejjetto. As economic boycotts intensified in Oromia between June 2016[5] and February 2018,[6] to suppress the peaceful protests the TPLF/EPRDF regime declared another

State of Emergency on February 16, 2018: "This is Ethiopia's second state of emergency in two years and it came a day after Prime Minister Hailemariam Desalegn resigned. The election of a new prime minister is expected early next week."[7]

The Oromo peaceful movement assisted the OPDO to empower itself and to negotiate with the EPRDF to appoint its member, Abyi Ahmed, to become the Prime Minister of Ethiopia on April 2, 2018. Abyi Ahmed served in the Ethiopian military and rose to the rank of Lieutenant Colonel, and directed the Information Network and Security Agency, which is responsible for cyber-security and control of the Internet. He has emerged as Chairman of the OPDO/EPRDF, and it is not yet clear whether he has total control on the apparatuses of the Security and the Military, which are still dominated by the TPLF military leaders. Our doubt of his power was increased by the displacement of 1.2 million Oromo and the killings of hundreds of them in the Ethiopian-Somali Regional State. Also, the Gumuz people from Benishangul killed many people and expelled more than eighty thousand Oromo from their region.

MAJOR EXTERNAL AND INTERNAL CHALLENGES

The Oromo national struggle still faces serious challenges from its external and internal enemies, despite the fact that it is progressing toward determining the political destiny of the Oromo nation. Although national *Oromummaa* is blossoming and the *Qerroo/Qaree*-led Oromia-wide movement is defeating the ideology of Ethiopianism or Amhara-Tigrayan supremacy and intensifying the crisis of the empire, the tottering Ethiopian regime is still in power claiming to reform itself under the leadership of Abiy Ahmed, the prime minister of Ethiopia, because of the absence of an Oromo national organizational capacity. At this historical moment, the commercialization and fragmentation of Oromo politics by Oromo political elites have undermined the development of the Oromo national organizational capacity. Oromo nationalists are divided and formed political organizations that are not yet capable of mobilizing all Oromo human, economic, and intellectual resources for building the Oromo national organizational capacity, despite the fact that the *Qerroo/Qarree*-led Oromo movement has laid the ground for the ideological unity of the Oromo national struggle.

In order to prevent the abortion of the transition to democracy, all progressive forces in general and the Oromo movement in particular should support the efforts of democratic transition. Since the Oromo movement is the backbone of this transition, all Oromo political forces including the progressive elements in the OPDO need to stop the commercialization and fragmentation of Oromo politics and combine their human, material, and ideological resources to build the Oromo national organizational capacity, which is absolutely necessary to protect the Oromo national interest at this historical period. The impact of Ethiopian colonialism, the erosion of Oromo national norms, political commercialization and fragmentation, the disconnection between local interests and national interests, and uneven development of Oromo nationalism (national *Oromummaa*) are the major challenges for building a unified Oromo national institution or organization. Without rebuilding strong national institutions, the Oromo cannot transform their numerical strength, abundant economic resources, and the determination of nationalists to national organizational power that can empower the nation.

The immediate challenge the Oromo face as a nation is accepting that they do not have strong national institutions and organizations that can empower the Oromo people at this moment. Another challenge that the Oromo nationalists face today is reshaping Oromo norms and behaviors toward building formidable national institutions and civic and political organizations. The Oromo do not have another model, except critically and thoroughly learning about the Oromo democratic traditions and rebuilding national consensus through honest, open, and democratic deliberations. The Oromo choice is either to reshape their current political norms and behaviors and the way they deliberate their politics in order to rebuild their democratic national institutions and organizations and to build an egalitarian multinational democracy or to perpetuate the existing status quo of fragmentation and disempowerment and suffer under the authoritarian-terrorist state of Ethiopia. The fragmented Oromo political organizations and national leadership should be challeneged by the Oromo people to negotiate and collaborate with one another on the Oromo liberation project in order to protect the Oromo national interest. The various forms of Oromo leadership must also be challenged to move from an initial reliance on a narrow political circle and borrowed political ideologies and practices, and to embrace Oromo-centric democratic values.

Futhermore, all Oromo nationalists should participate in revitalizing the Oromo national movement through the application of elements of *gadaa/siiqqee* principles by aiming at the establishment of a democratic Oromia state and/or shared sovereignty with others by implementing internal peace within the Oromo national movement and the Oromo society and by promoting peace (*nagaa* Oromoo) with Oromo neighbors.

The Oromo national movement needs to retrieve, refine, adapt, and practice the principles of *gadaa/siqqee*. The idea of building a national *Gumii Oromiyaa* must be given top priority by all Oromo and their political and civic organizations in order to revitalize, centralize, and coordinate the Oromo national movement and protect the Oromo national interest. Oromo nationalist leaders need to start to search for ways of enabling all Oromo to participate in the Oromo national movement by providing ideas, resources, expertise, and their labor. Despite the fact that the contemporary organizations of the Oromo national movement use *gadaa* names or concepts, they rarely apply the principles of the system to regulate their own political behavior and practices. According to the Oromo political traditions, rules and laws are made through serious debates, and once decisions have been made by the general assembly both leaders and citizens are obligated to implement them. Nobody is above the rule of law. Although it is challenging and difficult to implement all relevant *gadaa* principles while engaging in the liberation struggle, Oromo organizations must agree on certain principles and initiate pragmatic policies that embody Oromo democracy if they are struggling to restore Oromo statehood, sovereignty, and democracy.

Certain *gadaa* principles that Oromo political and civic organizations need to immediately adapt include the rule of democratic laws, periodic succession of leadership, moral and ethical integrity, honesty, democratic public deliberations, the sovereignty of the people and defeating the collaborator of the enemy, and building national political consensus. By mobilizing *gadaa/siiqqee* experts and Oromo intellectuals who are familiar with the Oromo democratic traditions, the Oromo national movement should start to formulate procedures, strategies, and tactics for the building of the supreme authority of a national assembly that may be called *Gumii Oromiyaa*. At this national *Gumii*, all Oromo liberation fronts and organizations that can carry out their national obligations, all representatives of Oromo civil and religious organizations, and representatives of all Oromo sectors must be included. This national *Gumii* can be modeled after the *Gumii Gayyo* (Huqqa 1998). The *Gumii Gayyo* is an expression of the exemplar model of the unwritten Oromo constitution. Reframing the unwritten Oromo constitution and transforming into a new national constitution based on Oromo democratic principles require absolute commitment from Oromo nationalists and their organizations rather than giving lip service to this idea. By establishing the National Assembly of *Gumii Oromiyaa,* Oromo nationalists and organizations of the Oromo national movement can initiate the process of framing a written Oromo constitution by adapting the received tradition to new circumstances while learning from other democratic traditions.

If Oromo nationalists and organizations are truly concerned about their people and if they want to win their national struggle, they need to show respect for their democratic traditions and practice civility in their political and ideological deliberations. Such responsible and courageous actions require taking accountability seriously and using a single standard for evaluating behavior and measuring performance in relation to the Oromo national struggle. To build *Gumii Oromiyaa*, the Oromo national movement needs to address five major issues. The first issue is to further develop national *Oromummaa* to its full capacity by overcoming its unevenness and deficiencies in order to strengthen the Oromo national organizational capacity. After Oromo were colonized and until Oromo nationalism emerged, Oromoness primarily remained on the personal and the interpersonal levels because Oromo were denied the opportunities to form national institutions and organizations.[8] Consequently, today the Oromo elites who have internalized these externally imposed regional or religious identities because of their low level of political consciousness or political opportunism, and the lack of clear understanding of national *Oromummaa*.

Without critically retrieving and restoring Oromo cultural and historical resources and using them in developing Oromo nationalism, it is difficult to build a national political agenda. Oromo who did not yet develop national political consciousness may confuse clan or regional or religious politics with the Oromo national politics because of the lack of the comprehension of the consequences of their political behaviors and actions. As one can learn from history, the Oromo political weakness mainly emerged as Oromo moved away from one *gadaa* republic and started to form autonomous *gadaa* governments in different parts of Oromia. Hence, the building of the Oromo national organizational capacity is only possible when national *Oromummaa* is fully developed and can be packaged into a generally accepted vision that energizes the entire Oromo nation to undertake a well-organized and coordinated collective action at the personal, interpersonal, and national levels. As an element of culture, and nationalism, national *Oromummaa* has the power to serve as a manifestation of the collective identity of the Oromo national movement. The basis of national *Oromummaa* must be built on overarching principles that are embedded within Oromo democratic traditions and culture and, at the same time, have universal relevance for all oppressed peoples. The main foundations of national *Oromummaa* are individual and collective freedom, justice, popular democracy, and human liberation, which are built on the concept of *safuu* (Oromo moral and ethical order) and are enshrined in *gadaa/siiqqee* principles. As the ideology of the Oromo national movement, national *Oromummaa* enables Oromo to retrieve their cultural memories, assess the consequences of Ethiopian colonialism, and give voice to their collective grievances.

As such, national *Oromummaa* can mobilize diverse cultural resources, interlink Oromo personal, interpersonal, and collective (national) relationships, and assists in the development of Oromo-centric political strategies and tactics that can mobilize the nation for collective action and empower the people for liberation. As the shared ideology of the Oromo national movement, national *Oromummaa* requires that the movement be inclusive of all persons operating in a democratic fashion. National *Oromummaa* enables the Oromo people to form alliances with all political forces and social movements that accept the principles of national self-determination and egalitarian multinational democracy in the promotion of a global humanity that is free of all forms of oppression and exploitation. The Oromo are struggling for national self-determination and an egalitarian multinational democracy because there are other peoples in Oromia and beyond with which they can share statehood and sovereignty based on Oromo democratic traditions. The Oromo movement respects the rights and political aspiration of other peoples beyond Oromia and invites them to create solidarity and form alliance with the Oromo nation.

Furthermore, Oromo civic, cultural, and religious institutions and other Oromo sectors should be partners in building the Oromo national assembly. Oromo nationalists do not need to wait to form the national *Gumii Oromiyaa* until liberation. *Gumii Oromiyaa* as a political and cultural platform can provide a mechanism for establishing a common understanding and consensus among the fragmented Oromo political forces provided that it will be wisely and carefully handled. Oromo nationalists should be clear that the Oromo national movement is not struggling to reinvent the *moottii* system or Oromo chiefdoms based on clans or regions. In some parts of the Oromo society, the emergence of the *moottii* system undermined the *gadaa* system and later facilitated the formation of those Oromo forces that collaborated with the Ethiopian colonial system. As other nationalisms, Oromo nationalism has two edges, the one edge cutting backward, and the other forward. The Oromo national movement should reconsider Oromo culture and history, and recognize the negative ones and avoid them. As the formation of different autonomous *gadaa* governments and the emergence of the *moottii* system contributed to the defeat of the Oromo people in the second half of the nineteenth century, the political fragmentation of the Oromo society will perpetuate the defeat of the Oromo nation in the twenty-first century. Without the coordination and the consolidation of the Oromo national movement, Oromo cannot effectively confront and defeat the Ethiopian colonial system and its Oromo collaborator class.

Oromo liberation organizations have a historic responsibility to cooperate with one another and participate in the Oromo national movement in order to reach larger audiences, share resources as well as experiences, and gain political legitimacy. It is essential that they end their internecine squabbles and negative political propaganda against one another. This does not mean that Oromo organizations should not be scrutinized and evaluated in relations to their objectives, ideologies, and performance. While consolidating the Oromo national movement, it is necessary to build political alliances with peoples who are interested in the principles of national self-determination and egalitarian multinational democracy. Although the priority of the Oromo national movement is to liberate the Oromo people, the movement has moral and political obligations to promote social justice and democracy for the peoples who have suffered under the successive authoritarian-terrorist governments of the Ethiopian Empire. Therefore, the Oromo movement needs to build a political alliance with national groups that endorse the principles of national self-determination and egalitarian multinational democracy. A democratic sovereign Oromia should play a central role in a multinational democratic state because of its democratic tradition, the size of its population, geopolitics, and abundant economic resources.

Every Oromo has moral, political, and national obligations to actively participate in the Oromo national struggle to enable the Oromo nation to achieve its political, social, and economic objectives. Particularly, Oromo intellectuals have great responsibility to mobilize all Oromo and others on the principles of self-determination, social justice, and egalitarian multinational democracy, and to expand the leadership capacity of the Oromo movement. The responsibilities of Oromo intellectuals also include developing pragmatic policies that will lay the foundation of both an Oromian democratic state and an egalitarian multinational state, establishing special relationship with the colonized nations in the Ethiopian Empire, expanding public diplomacy by consolidating the support of the Oromo diaspora, and influencing world powers by using the principles of global *Oromummaa* to support the just cause of the Oromo for social justice, liberation, and democracy.

CONCLUSION

The protection of the Oromo national interest requires restoring the best elements of the *gadaa/siqqee* principles, building national organizational capacity, reinventing an Oromia democratic state in a multinational context, and building an Oromia formidable defense force, which incorporates the Oromo Liberation Army. These are important political steps that are required to stop the systematic attack and terrorism on the Oromo people in Oromia and in different regional Ethiopian states, such as the Somali, Afar, Amhara, the Southern Nations and Nationalities and Peoples Regional State, and Benishangul, as well as in Finfinnee (Addis Ababa) and its surroundings. The first subset of the Oromo national interest is the protection of what the Oromo struggle has achieved up to now. These achievements include the restoration of Oromo national identity and nationalism; the development of *qubee* (the Oromo alphabet) and the restoration of the Oromo language; the geopolitical demarcation of Oromia and the creation of the Oromia Regional State through federalism; the revival of Oromo culture and national unity through restoring certain elements of *gadaa/siqqee;* the efforts of protecting Oromo lands and other resources; and the efforts of liberating Oromo collaborators from the yoke of the enemy by empowering them through developing the psychology of liberation and victorious consciousness to overcome their inferiority complex. The second subset of the Oromo national interest is to maintain the commitment of the Oromo people, which is demonstrated under the leadership of *Qeerroo/Qarree* to achieve popular sovereignty, statehood, and egalitarian multinational democracy. The protection of these achievements is absolutely necessary to move toward protecting the Oromo national interest.

The immediate task for the Oromo political and civic institutions and organizations should be to agree upon creating the democratic rules of the game based on acceptable national norms and behaviors and values that reflect *safuu* and Oromo democracy in order to protect the Oromo national interest. The next task is to build formidable national institutions and organizations that will empower the Oromo nation to determine its national destiny. All concerned Oromo are agents who can contribute something to change the deplorable condition of their people. It is wrong to be neutral and silent when the Oromo people are facing terrorism and genocidal massacres by the colonial elites and their collaborators. Particularly, the diaspora Oromo have moral and ethical responsibilities to maintain *safuu* and to get organized to support the struggle of their people; they must also stop those who engage in divisive activities that facilitate the perpetual suffering of their people. History aptly demonstrates that people can revolt and overthrow regimes, but they cannot form their own democratic government without having their strong national institutions and organizations. All Oromo nationalists and organizations are required to be united for building the Oromo national organizational capacity, which insures the survival of the Oromo nation and protects its national interest.

NOTES

1. As Pierre Bourdieu notes: "as *economic capital*, which is . . . directly convertible into money and may be institutionalized in the forms of private property rights; as *cultural capital*, which is convertible . . . into economic capital and may be institutionalized in the forms of [position of power] and educational qualifications; and as *social capital*, made of social obligations ('connections'), which is convertible . . . into economic capital and may be institutionalized in the form of a title of nobility." His theories of cultural capital should not be limited to formal education, and it must also include informal education, which plays a significant role in maintaining status quo in class, gender, and ethnonational hierarchies. See, https://www.marxists.org/reference/subject/philosophy/works/fr/bourdieu-forms-capital.htm, accessed on 11/09/17.

2. *Gadaa* was a form of constitutional government of the Oromo. It was practiced through the election of political leaders by adult male suffrage every eight years; corrupt leaders would be removed from power through *buqisu* (recall) before their official tenure. See Asmarom Legesse, *Oromo Democracy: An Indigenous African Political System* (Trenton, NJ: Red Sea Press, Inc., 2006). *Siqqee* is a sub-set of *gadaa*, and I use the terms *gadaa/siqqee* to designate the concept of Oromo democracy.

3. The accumulated grievances, the recent intensification of land grabbing policies, massive poverty, gross human rights violations, and the broadening of the political consciousness of the Oromo in general and the youth, in particular, have resulted in the Oromia-wide peaceful youth protest movement. The *Qeerroo/Qarree* protest movement erupted in Ginchi, near Ambo, not far from Finfinnee (Addis Ababa—the capital city), on November 12, 2015, and shortly covered all of Oromia like wildfire. The Oromo elementary and secondary students of this small town ignited the peaceful

protests because of the privatization and confiscation of a small soccer field and selling of the nearby Chilimoo forest to be cleared and deforested. Supporting the peaceful protests of these students and opposing the so-called Addis Ababa master plan, the entire Oromo population from all walks of life joined the peaceful protests.

4. https://www.garda.com/crisis24/news-alerts/90136/ethiopia-three-day-strike-in-amhara-and-oromia-regions-feb-12-14, accessed on 7/16/2018.

5. https://bawza.com/2018/03/05/boycott-oromia-protest-state-emergency/, accessed on 7/16/2018.

6. https://bawza.com/2018/03/05/boycott-oromia-protest-state-emergency/, accessed on 7/16/2018.

7. https://www.washingtonpost.com/world/africa/ethiopian-lawmakers-approve-state-of-emergency/2018/03/0, accessed on 7/16/2018.

8. Oromoness was targeted for destruction and colonial administrative regions that were established to suppress the Oromo people and exploit their resources were glorified and institutionalized. As a result, Oromo relational identities have been localized, and not strongly connected to the collective identity of national *Oromummaa*. Oromo have been separated from one another and prevented from exchanging goods and information for more than a century. They were exposed to different cultures (i.e., languages, customs, values, etc.) and religions and adopted some elements of these cultures and religions.

NINE

The Challenges of Building Oromo National Institutions

HISTORICAL BACKGROUND

A brief historical background of the Oromo and their institutions and organizations is necessary to provide context for the issues discussed in this chapter. The colonization of the Oromo destroyed their cultural and political institutions. More than half a century later a young Oromo generation began to create national institutions and organizations such as the Macha-Tulama Self-Help Association (MTA) and the Oromo Liberation Front (OLF) in the early 1960s and in the 1970s respectively (Jalata 2005). In response, the Ethiopian totalitarian political apparatus violently repressed the development of the MTA and the OLF. The former was banned in 1967 after attracting more than three million members, and the OLF, an armed politico-military insurgency seeking to reverse the earlier colonization and to establish an independent democratic government based on traditional Oromo values, only functioned legally and openly between 1991 and 1992. In 1991 the OLF joined the Transitional Government of Ethiopia led by the Tigrayan Liberation Front (TPLF) by contributing to the overthrow of the Amhara-led Ethiopian military junta. In the same way that the Amhara-dominated government destroyed the MTA because of its popularity, their successor, the Tigrayan-led regime, declared war on the OLF in 1992 because most of the Oromo supported the organization (Jalata 2010a) and that support threatened the dominance of the TPLF in the government. The OLF has functioned as an "illegal" and clandestine organization for more than four decades, with the exception of the Transitional Government of Ethiopia period, and has not had the opportunity to openly educate, mobilize, and organize the Oromo people. Thousands of Oromo have been brutalized, repressed, killed, or exiled after being labeled as OLF members and terrorists.[1]

The Oromo people have been repressed, oppressed, and exploited, and denied the legal right to openly build their national institutions and organizations for more than a century. As a result, Oromo nationalists have been forced to organize themselves clandestinely, which has been risky and suicidal because any Oromo who has been suspected in organizing people could be automatically imprisoned, tortured, or executed (Jalata 2005). The colonization and subsequent repression of the Oromo people have occurred in relation to global capitalism. In general, global capitalism, through colonialism and incorporation, brought together various population groups in a political unit called the nation-state in which the dominant or colonizing ethnonations either destroyed through violence or absorbed subordinate ethnonations through structural assimilation or created a system that perpetuates exploitation and oppression by practicing racist policies and by denying political rights and civil equality (Jalata 2010a). For political expediency, Ethiopianist scholars such as Teshale Tibebu (1995) and Merera Gudina (2003) argue that modern Ethiopia was not formed through colonialism, and assert that it was created through territorial expansion and incorporation of various Ethiopian peoples. In reality, proper Abyssinia/old Ethiopia only included some parts of Gojjam, Gondar, Tigray, and small parts of Shawa before the Scramble for Africa.

In actuality, during the last decades of the nineteenth century, Menelik terrorized and colonized the Oromo and others with the help of France, Italy, and England to obtain commodities such as gold, ivory, coffee, musk, hides and skins, and slaves and lands.[2] Menelik became one of the richest capitalists in the world and invested in American Railway Stock; "the Abyssinian ruler had extended the range of his financial operations to the United States, and [was] a heavy investor in American railroads . . . with his American securities and his French and Belgian mining investments, Menelik [had] a private fortune estimated at no less than twenty-five million dollars" (*New York Times*, November 7, 1909). Historical facts demonstrate that modern Ethiopia has been a colonial empire, and the colonial terrorism and massive killings that started during the last decades of the nineteenth century continues into the twenty-first century with the support of global powers (Jalata 2010a). The creation of the Ethiopian Empire and the emergence of the Oromo national movement occurred in the context of these complex processes. Therefore, the development of Oromo nationalism is not the result of a naturally given process, but is a historical and political product, which has developed in response to large-scale and long-term social change. Consequently, oppressed Oromo nationalism has developed as the result of human agency, and social and structural factors such as the immortality of cultural memory, transformations in social structures resulting from economic and political changes, urbanization, community formation, the emergence of an educated class, politicized collective grievances, and the dissemination of scientific knowledge through global and local networks (Jalata 2010a, 12–13). The issues of Oromo institutions and organizations cannot be adequately addressed without recognizing these complex historical and political issues. Before explaining the current challenges of building Oromo national institutions and organizations, it is necessary to examine the conceptual, empirical, and theoretical aspects of institutions.

THE CONCEPTUAL, PRACTICAL, AND THEORETICAL UNDERSTANDING OF INSTITUTIONS

The complexity and diversity of social institutions make an understanding of their conceptual, practical, and theoretical characteristics cumbersome. Although social scientists have yet to establish a consensus on the definition of a typical social institution (Hechter 1990, 13), there are empirical and theoretical deliberations on the concepts that are helpful in comprehending social institutions. Sometimes, the term social institution can be referred to ideal types such as the family or religion or the polity or the economy. Other times, it can be referred to laws, norms, or informal rules in a society. People also use the concept of institution to refer to particular organizations such as Howard University or CNN. Since an institution is a complex interaction among social, cultural, political, economic, and organizational factors in a society (Aoki 2005), it cannot be defined and theorized with precision. Therefore, a clear understanding of social institutions and their consistent changes require knowing the difference between institutions and organizations and their roles and interactions. Institutions are "the rules of the game," and organizations are the players or the agents in a society (North 1995, 15). In other words, social "institutions are the constraints that human beings impose on human interaction. They consist of formal rules (constitutions, statute law, common law, and regulations) and informal constraints (conventions, norms, and self-enforced codes of conduct) and their enforcement characteristics. These constraints define (together with the standard constraints of economics) the opportunity set in the economy" (North 1995, 15).

Ethiopian colonialism suppressed Oromo institutions such as the *gadaa/siiqqee* system (Oromo democracy), which established the rules of the game in organizing and ordering the Oromo society before colonization. Without strong institutional foundations, Oromo political organizations have faced internal and external challenges that have undermined their development, as we will see below. At this historical moment, the Oromo society does not have political power and an institutional mechanism, which can be mobilized to effectively organize its members by constraining those Oromo collaborators of the enemy. Because of its colonization and subordination, the Oromo society lacks formal and informal rules to effectively control the norms, values, and actions of its members to promote its welfare. Without establishing their formal and informal rules, the Oromo people could not build their strong political organizations, which are necessary to liberate and develop them. Generally speaking, social institutions produce and maintain *"some regularity in collective behavior"* in a society in order to influence individuals to behave similarly in the same social condition (Hechter 1990, 14).

There are two theoretical assumptions about the emergence and maintenance of social institutions: One of the assumptions is the *invisible-hand* approach, and the other one is the *solidarity* perspective. The first one considers "the emergence of institutions as a spontaneous by-product of the voluntary actions of self-interested individuals who share *no common ends or values*" (Hechter 1990, 14). According to this perspective, institutions are self-regulating entities because they have self-enforcing equilibriums, and they do not need another enforcement agency. This assumption is based on evolutionary theories: "Evolutionary theories generally rely on one of the mechanisms originally formulated by classical theory: spontaneous emergence, market-coordinated exchange, or social selection" (Knight and Sened 1995, 2–3). This perspective wrongly denies the intervention of the state in the economy, and how politics and economics are dialectically integrated. States frequently intervene in the economy through colonialism, war, labor control, and liberalism/neo-liberalism to transfer capital/wealth from the colonized and subaltern groups and classes to the dominant classes or capital accumulators. Therefore, the notion of "self-enforcing equilibriums" and the denial of the necessity "another enforcement agency" in "market-coordinated exchange" are, at least, not accurate. All rich countries and their elites have enriched themselves through colonialism, war, neoliberalism, exploitation of free or wage labor, dispossession of valuable resources such as land, and not necessarily through mark-oriented exchange (Jalata 2016). For example, the Ethiopian colonial state has dispossessed Oromo lands and other economic resources and exploited Oromo labor to enrich the colonial bureaucrats and their collaborators. The principles of "self-regulating entities" and "self-enforcing equilibriums" are not applicable because force is used, not market, to intensify the process of wealth/capital accumulation at the cost of the Oromo society.

"From the solidarity perspective, institutions persist not because they constitute self-enforcing equilibriums, but they are supported by consciously-designed controls" (Hechter 1990, 14–15). Social institutions enable a society to solve their collective problems by establishing collectivity and solidarity among groups of individuals: "Social institutions provide groups of individuals with the means of resolving collective action problems and provide benefits for collective activity. On these accounts, institutional maintenance and stability are primarily explained by the capacity of institutions to produce collective goods or benefits for social groups" (Knight and Sened 1995, 2). However, evolutionary theories claim that social forces including population, production, reproduction, regulation, and distribution have pushed individuals and collective actors to organize certain ways to satisfy their needs; these forces led to the development of core human institutions such as economy, kinship, religion, polity, law, and education (Turner 2003). As Jonathan H. Turner (2003, 2) asserts, "social institutions . . . [are] *those population-wide structures and associated cultural (symbolic) systems that humans create and use to adjust to the exigencies of their environment.* Without institutions, humans cannot survive, and societies cannot exist." Social "institutions are generated, sustained, and changed by population, production, reproduction, regulation, and distribution. Each of these forces constitutes a basic contingency of human existence, pushing individual and collective actors to build particular kinds of social structures and cultural systems" (Turner 2003, 7). Production involves resources from the environment that are needed to sustain life.

The activities of the economy develop from these resources and depend on technology, physical capital or implements, human capital or the knowledge/skill, property, and entrepreneurship or the mechanisms for organizing technology, physical capital, and property systems (Turner 2003, 7). Above all, evolutionary and functionalist theories are incapable of critically and thoroughly explaining modern institutions and the crimes that some of them have committed against the cultures and institutions of indigenous peoples. Both theories have assumed that a society develops from primitive to modernity, and social change is necessarily progress by denying or ignoring the destruction of indigenous peoples and their cultures and institutions by the forces of modernity and global capitalism. Furthermore, they are inherently social Darwinists and they dismiss the institutions of indigenous peoples as primitive and useless. The West and dominant ethnonations and their institutions developed and enriched themselves at the cost of indigenous peoples in the Americas, Australia, Africa, and other places (Jalata 2016). Without any question, social institutions play central roles in the processes of socioeconomic reproduction, socialization, preservation or change of social order, transmission of culture, and personality development. In satisfying human needs, social institutions create and maintain social solidary and cohesion among members of a society to facilitate collective action. Human beings need to reproduce themselves by producing material goods and services through their institutional frameworks. All institutions produce and preserve social norms and transmit them to members of a given society. This is called the process of socialization.

Every society establishes its norm as a property of its social system at micro and macro levels to differentiate proper or correct behaviors and actions from improper or incorrect behaviors and actions by rewarding the former and punishing the latter (Coleman 1990, 37). "The concept of a norm at a macro-social level, governing the behavior of individuals at a micro-social level, provides a convenient device for explaining individual behavior, taking a social system as a given" (Coleman 1990, 36). As James S. Coleman (1990, 35) notes, "the emergence of norms can be accounted for by two simple principles. The first of these concerns the conditions in which a demand for effective norms will arise; the second concerns the conditions under which the demand will be satisfied. Both sets of conditions may be described as a social structural." Social norms and state institutions, such as the military, assist to maintain a social order or a social system. "Conceptualizing social institutions as one of multiple possible stable cultural equilibrium allows a straightforward explanation of their properties. The evolution of institutions is partly driven by both the deliberate and intuitive decisions of individuals and collectivities. The innate components of human psychology coevolved in response to a culturally evolved, institutional environment" (Boyd and Richerson 2008, 305). Institutions "have the capacity to change the world [positively or negatively] . . . [and] they are . . . our best instrument for changing the world" (Soltan 1998, 49). As the case of the Oromo demonstrates below, colonial institutions have negatively changed the colonized people to exploit their economic and labor resources.

It is important to realize that the colonized people need autonomous or independent institutions to solve their externally imposed and internally generated problems. Whether collective behaviors or norms are produced spontaneously or designed consciously or both, all societies need independent institutions to collectively solve their problems. New institutionalists assert that "institutions must be grounded in the social fabric and thus that rational choice by individuals must be combined with historical and cultural variables" (Soltan, Uslaner and Haufler 1998, 3). It is necessary to clearly comprehend the differences between the institutions of the colonizers and the colonized. In the capitalist world system, the elites and their supporters "have . . . perceived the game as one where the highest rewards accrued to military conquest, exploitation (such as enslavement [and colonization]), formation of monopolies, and so forth; in consequence, the kinds of skills and knowledge invested in have been aimed at furthering such policies" (North 1995, 19). It is demonstrated below that Ethiopian colonialism and its institutions have destroyed and/or suppressed Oromo national institutions in order to make the Oromo society powerless and to exploit its economic and human resources. Without challenging and defeating Ethiopian colonial institutions and organizations and without building the Oromo independent national institutions and organizations, the Oromo national movement cannot be victorious.

THE IMPACT OF ETHIOPIAN COLONIALISM ON OROMO INSTITUTIONS

The colonization of Oromia involved human tragedies and institutional destructions. The repression of Oromo lives and institutions were aspects of Ethiopian colonial violence. The Oromo who survived from initial colonial violence and who previously enjoyed an egalitarian democracy known as the *gadaa/siiqqee* system were forced to live an impoverished life under political repression. Alexander Bulatovich (2000, 68) describes the *gadaa* administration, and how it was destroyed by Ethiopian colonialism: "The peaceful free way of life, which could have become the ideal for philosophers and writers of the eighteenth century, if they had known it, was completely changed. Their peaceful way of life [was] broken; freedom [was] lost; and the independent, freedom loving [Oromo] find themselves under the severe authority of the Abyssinian conquerors." Furthermore, the other political system that was suppressed and co-opted to the Ethiopian colonial system was called the *mooti* system (Jalata 2005, 26–36). The *mooti* system emerged in a few branches of the Oromo, and it was hierarchical and the opposite of Oromo democracy. The historical legacy of Oromo political leadership is the sovereignty the Oromo experienced under the *gadaa/siiqee* government and its egalitarian framework. Long before democracy was the norm in Europe and North America, the design of *gadaa/siiqqee* as a social and political institution worked to prevent political domination and economic exploitation in the Oromo society.

Consequently, under the *gadaa/siiqee* system, the Oromo society enjoyed relative peace, stability, sustainable development, and political sovereignty although technologically and bureaucratically it was not well developed. Discussing the philosophy of Oromo democracy, Asmarom Legesse (1973, 2) notes: "What is astonishing about this cultural tradition is how far Oromo have gone to ensure that power does not fall in the hand of war chiefs and despots. They achieve this goal by creating a system of checks and balances that is at least as complex as the systems we find in Western democracies." The imposition of the Ethiopian colonial system and the emergence of an Oromo collaborative class have denied the Oromo the opportunity of building strong national institutions and organizations. As a result, the Oromo continue to face monumental challenges in building national institutions that could have helped them in establishing the rules of the game, and in building strong national organizations that could have effectively mobilized them to successfully carry out the national projects of liberation, development and egalitarian democracy. The Ethiopian colonial state gradually established settler colonialism and developed five major types of colonial institutions, namely, slavery, the colonial landholding system, the *nafxanya-gabbar* system (semi-slavery), the Oromo collaborative class, and garrison and non-garrison cities (Jalata 2005). These colonial institutions were created to effectively dominate and control the Oromo and their country in order to intensify the exploitation of their economic and human resources. The Ethiopian colonial state partitioned the Oromo society physically and mentally, and the Oromo national movement has yet to fully destroy the foundations of these divisions.

These divisions have undermined *safuu* (Oromo moral and ethical order) and the rules of the game that they used to have in building and consolidating their institutions. Consequently, in the absence of strong institutions and organizations in the Oromo society, some Oromo individuals and groups have become the agents of the colonial system to benefit themselves and their colonial masters. That was why millions of Oromo joined the Oromo People's Democratic Organization (OPDO), a puppet organization that was formed in March 1982 by the Tigrayan People's Liberation Front (TPLF) with the support of the Eritrean People's Liberation Front to counter the Oromo Liberation Front (OLF), which has struggled for the liberation of the Oromo people and their country, Oromia, since the early 1970s. OPDO members were originally recruited from Oromo and Oromo-speaking non-Oromo war captives, and later many opportunist Oromo joined the organization for money and power. Some members of this organization have become colonial agents for the Tigrayan-led Ethiopian colonial state and have been involved in terrorizing, killing, imprisoning, torturing, and suppressing members of the Oromo society. The majority of the Oromo who joined the regime in recent years did so for economic reasons because the TPLF regime has controlled the political economy of the empire. The Ethiopian colonial state has used brute force and developed elaborate mechanisms to prevent the Oromo people from building independent national institutions, organizations, and leadership (Jalata 2007, 33). Understanding the key roles of leaders in building institutions and organizing people, the colonial system has eliminated intelligent and farsighted leaders and assimilated the others through religion, education, and political marriage (Dugassa 2012, 145–160).

Oromo institutions, except families or extended families, kinships or lineages, have been destroyed or suppressed during the years since the imposition of Ethiopia colonialism. Institutions can be imposed by powerful forces on conquered populations or can be created voluntarily by individuals who have roughly equal power (Hechter 1990, 15). The suppression of *Waaqeffannaa*, an indigenous Oromo religion, and the imposition of the imperial religions of Christianity and Islam have also undermined the development of Oromo national norms and values. In addition to brutal force, the absence of Oromo national norms has led most Oromo to focus on their kinships or lineages or localities while failing to understand the importance of building national organizations and institutions; that is why most Oromo in the diaspora are organized in kinship-based and local self-help or religious-based associations to help one another during death or wedding or other specific activities and less organized in national institutions and organizations. This reality is currently demonstrated by the existence of many kinship-based and local self-associations in the diaspora that do not have strong relationships with national institutions and organizations. Consequently, some Oromo in the diaspora are more familiar with their personal and relational selves than they are with their Oromo collective self because their level of Oromo nationalism is rudimentary. Oromo individuals have intimate relations with their family members, friends, and local communities. These interpersonal and close relations foster helping, nurturing, and caring relationships. However, without developing these micro-relationships into the macro-relationships of national *Oromummaa* (Oromo national culture, identity and nationalism) through national institutions, the building of Oromo national organizational capacity is illusive. Organizing the Oromo requires learning about the multiplicity and flexibility of Oromo identities and fashioning from them a collective national identity that encompasses the vast majority of the Oromo populace.

Having kin-based and local-based self-help associations could have been beneficial had they worked toward building Oromo national institutions and organizations. These problems are further complicated by the fragmentation of Oromo political and civic organizations. A few Oromo nationalist elements in the diaspora have tried to create and build national civic institutions and political organizations. For instance, in North America these elements created the Union of Oromo in North America, the Oromo Studies Association, Oromo communities in various cities and the Global Gumii Oromia that have kept the spirit of Oromo nationalism. However, these associations and organizations have yet to coalescence into formidable national institutions because they have been easily influenced by parochial norms and the presence of individuals surreptitiously collaborating with Ethiopian colonial structures. As mentioned above, in Oromia, the attempt by a few Oromo nationalists to build an Oromo polity in the period following the 1960s has faced many dangers because of the brutality of Ethiopian colonialism that has killed or imprisoned farsighted leaders and denied the Oromo the freedom of political organization, association, and expression. The political opportunism and/or naiveté of some Oromo political elites have also contributed to the political fragmentation and the disempowerment of the Oromo society. Recently, however, the political/organizational situation in Oromia has been undergoing fundamental changes. The accumulated grievances, the recent intensification of land grabbing policies, particularly the so-called Integrated Addis Ababa Master Plan, and the development of the political consciousness of the Oromo people beginning with the national struggle of the 1960s have resulted in the Oromia-wide peaceful protest movement that emerged in 2015. The Oromo protest movement that erupted in

Ginchi, near Ambo, on November 12, 2015, quickly covered all Oromia like wildfire. The sporadic Oromo student protests, however, started in 2005 with the influence of the OLF.

The Oromo students in Ginchi town ignited peaceful protests because of the privatization and confiscation of a small soccer field and the selling of the nearby Chilimoo forest to be cleared and deforested. Supporting the peaceful protests of these students, Oromo from all walks of life joined the peaceful protests all over Oromia by opposing the so-called Integrated Addis Ababa Master Plan. The so-called master plan was intended to expand Finfinnee (Addis Ababa) to 1.5 million hectares of surrounding Oromo lands by evicting Oromo farmers and by destroying Oromo identity, culture and history (Thomson and López 2015) and by replacing them with Tigrayans and their collaborators. Through the accumulated experiences of the past twenty-seven years, the Oromo people had realized that the Tigrayan colonial elites with the help of their Oromo collaborators had been expropriating Oromo lands and other resources and transferring them to themselves and their domestic and global supporters. In these processes, the Oromo people have become aliens in their own country, and Oromia had been owned by Tigrayans. Educated and evicted Oromo have become jobless while most Tigrayans and their collaborators dominated and controlled the political economy of Oromia and Ethiopia. At the same time, the Oromo national struggle that emerged in the 1960s has been penetrating the psyche of the Oromo people. This struggle has been revitalizing the Oromo national culture, history, and nationalism as national *Oromummaa*, which has blossomed and become a revolutionary flame.

It is believed that underground activist networks known as *Qeerroo/Qarree* (youth)[3] organized the Oromo community. The *Qeerroo/Qarree* first emerged in 1991 with the participation of the OLF in the transitional government of Ethiopia. In 1992 the Tigrayan-led minority regime pushed the OLF out of the transitional government and the activist networks of *Qeerroo/Qarree* gradually blossomed as a form of Oromo nationalism.[4] It took more than two decades for the Oromo struggle to transform into a broad-based social movement. The OLF learned, through trial and error, how to build secret activist cells or nuclei through which it has disseminated its directives and policies among Oromo students in colleges and high and elementary schools.[5] In 2005, it declared what it called *Fincila Dida Garbummaa* (Revolt Against Political Slavery) in which it invited all Oromo students and others to peacefully and clandestinely participate in the Oromo national struggle.[6] Today the *Qeerroo/Qarree* are made up of Oromo youth and other nationalist elements. These are predominantly students from elementary school to university, organizing collective action through social media networks and personal relations. The *Qeerroo/Qarree* clandestine groups have clearly articulated that the

OLF should replace the Tigrayan-led regime and recognized the OLF as the origin of the recent outbreak of Oromo nationalism.

The government reaction to the *Qeerroo/Qarree* has been violent and repressive. Despite the fact that Oromia is the largest regional state in Ethiopia,[7] it has been under state of emergency laws[8] since the protests began. The regime has used these laws to silence Oromo protesters and political organizations[9] by arbitrarily imprisoning and killing activists and politicians.[10] The Tigrayan-led government had been able to use these laws to detain thousands of Oromo, holding them in prisons and concentration camps.[11] Security structures called *tokkoo-shane* (one-to-five), *garee* and *got* had also been implemented.[12] The *gott* is a village-level political and security structure, and *garee* is a subset of *gott* and consists 30 people. Their responsibilities include spying, identifying, exposing, imprisoning, torturing and killing Oromo who are not interested in serving the regime. There had been deaths and reports of thousands of Oromo who had been maimed as a result of torture and beatings during the suppression of protests.[13] The Tigrayan elites and their Oromo collaborators who used to think that the Oromo people were collections of "tribes" who could be used as raw material and firewood have failed to understand the essence of the ongoing Oromo movement. They have believed that by beating, torturing, castrating, decapitating, raping, and murdering Oromo students, farmers, educators, and merchants could stop the Oromo struggle for statehood, sovereignty, and the establishment of an egalitarian multinational democracy.[14]

Nevertheless, the Oromo protest movement has opened a new chapter in the history of Oromia and Ethiopia. This history is being written by Oromo blood, and the relationship between the Oromo and their colonizers has been changed forever. The final chapter of this history has yet to be written. Many things have changed as the result of the Oromo protest movement. The costs the Oromo have paid in lives and suffering is very high. Within five months more than 500 Oromo including school children, pregnant women, and elderly people were massacred, and tens of thousands of Oromo were imprisoned, kicked, beaten, tortured, and decapitated.[15] In fact, at this time, we lack full data on the killings, imprisonments, and other crimes that have been committed against the Oromo. Despite all these tragedies, the Oromo people have restored the national pride, patriotism, and bravery that they enjoyed prior to mid-nineteenth century. The protests gained further traction as the state's reaction became violent. For example, in early October 2016 millions of Oromo gathered at Hora Arsadii, south east of Finfinnee, for "Irreechaa"—the Oromo national holiday of thanksgiving. The Tigrayan-led government's army killed more than 700 Oromo and injured and imprisoned thousands.[16] This was sparked by peaceful, anti-government chants by young Oromo.[17] After the massacre, Oromo protesters burned properties including both locally and internationally owned businesses that had been built on the land seized from the Oromo by Tigrayan political and business elites.[18] As the Oromo protest movement intensified, the Amhara, Konso, Sidama, Gurage, and Gedeo joined the protest movement.

The Ethiopian government's response was to declare states of emergency.[19] The first state of emergency was set at six months, and later extended by three months. It was aimed at curbing the growing antigovernment protest movement. The second state of emergency was the last attempt by the Tigrayan-led government to stop the Oromo protests so they could remain in power. The government therefore used the states of emergency to gain total control over the people and information;[20] it also used a heavy force by denying the people the freedom of organization and association. As a result, the regions of Oromia, Amhara, Konso, Gurage, and Gedeo had become conflict zones[21] with the regime indiscriminately imprisoning, looting, and killing protesters.[22] According to the state of emergency rules, Oromo, Amharas, Konsos, and others had been restricted from access to the media. The people were not allowed to listen to diaspora-based media such as the Voice of Oromo Liberation Radio or to watch media channels, like the Oromia Media Network, the Oromia News Network, and the Ethiopian Satellite Television and Radio. Ethiopian soldiers were enforcing these rules and continued to seize or vandalize the satellite dishes of citizens. The emergency rules also prevented citizens from associating with political organizations that the regime had branded as "terrorist." One of these was the Oromo Liberation Front. For several years, the Oromia region had been under a crackdown enforced by special police groups and the army known as "Agazi."[23] After the protest movement started, according to rights organizations, more than 2,000 Oromo were killed in eleven months,[24] and in 2018 alone about 7,000 Oromo were murdered in Oromia. Several thousands more had been imprisoned, tortured, blinded, and raped. To hide its crimes from the international community, the regime frequently blocked the Internet and collected phones from thousands of Oromo.[25]

The Oromo engaged in peaceful protests all over Oromia for more than three years, and the regime continued to kill and imprison people *en masse*. They were denied state support in relation to protection, food, shelter, clothing, medicine, and other necessary services.[26] Because the regime feared the size of the Oromo population—the Oromo are the largest ethnonational group in Ethiopia—it attempted to reduce their influence through hidden policies and war.[27] The regime had prevented Oromo representatives from coming into political power through systematic killings, imprisonment, or exile.[28] For these reasons, the Oromo were very concerned about their future. In addition, there was little hope for things to change as a result of external pressure because international powers such as the United States[29] as well as organizations such as USAID had a close relationship with the government.[30] This gave rise to concerns within the Oromo community that their grievances would not be heard and that they would not be given support.

Nevertheless, the Oromo people are determined to change the status quo and better their future. That is why they are continuing with their movement, despite massive incidents of deaths and imprisonments. At the same time, the Ethiopian regime has demonstrated that it will dictate everything to the Oromo people and its leadership through the barrel of a gun. The Oromo people are rejecting this heavy-handed approach. So, in this conflict, there are two options—either the regime must go, and the Oromo be victorious, or the Oromo people must be politically and economically enslaved to serve the interest of the regime. Despite the fact that the regime has intensified its violence, the Oromo protest movement has started to change the political landscape of Ethiopia and shaken the regime's foundations. Erupting like "a social volcano," it has sent ripples through the empire with different groups changing their attitudes and standing in solidarity with the Oromo.[31] The support of the Ahmaras had been particularly significant as they are the second-largest ethnonational group in Ethiopia. For the first time in history, the plight of the Oromo people has also received worldwide attention. International media outlets have reported on the peaceful protests and subsequent government repression. This has resulted in diplomatic repercussions.

In January 2016 the European Parliament condemned the Ethiopian government's violent crackdown.[32] It also called for the establishment of a credible, transparent, and independent body to investigate the murder and imprisonment of thousands of protesters. Similarly, the UN Human Rights Experts demanded that Ethiopian authorities stop the violent crackdown.[33] Not all global actors are taking a strong stance. Some are concerned with maintaining good relations with the government. Nevertheless, the momentum of the Oromo movement has been continuing. The protests, and subsequent support, have seen the further development of activist networks and Oromo leadership, doubling their efforts to build their national institutional and organizational capacity. There are reasons why the Oromo movement has yet to dismantle Ethiopian colonial structures after shaking their foundations. The absence of the national institutional and organizational capacity, which is a prerequisite to capture state power, is the main reason. This fundamental problem should be recognized and solved, if the Oromo are to achieve their national political objectives of liberation and egalitarian multinational democracy for all ethnonations within the Ethiopian empire.

MAJOR OBSTACLES IN BUILDING OROMO NATIONAL INSTITUTIONS

The political legacy of Ethiopian colonialism, the erosion of Oromo national norms, political fragmentation, the disconnection between local interests and national interests, and uneven development of national *Oromummaa* are the major challenges for building Oromo national institutions and organizations. Successive Ethiopian colonial governments have prevented the Oromo society from developing autonomous national institutions and organizations through violence and other policies (Jalata 2007, 2010; Dugassa 2012). These chains of factors have negatively affected the Oromo elites and the other sectors of the Oromo society psychologically, ideologically, culturally, and politically. As a result, most of the time, most Oromo elites spend their intellectual and material resources, energies, and time on peripheral projects such as changing of the Ethiopian Empire through introducing "socialism" or "democracy" or focus on the differences among Oromo branches and localities rather than learning critically and rigorously about Oromo national history, culture, and tradition in order to build Oromo national institutions and organizations. As Robert Boyd and Peter J. Richerson (2008, 322) state, "The visibility of politically driven institutional change might suggest that every institutional feature of a society is subject to strong political influences. History, however, teaches us that institutions have deep roots that guide politics via unexamined attitudes, intuitions, and emotions."

It is obvious that the absence of national institutions has hindered the progress of the Oromo national struggle. Oromo political organizations could not be effective without national institutions that could have responded to the onslaught of the colonial state by mobilizing the Oromo society. Without building strong national institutions, the Oromo will not be able to transform their numerical strength, abundant economic resources, and the determination of nationalists into national organizational power that can empower the Oromo people. By the way, even the developed societies, which have complex national institutions, face the problem of institutional renewal to catch up with the global movement of large numbers of people for economic and humanitarian situations as well as to advance in science and technology. For instance, countries that are very rich have yet to solve the problem of poverty; societies that have advanced in medicine by replacing damaged hips, livers, kidneys, knees, and other parts of human body, and in biology by mapping the human genome and understanding the structure of the human brain, and in computer science by improving the acquisition of knowledge, the storage of information, and the speed of communication have failed to solve the major problems of humanity. As Lawrence S. Wittner (2017, 1) points out, "there is a glaring discrepancy between these kinds of advances and the social institutions that can ensure that they are used for the benefit of humanity. Despite very substantial progress in modern science, vast numbers of people receive no medical treatment or, at best, inferior medical care. Television's marvelous ability to transmit knowledge, culture, and understanding around the world is employed primarily to distribute mindless, coarse entertainment and peddle commercial products."

Powerful countries and their clients are still engaged in violent development that destroys humanity and the environment to benefit a few capital accumulators and their agents around the globe. The following point that Wittner raises for powerful groups and countries also applies to the Oromo case: "The real question is whether people and nations can muster the political will to reshape their behavior and social institutions to meet the challenges of today and tomorrow." The challenge the Oromo nationalists face today is reshaping their norms and behaviors toward building formidable national institutions and political organizations by transforming their kin-based or local-based institutions and fragmented political organizations. The transformation of norms and behaviors is required on micro- and macro-levels. A key model for this transformation includes to critically and thoroughly learning about the Oromo democratic traditions and to build a national consensus through honest, open, and democratic deliberations. As Robert Boyd and Peter J. Richerson (2008, 322) note, "Every human social group has politics. Ongoing environmental changes will probably destabilize existing institutional equilibriums and make other potential equilibriums attractive. Deliberate, collective decision making is a means to escape failing equilibriums and to negotiate a path to a superior new one. In these often-controversial domains, we are extremely well aware that there are choices to be made. The art of reason, empirical science, and rhetoric are deployed to persuade others that some change in an institution is necessary or not." If they are to be successful in the task of liberating and democratizing the Oromo society, Oromo nationalists need to understand the complexities and possibilities where local or kinship or regional and national institutions are mutually and dialectically integrated in building institutions and organizations at micro, meso- and national levels.

The Oromo choice is either to reshape their current norms and behaviors and the way they deliberate their politics in order to build their democratic national institutions and organizations to liberate themselves or to perpetuate the existing status quo of fragmentation and disempowerment and suffer under the colonial state of Ethiopia. Understanding this reality, some Oromo activist scholars and nationalists have recently established a national civic platform in North America known as the Global Gumii Oromia based on *gadaa/siiqqee* principles and invited all Oromo institutions and organizations including religious ones, political organizations, professional associations, civic institutions, groups and individuals to openly, honestly, and democratically deliberate with this new national civic institution to collectively build Oromo national institutions and organizations in order to make collective decision on Oromia's national affairs. All Oromo nationalists need to recognize that Oromo "indigenous organizational structures are framed in an Oromo paradigm of thinking and they are in a better position to understand the social problems of the Oromo people. In addition, they foster the participation of people, create a stable, transparent and dynamic society and help to continuously improve the social environment in which the Oromo work and live" (Dugassa 2014, 23).

THE WAY FORWARD

The immediate task Oromo nationalists need to accomplish is agreeing to create the democratic rules of the game based on acceptable national norms, behaviors, and values that reflect *safuu* (Oromo ethical and moral order) and Oromo democracy. The next task is to fashion and build formidable national institutions and organizations that will empower the Oromo nation to determine its national destiny. All concerned Oromo are agents who can contribute something to change the deplorable condition of their people. It is morally wrong to be neutral and silently standby when the Oromo people are facing state violence and massive killings. Particularly the diaspora Oromo have moral and ethical responsibilities to maintain *safuu* and to get organized to support the struggle of their people; they need also stop those who engage in divisive activities that facilitate the perpetual suffering of their people. The Tigrayan-led Ethiopian government was challenged by the Oromo protest movement and other similar movements. After sacrificing thousands of precious lives of Oromo nationalists and revolutionaries for many decades, are the Oromo going to allow those who have better national institutions to bypass them for the fifth times and capture state power in Oromia and beyond? History aptly demonstrates that people can revolt and overthrow regimes, but they cannot form their own democratic government without having strong national institutions and organizations based on their traditions and values.

Without building strong national institutions the Oromo will be unable to build strong national political organizations. As Douglass North (1995, 18) says, "The viability, profitability, and survival of the organizations of a society typically depend on the existing institutional matrix." From all Oromo corners, the slogan of unity is articulated without explaining the meaning of this unity. All Oromo branches are historically, culturally, and linguistically united and nobody can dismantle this unity. The unity that the Oromo need to articulate now is not a general and abstract unity, but an institutional and political unity that their enemies have constantly suppressed. This institutional and political unity requires honest deliberations, rigorous social scientific knowledge, strong will-power, sacrifice, and tolerance from all Oromo elites—political, religious, economic, and academic—and from all sectors of the Oromo society. The Oromo need to unlearn the norms and behaviors that they have learned from alien cultures and develop democratic rules of the game consistent with their long-standing cultural values. This requires recognizing that, among other meanings "institutions are the laws, informal rules, and conventions that give durable structure to social interactions in a population" (Boyd and Richerson 2008, 305). Most of the time, human beings have deep loyalty for their relatives and friends, but national institutional and organizational building requires larger loyalties to a nation and a country. The Oromo in the diaspora in particular and the Oromo people in general can learn from the positive experiences of Jewish and Palestinian peoples and others who had faced difficult conditions and seriously struggled for their survival and liberation.

The diaspora Oromo can learn some lessons from the Jewish and Palestinian diaspora groups in the process of national institutional and organizational building. Because of the repressive nature of the Ethiopian state, the Oromo in Oromia could not openly and peacefully build their national institutions and organizations. Like the Jewish and Palestinian peoples, the Oromo in the diaspora can build their national institutions and organizations and support the Oromo national struggle in their homeland. The impact of European anti-Semitism and the attacks on Jewish individuals and groups from all sides induced a few Jewish thinkers and ideologues to propose the development of Zionism and the establishment of a Jewish national state (Milton-Edwards 2009, 13). After living in exile for thousands of years in different countries, the Jewish Diaspora gained more political consciousness, skills, and knowledge to organize and become a strong people through integrating into the world system. These global experiences helped the Jewish Diaspora in playing a decisive role in creating the World Zionist Organization in 1887, and in forming a unified national leadership known as the Jewish Agency in 1929 in Zurich and to bring together and unify organizations and institutions such as Haganah, Palmach, Histadrut, Mapai and even Herut (Adelman 2008, 31–34). The Jewish Agency, within two decades, facilitated the creation of the Jewish state by settling millions of Diaspora Jews in Palestine, and, for over 80 years, by serving as the link between the Diaspora Jewish community and Israel.

Theodor Herzl, an Austro-Hungarian journalist, writer, and political activist, began to develop the idea of a Jewish state in Palestine and launched a movement aiming at "the immediate return of the Jews to Palestine on a mass scale, from every one of countries of the Diaspora, to land which would be theirs as a Jewish homeland, recognized as such by the Great Powers of the world" (Gilbert 2008, 10). He founded the World Zionist Organization, and the concept of Zionism was coined six years before the formation of this organization. In the same year, he published a book entitled *Der Judenstaat* (*The Jewish State*) and fashioned political Zionism by proposing a national identity and a national homeland for the Jews. Max Nordau, his ardent supporter who was also a Jewish newspaper correspondent in Paris, drafted a document known as the Basel Program in 1897 for the First Zionist Congress at Basel, Switzerland. This program was the manifesto of the Zionist movement, and its key objective was "establishing for the Jewish people a publicly and legally assured home in Eretz Yisrael [Palestine]."[34] Herzl was "a practical man who understood that to succeed Zionism needed a permanent institutional structure that could speak in the name of the movement and move its diverse adherents toward consensus" (Gelvin 2007, 52). He organized the First Zionist Congress with about two hundred Zionists that issued the Basel Program with clear nationalist objectives. Recognizing the importance of these tasks, Herzl wrote in his diary on September 3, 1897, the following: "Were I to sum up the Basel Congress in a word—which I shall guard against pronouncing publicly—it would be this: At Basel I founded the Jewish state. If I said this out loud today, I would be answered by universal laughter. Perhaps in five years, and certainly in fifty, everyone will know it."

Unfortunately, Herzl's racist worldviews and the lack of concern for the Palestinians facilitated the emergence of "a social cancer" between the two related peoples who could have formed a bi-national democratic state in a shared sovereign Palestine. Herzl and his colleagues ignored the existence of 650,000 Palestinians although Leo Motzkin recognized this fact after he visited Palestine (Gilbert 2008, 17). Considering the racist aspects of Zionism and the consequence of establishing an exclusive state in a bi-national society, many leading Jewish intellectuals and thinkers, such as Herman Cohen and Franz Rosenzweig and later on Martin Buber, Gershom Scholem, Hannah Arendt, Albert Einstein, and Hans Kohn opposed the goal of creating an exclusive Jewish state (Hazony 2001, xxiv). Although the Zionists were fighting against European racism and fascism, they decided to practice similar evils on the Palestinians. Since its inception, the Israeli state has been engaging in state terrorism against the Palestinians. The Oromo nationalists need to carefully avoid the mistakes of the Zionists and the Israeli state and intensify their national struggle for genuine national self-determination and egalitarian multinational democracy. Similarly, after the mid-twentieth century, some Palestinians in the diaspora achieved modern education and developed intellectual capacity and skills through the exposure to the capitalist world system that enabled them to overcome their lack of modern political structures and leadership that were necessary to better organize and confront the Jewish state and its supporters.

Gradually the leaders of the Palestinian Student Union in Egypt such as Yasser Arafat, Khalil al-Wazir, and Salah Khalaf formed Fatah in 1959. The newly emerged leaders of this organization focused on Palestinian nationalism rather than Arab nationalism. Fatah, the movement for the Liberation of Palestine, declared the revival of the Palestinian political awareness and launched armed struggle against the Israeli state. On its part, the Israeli state continued to expropriate more lands and other resources and decided to "channel the waters of the River Jordan down to the Negev" (Fraser 2008, 75). Arab states were very angry at this decision, and understanding that Israel could not be stopped militarily, Gamal Abdel Nasser of Egypt convened an Arab summit in Cairo in January 1964; this summit decided to form a political organization known as the Palestinian Liberation Organization (PLO). Gamal Abdel Nasser was mainly responsible for the formation of the PLO in 1964, and he picked its first leader, Ahmad Shuqairy (Gelvin 2007, 198). Yasir Arafat was elected its chairman in 1969; he held the position until his death. When Egypt controlled the PLO through Shuqairy's leadership, the organization remained ineffective and made the Palestinians bitter (Fraser 2008, 75). The Palestinian Liberation Army initiated its military operations in January 1965 by raiding the Israeli water networks and causing a new threat and crisis to Israeli's security. These conditions alarmed Israel to declare a pre-emptive war against Arab states. Israel defeated Arab states in 1967, and occupied the remaining Palestinian territories, including the West Bank, the Gaza Strip, and Eastern Jerusalem. Considering all these situations, the Palestinian nationalists decided to lead and fight their liberation war.

Fatah and a coalition of other Palestinian organizations and groups took over the PLO leadership and Arafat was elected as its Chairman. Since then it became clear that the Jewish state could not have absolute monopoly over violence, the PLO and other Palestinian organizations started to use all forms of violence, including oppositional terrorism, to be able to survive as a nation and to achieve their national sovereignty. There were a number of Palestinian liberation organizations that were members of the PLO, including the Popular Front for the Liberation of Palestine (PFLP), Fatah, and the Popular Democratic Front for the Liberation of Palestine (PDFLP). The PFLP and the PDFLP frequently engaged in oppositional terrorist acts such as hijacking airplanes, and brought the question of Palestine to international attention (Harms and Ferry 2008, 119–120). With the strengthening of the PLO and the emergence of Arafat as its chairman, some Palestinians convinced themselves that the only alternative was to liberate their county by all means. The PLO initiated guerrilla tactics and Palestinian commandos operating from neighboring countries engaged in cross-border raids, airplane hijackings, and hostage-takings. The Palestinian armed struggle "brought mixed results. On the one hand, in targeting Israeli civilians as well as soldiers, Palestinians were branded as 'terrorists' in the Western press, and accorded little sympathy after Israeli reprisals. On the other hand, their resistance not only restored a measure of self-respect and confidence among the Palestinian people, but it also publicized their grievances after 20 years of neglect by the world community, and gained them official recognition" (Halwani and Kapitan 2008, 7).

Claiming that the PLO was a terrorist organization, the Israeli state continued its terrorist activities on the Palestinians in the occupied territories. The support of the West, particularly the United States, Israeli racist arrogance, over-confidence in military and technology, military adventures, and various forms of violence in the West Bank and the Gaza Strip led to the outbreak of the *Intifadas* (shaking off) in the 1980s and the creation of Hamas. Learning from the positive experiences of the Jewish and Palestinian peoples, the Oromo in the diaspora and in Oromia need to immediately build their strong national institutions and political organizations to insure their survival as a nation and to form a state that is democratic and multinational. The Oromo nationalists need to demonstrate that their national *Oromummaa*, which embraces rich Oromo culture, identity, and nationalism of Oromo democracy, is inclusive or multicultural-centric and egalitarian, and different from oppressor Ethiopian nationalism and Zionism. Oromo national institutions and organizations should avoid the pitfalls of Zionists who fought against racism and fascism and gradually ended up perpetrating state violence against Palestinians before and after they captured state power. In order to avoid the mistakes of the PLO, the Oromo liberation organizations should also avoid engaging in any form of terrorism.

Furthermore, the Oromo movement can also learn from the political experiences of Hutu and the Tutsi peoples that led to the Rwandan genocide of 1994. There were historical and momentous factors for this genocide: The mishandling of the political contradictions between the Hutu and Tutsi peoples by political elites for many decades, the civil war between the two ethnonations, and the assassination of President Juvenal Habyarimana of Hutu origin on April 6, 1994, contributed to the genocide (Sambou 2016; Straus 2007). These contradictions emerged from the Tutsi monarchical political system and German and Belgian colonial legacies, which established the racialized/ethnicized political identities that glorified the Tutsi at the cost of the Hutu (Nikuze 2014; Sambou 2016). Before WWI, the German colonialists and after the war Belgian colonialists sided with the Tutsi monarchy (Clark 2006) and intensified the oppression and exploitation of the Hutu majority during the colonial era. These factors had created animosity between the Hutus and Tutsis that would later contribute to "a cascade of violent events leading to the genocide" (Sambou 2016, 6). During the 1959 revolution and decolonization, the Tutsi absolute monarchy, which was collaborating with the Belgian colonial government, was overthrown and the new government controlled by the Hutu was established. According to Joseph Sambou (2016, 6), the "demand for decolonization and liberation ushered in a restructuring that vested the majority Hutu with absolute control and enforced their identities as the 'rightful native' of Rwanda and the minority Tutsi as 'nonindigenous.' [T]he invasion of the RPF [the Rwandan Patriotic Front] in 1990, which Hutu extremists viewed as a challenge to 'Hutu Power' and a signal of the return to the days of servitude, was the last straw."

Both the Hutu and the Tutsi political elites were not willing to share state power democratically, and they practiced political exclusivism that facilitated political extremism (Clark 2006). The assassination of the president, the civil war, and the political crisis were momentous factors to trigger the genocide:

> The assassination ruptured Rwanda's political order and thereby created a temporary gap in authority. The president's death independently caused anger, leading to calls for violent revenge; the assassination augmented the anxiety, fear, and confusion of the war; and the rupture in political order also set the stage for local power struggles. This last factor is particularly important. After the president's death, Hutu hardliners succeeded in gaining control of the state and urged war against the Tutsi "enemy." That idea—war against the Tutsi—then became the terms around which local actors asserted power and authority in their communities. The hardliners and those who adhered to the program of genocide ultimately won the upper hand in almost all areas not yet lost to the rebels. But such would not likely have happened outside a context of war, including the president's assassination. (Straus 2007, 262)

Despite the fact that the Tutsi were the main victims of the genocide, the RPF, the movement of the Tutsi, defeated the genocidal government-led by the Hutu and formed the Tutsi-led government. But the new government has not yet resolved the racialization/ethnicization of political power in Rwanda. As Filip Reyntjens (2015, 21) states, starting from early 1995 "the RPF was pushing a 'Tutsification' of the country. While officially rejecting ethnic discrimination and even the notion of ethnicity, the RPF reserved access to power, wealth, and knowledge to Tutsi elites. By the end of the 1990s, about two-thirds of the major state jobs were filled by Tutsi RPF members; the military and intelligence services were almost exclusively in their hands." So, the political problem of Rwanda has yet to be resolved and the future of Rwanda is threatened by a serious danger. The Oromo national movement needs to critically and thoroughly understand the complexity of racialization/ethnicization political power in a multinational country and the ideological extremism associated with it in order to avoid such dangerous problems. While building their national institutions and organizations, Oromo political elites and the Oromo people need to increase their political maturity based on the principles of national self-determination and egalitarian multinational democracy and continue to struggle against all forms of political extremism in Oromia, Ethiopia, and beyond.

CONCLUSION

In their struggle against the Tigrayan-led Ethiopian government, the Oromo had paid heavily in human lives and economic resources for almost three decades. Despite the fact that the development of national *Oromummaa* has blossomed and the unity of the Oromo in protest movement has been solidified recently, the Oromo nation has been unable to capture state power by overthrowing the Tigrrayan-led authoritarian regime. It is self-evident that the capturing of state power by the Oromo to regain their freedom and sovereignty is only possible by building national institutions and organizations. This is a very difficult and complex task despite the fact that the Oromo have numerical strength and abundant economic resources.[35] The political potential, the size of the Oromo population, and the richness of their economic resources have created many enemies for the Oromo people. The Tigrayan-led regime had successfully mobilized their neighbors, particularly the paramilitary force known as the "Liyu Police" of the Ethiopian Somali regional state against the Oromo, and uprooted about 1.2 million people from this regional state and Eastern and Southern Oromia between 2016 and November 2018.[36] The Somali paramilitary force has raped hundreds Oromo girls and women and massacred thousands of Oromo. The Tigrayan colonial force also mobilized the Gumuz people against the Oromo in Western Oromia and caused the killing of 40 people and displacement of 70,000.[37] The Oromo have only themselves and they need to realize this and honestly and democratically deliberate to establish the democratic rules of the game and build formidable national institutions and organizations in order to survive and successfully achieve their political objectives.

If the Oromo continue to fail as they did in 1974, when the military overthrew the Haile Selassie government, and as in 1991, when the Tigrayan People's Liberation Front replaced the military regime because of its relative national institutional and organizational strength, the better-organized ethnonation may capture the state power and continue Ethiopian colonialism, state violence, and massive killings. The Habasha groups (mainly Amhara and Tigray ethnonational groups, previously known as Abyssinians) that advocate democracy now cannot practically accept the principles of democracy and implement them because of their political culture and historical background (Jalata 2010a). The Amhara-led military regime claimed to implement socialism, but eradicated all socialists and democrats and reinstituted a dictatorship. Similarly, the Tigrayan-led regime promised national self-determination, federalism, and democracy, but practiced a continuation of colonialism, violence, and political repression. Therefore, only naïve individuals, groups, or organizations are persuaded by the slogans of the Habasha political groups, which claim to promote democracy while ardently opposing the principles of self-determination and multinational democracy. Overall, genuine Oromo nationalists, activists and organizations need to recognize that without creating the democratic rules of the game among all independent Oromo institutions and organizations in conjunction with similar institutional building within other oppressed ethnonations, there cannot be a political resolution in the Ethiopian Empire. Without this multi-ethnonational institutional building, the oppressed peoples in this empire cannot build strong national institutions and organizations that are absolutely necessary for the survival of the Oromo nation and all other ethnonations and for transforming the Ethiopian colonial state into an egalitarian multinational democracy in the Horn of Africa that respects the rights and traditions of all.

NOTES

1. "Ethiopia: 'Because I Am Oromo': Sweeping Repression in the Oromia Region of Ethiopia," https://www.amnesty.org/en/documents/afr25/006/2014/en/, accessed on 10/23/2017.
2. Menelik controlled slave trade (an estimated 25,000 slaves per year in the 1880s); with his wife he owned 70,000 enslaved Africans (Jalata 2005).
3. *Qeerroo/Qarree* means "youth" in the Oromo language; *Qerroo* is an unmarried young man, and *Qarree* is an unmarried young girl. Currently, these terms are the name of the revolutionary youth wing of the Oromo national movement organized clandestinely by the Oromo Liberation Front.
4. Telephone interview with Abbaa Caalaa Lataa on June 18, 2017; he was responsible for the Political Department of the Oromo Liberation Front.
5. Abbaa Caalaa Lataa, *ibid*.
6. *Ibid*.
7. https://www.hrw.org/news/2016/02/21/ethiopia-no-letcrackdown-protests, accessed on 06/09/2017.
8. https://Oromianeconomist.com/2016/03/23/martial-law-in-Oromia-the-stat-is-now-under-8-military-divisions-controoled-by-fascist-tplf-warlords-from-tigray/, accessed on 06/09/2017.
9. https://www.tesfanews.net/us-concerned-ethiopia-using-martial-law-silence-dissent/, accessed on 10/19/2017.
10. https://www.amnesty.org/en/documents/afr25/006/2014/en/, accessed on 10/19/2017.
11. https://www.hrw.org/report/2016/06/16/such-brutal-crackdown/killings-and-arrests-response-ethiopias-Oromo-protestsholding them in prisons and concentration camps, accessed on 06/09/2017.
12. https://www.hrw.org/reports/2005/ethiopia0505/2.html, accessed on 06/09/2017.
13. https://www.hrw.org/reports/2016/06/16/such-brutal-crackdwon/killings-and-arrests-response-ethiopias-oromo-protests, 06/09/2017.
14. http://amharic.voanews.com/a/what-is-the-current-situation-in-oromia-region/3331322.html, accessed on 05/17/2016.
15. Oromiamedianetwork, https://vimeo.com/166427775?from=outro-embed, accessed on 05/13/2016.
16. https://www.opride.com/2016/10/02%20irreecha-massacre-several-dozens-feared-dead-bishoftu/, accessed 06/09/2017.
17. https://www.opride.com/2016/10/02%20irreecha-massacre-several-dozens-feared-dead-bishoftu/, accessed 06/09/2017.
18. http://nazret.com/blog/index.php/2016/02/14/ethiopia-oromo-protests-burned-down, accessed on 06/09/2017.

19. http://www.aljazeera.com.news/2016/10/ethiopia-declares-state-emergency-protests-161009110506730.html, accessed on 06/09/2017.
20. http://www.yahoo.com/news/ethiopia-declares-state-emergency-101402878.html, accessed on 06/09/2017.
21. http://www.aljazeera.com/news/2016/09/firms-attacked-ethiopia-protests-continue-160902064459286.html, accessed on 06/09/2017.
22. http://www.aljazeera.com/news/2016/09/firms-attacked-ethiopia-protests-continue-160902064459286.html, accessed on 06/09/2017.
23. http://www.ayyaantuu.net/ethiopia-oromia-regional-state-under-siege/, accessed on 06/10/2017.
24. https://www.hrw.org/reports/2005/ethiopia0505/, accessed 06/10/2017.
25. http://ecadforum.com/2016/10/06/internet.blocked-in-ethiopia/, accessed on 06/10/2017.
26. http://agensir.it/mondo/2016/10/12/ethiopia-state-of-emergency-the-repression-of-the oromo-people-in-broad-daylight/, accessed on 06/10/2017.
27. https://www.amnesty.org/en/documents/afr25/006/2014/en/, accessed on 06/10/2017.
28. https://www.change.org/p/united-nations-human-rights-committee-humanriths-campaign-stop-massacre-of-oromo-people-and-suppression-of-human-rights-in-ethiopia, accessed on 06/10/2017.
29. http://www.voanews.com/a/us-ethiopia-relationship-strong-but-complicated-2880154.html, accessed on 06/10/2017.
30. https://www.usaid.gov/ethiopia, accessed on 06/10/2017.
31. http://africanaarguments.org/2016/08/06/ethiopia-unprecented-nationwide-oromo-protests-who-what-why/, accessed on 06/10/2017.
32. http://www.news24.com/africa/news/www.europarl.europa.eu/sides/getdoc-do?type-motion&refer, accessed on 06/10/2017.
33. http://www.ohchr.org/en/newsevents/pages/displaynews.aspx?newssid=16977&langid=e, accessed on 06/10/2017.
34. https://www.knesset.gov.il/lexicon/eng/bazel_eng.htm, accessed on 10/19/2017.
35. The Oromo are the largest ethnonational group in the Ethiopian Empire, and Oromia is the richest regional state on which other states depend on economically.
36. "https://ethsat.com/2018/07/ethiopia-regions-beset-by-violence-agree-for-federal-forces-intervene-to-restore-calm/, accessed on 10/5/2018.
37. "'Thousands Flee' ethnic conflict in western Ethiopia," https://www.bbc.com/news/world-africa-45724440, accessed on 10/5/2018.

References

Adelman, Jonathan. 2008. *The Rise of Israel*. New York: Routledge.
Adolfo, Gilly. 1967 [1965]. "Introduction." In *A Dying Colonialism*, translated by Haakon Chevalier. New York: Grove Press, Inc.
Agyeman-Duah, Baffour. 1984. *United States Military Assistance Relationship with Ethiopia, 1953–77: Historical and Theoretical Analysis*. PhD Dissertation. University of Denver.
Akbar, Na'im. 1996. *Breaking the Chains of Psychological Slavery*. Tallahassee, FL: Mind Productions and Associates.
Ali, Tariq. 2003. *The Clash of Fundamentalisms: Crusaders, Jihads and Modernity*. London: Verso
Amnesty International, Human Rights Watch/Africa. 1991–2007. Series
Aoki, Masahiko 2005. "Institutions and Institutional Change." *Paper presented at the 2005 World Congress of the International Economic Association held in Morocco*, pp. 1–39.
Arrighi, Giovanni Terence K. Hopkins, and Immanuel Wallerstein. 1989. *Anti-systemic Movements*. London: Verso.
Associated Press, 2009.
———. 2014. "Ethiopia: 'Because I am Oromo': Sweeping Repression in the Oromia Region of Ethiopia,"https://www.amnesty.org/en/documents/afr25/006/2014/en/, accessed on 7/17/2018.
Baissa, Lemmu. 1971. *The Democratic Political System of the [Oromo] of Ethiopia and the Possibility of Its Use in Nation-Building*. MA Thesis. George Washington University.
———. 1993. "The Political Culture of *Gada*: Building Blocks of Oromo Power." Paper presented at the Oromo Studies Association Conference, University of Toronto, Canada, 31 July–1 August.
———. 2004. "The Oromo *Gadaa* System of Government: An Indigenous African Democracy." In Asafa Jalata, ed., *State Crises, Globalization and National Movements in Northeast Africa*. New York: Routledge, pp. 101–121.
Balibar, Etienne and Immanuel Wallerstein 1991. *Race, Nation, Class: Ambiguous Identities*. New York: Verso.
Barker, Colin. 2001. "Robert Michels and the 'Cruel Game.'" *Leadership and Social Movements*. Manchester: Manchester University Press.
Barta, Tony. 2007. "On Pain of Extinction: Laws of Nature and History in Darwin, Marx, and Arendt." In *Hannah Arendt and the Uses of History: Imperialism, Nation, Race and Genocide*, edited by Richard H. King and Dan Stone. New York: Berghahn Books, pp. 87–108.
Bates, Darrel. 1979. *The Abyssinian Difficulty: The Emperor Theodorus and the Maqdala Campaign, 1867–1868*. Oxford: Oxford University Press.
Baxter, P. T. W. 1978. "Boran Age-Sets and Generation-Sets: Gada, a Puzzle or a Maze?" In P.T.W. Baxter and U. Almagor (eds.), *Age, Generation and Time: Some Features of East African Age Organizations*. New York: St. Martin's Press, pp. 151–182.
Berberoglu, Berch. 2003. *Globalization of Capital and the Nation-State*. Lanham, MD: Rowman & Littlefield Publishers, Inc.
Bourdieu, PIerre. 1986. "The Forms of Capital." https://www.marxists.org/reference/subject/philosophy/works/fr/bourdieu-forms-capital.htm, accessed on 11/09/2017.
Boyd, Robert and Peter J. Richerson. 2008. "Gene-Culture Coevolution and the Evolution of Social Institutions." In *Better Than Conscious? Decision Making, the Human*

Mind, and Implications for Institutions, edited by Christoph Engel and Wolf Singer. Boston: MIT Press, pp. 305–323,

Budge, A. Wallis, (tr.). 1932. *The Queen of Sheba and Her Only Son Menyelek I.* London.

Buechler, Steven. 1993. "Beyond Resource Mobilization Theory? Emerging Trends in Social Movement Theory." *The Sociological Quarterly* 34: 217–235.

———. 2011. *Understanding Social Movements: Theories from the Classical Era to the Present.* Boulder: Paradigm Publishers.

Bulatovich, Alexander. 2000. *Ethiopian through Russian Eyes: Country in Transition, 1896–1898,* translated by Richard Seltzer. Lawrenceville, NJ: Red Sea Press.

Bulcha, Mekuria. 2016. *Contours of the Emergent & Ancient Oromo Nation.* 2nd rev. ed. Cape Town, South Africa: CASAS.

Bulhan, Hussein Abdilahi. 1985. *Frantz Fanon and the Psychology of Oppression.* New York: Plenum Press.

Cabral, Amilcar. 1973. *Return to the Source.* New York: Monthly Review Press.

Cairns, James and Alan Sears. 2012. *The Democratic Imagination: Envisioning Popular Power in the Twenty-First Century.* Toronto: The University of Toronto Press.

Chalk, Frank and Kurt Jonassoh. 1990. *History and Sociology of Genocide: Analyses and Case Studies.* New Haven: Yale University Press.

Clark, John F. 2006. "Rwanda: Tragic Land of Dual Nationalisms." In *After Independence: Making and Protecting the Nation in Postcolonial and Post-communist States.* Ann Arbor: The University of Michigan Press, pp. 71–106.

Coleman, James S. 1990. "The Emergence of Norms." In *Social Institutions: Their Emergence, Maintenance and Effects.* New York: Aldine de Gruyter, pp. 35–59.

Collins, Patricia Hill. 1990. *Black Feminist Thought.* New York: Routledge.

Connell, Raewyn. 2007. "The Northern Theory of Globalization." *Sociological Theory* 25: 368–385.

Cormack. Mike. 1992. *Ideology.* Ann Arbor: The University of Michigan Press.

Dallin, Alexander and George W. Breslauer. 1970. *Political Terror in Communist Systems.* Stanford: Stanford University Press.

de Salviac, Martial. 2005 [1901]. *An Ancient People, Great African Nation,* translated by Ayalew Kano. East Lansing: Michigan State University Press.

Dugassa, Begna F. 2011. "Colonialism of Mind: Deterrent of Social Transformation." *Sociology Mind* 1(2): 55–64.

———. 2012. "Denial of Leadership Development and the Underdevelopment of Public Health: The Experience of the Oromo People in Ethiopia." *Journal of Oromo Studies* 19(1–2): 139–174.

———. 2014. "Reclaiming Oromo Indigenous Organizational Structures and Fostering Supportive Environments for Health." *Archives of Business Research* 2(1): 23–45.

Easterly, William. 2006. *The White Men's Burden: Why the West's Efforts to Aid the Rest Have Done So Much Ill and So Little Good.* London: Oxford University Press.

Etefa, Tsega. 2008. "Pan-Oromo Confederations in the Sixteenth and Seventeenth Centuries." *The Journal of Oromo Studies* 15(1): 19–40.

———. 2010. "A Great African Nation: The Oromo in European Accounts." *Journal of Oromo Studies* 17(1): 87–110.

———. 2012. *Integration and Peace in East Africa: A History of the Oromo Nation.* New York: Palgrave.

Fanon, Frantz. 1963 [1961]. *The Wretched of the Earth,* translated by Constance Farrington. New York: Grove Press, Inc.

———. 1967 [1965]. *A Dying Colonialism,* translated by Haakon Chevalier. New York: Grove Press, Inc.

———. 2005 [1952]. *Black Skin, White Masks,* translated by Richard Philcox. New York: Grove Press, Inc.

———. 2008 [1952]. *Black Skin, White Masks,* translated by Richard Philcox. New York: Grove Press, Inc.

Fossati, Bruna, L. Namarra, and Peter Niggli. 1996. *The New Rulers of Ethiopia and the Persecution of the Oromo: Reports from the Oromo Refugees in Djibouti*. Dokumentation, Evangelischer Pressedienst Frankfurt am Main.
Frank, André Gunder. 1996. *The Development of Underdevelopment*. New York: Monthly Review Press.
Fraser, T. G. 2008. *The Arab-Israeli Conflict*. 3rd ed. New York: Palgrave Macmillan.
Gamson, William, Bruce Fireman, and Steven Buechler. 1982. *Encounters with Unjust Authority*. Homewood, IL: Dorsey Press.
Geertz, C. 1994. "Primordial and Civic Ties." In *Nationalism*, edited by J. Hutchinson and A. D. Smith. Oxford: Oxford University Press.
Gelvin, James L. 2007. *The Israel-Palestine Conflict*. New York: Cambridge University Press.
Gilbert, Martin. 2008. *Israel: A History*. London: Transworld Publishers.
Gilkes Patrick. 1975. *The Dying Lion: Feudalism and Modernization in Ethiopia*. New York: St. Martin's Press.
Giorgis, Tamrat G. 2009. "A Stranger Comes to Town." *Addis Fortune* 10, no. 486. http://www.addisfortune.com/Vol%2010%20No%20486%20Archive/agenda.htm.
Golocha, T. 1998. *The Politico-legal System of the Guji Oromo*. Unpublished LLB Thesis. Addis Ababa University, Addis Ababa, Ethiopia.
Gramsci, Antonio.1971. *Selections from the Prison Notebook*. London: Lawrence and Wishart.
———. 1985. *Prison Notebooks*, edited by Quinin Hoare and G. N. Smith. New York: International Publishers.
Gudina, Merera. 2003. *Ethiopia: Competing Ethnic Nationalisms and the Quest for Democracy 1960–2000*. The Netherlands: Shaker Publishing.
Hall, Budd. 1993. "Introduction." In *Voices of Change: Participatory Research in the United States and Canada*, edited by Peter Park, Mary Brydon-Miller, Budd Hall, and Ted Jackson. Westport: Praeger, pp. xiii-xxii.
Halliday, Fred and Maxine Molyneux. 1981. *The Ethiopian Revolution*. London: Verso.
Halwani, Raja and Tomis Kapitan. 2008. *The Israeli-Palestine Conflict*. New York: Palgrave Macmillan.
Harding, S. (1993). "Introduction: Eurocentric Scientific Illiteracy—A Challenge for the World Community." In S. Harding (ed.), *The "Racial" Economy of Science: Toward a Democratic Future*. Bloomington: Indiana University Press, pp. 1–22.
Harms, Greg and Todd M. Ferry. 2008. *The Palestine-Israel Conflict: A Basic Introduction*. London: Pluto Press.
Harvey, David. 2005. *A Brief History of Neoliberalism*. Oxford: Oxford University Press.
Hasselblatt, Gunnar. 1992. "After Fourteen Years: Return to Addis Ababa—and to a Free Oromia, December 1991–January 1992." A Travel Diary, Berlin.
Hassen, Mohmmed. 1990. *The Oromo of Ethiopia: A History 1570–1860*. Cambridge: Cambridge University Press.
———. 1991. "The Historian Bahrey and the Importance of His "History of the Galla." *Horn of Africa* 13(3–4), 14(1–2): 90–106.
———. 1998. "The Macha-Tulama Association 1963–1967 and the Development of Oromo Nationalism." In *Oromo Nationalism and the Ethiopian Discourse*, edited by Asafa Jalata. Lawrenceville, NJ: Red Sea Press.
———. 2001. "Is Genocide Against the Oromo in Ethiopia Possible?" Paper presented at the Fourth International Biennial Conference of the Association of Genocide Scholars, Radisson Hotel, Minneapolis, June 10.
———. 2002."Conquest, Tyranny, and Ethnocide against the Oromo." *Northeast African Studies* 9(3): 15–49.
———. 2005. "Pilgrimage to the Abba Muuda." *Journal of Oromo Studies* 12(1–2): 142–157.
———. 2015. *The Oromo & the Christian Kingdom of Ethiopia 1300–1700*. London: James Currey.

Hazony, Yoram. 2001. *The Jewish State: The Struggle for Israel's Soul*. New York: Basic Books.
Hechter, Michael. 1990. "The Emergence of Cooperative Social Institutions." In Michael Hechter, Karl-Dieter OPP, and Reinhard Wipper, eds., *Social Institutions: Their Emergence, Maintenance and Effects*. New York: Aldine de Gruyter, pp. 13–33.
Hechter, Michael, Karl-Dieter OPP, and Reinhard Wipper (eds.). 1990. *Social Institutions: Their Emergence, Maintenance and Effects*. New York: Aldine de Gruyter.
Herbert, Edwin. 2003. *Small Wars and Skirmishes 1902–1918*. Nottingham: Foundry Books.
Herman, E. S. 1982. *The Real Terror Network: Terrorism in Fact and Propaganda*. Boston: South End Press.
Hinnant, J. 1978. "'The Guji': Gada as a Ritual System." In P. T. Baxter & U. Almagor (eds.), *Age, Generation and Time: Some Features of East African Age Organizations*. London: C. Hurst & Co., pp. 201–242.
Hirst, Paul. 2001. *War and Power in the 21st Century*. Cambridge: Polity.
Hizbawi Adera. 1996, 1997. A TPLF/EPRDF (government) Political Pamphlet, Dec. 1996–Feb. 1997, Vol. 4. No. 7. It has been printed and disseminated by party officials of the TPLF.
Hochschild, Adam. 1998. *King Leopold's Ghost: A Story of Greed, Terror, and Heroism in Colonial Africa*. New York: Houghton Mifflin Company.
Hoffman, Bruce. 2006 [1998]. *Inside Terrorism*. New York: Columbia University.
Holcomb, Bonnie K. 1991. "Akka Gadaatti: The Unfolding of Oromo Nationalism–Keynote Remarks." *Proceedings of the 1991 Conference on Oromia*, University of Toronto, Canada, 3–4 August, pp. 1–10.
———. 2002. "*Oromummaa* as a Construct or Peace through Balance: *Oromummaa* in the Twenty-first Century." Presentation prepared for the Oromo Studies Association Conference Roundtable," Washington, DC, July 27–28, 2002.
Holcomb, Bonnie and Sisai Ibssa. 1990. *The Invention of Ethiopia*. Trenton: Red Sea Press.
Human Rights League of the Horn of Africa. 2009. "Refugees Poisoned to Death in Puntland, Somalia," December 19, 2009. http://www.humanrightsleague.com/press_Releases.html
Human Rights Watch. 2005a. May, vol. 17, no. 7 (A).
———. 2005b. "Human Rights."www.genocidewatch.org.
———. 2009. "An Analysis of Ethiopia's Draft Anti-Terrorism Law," updated June 30.
Huqqa, Gollo. 1998. *The 37th Gumii Gaayo Assembly*. Addis Ababa: The Norwegian Church Aid.
Hybel, Alex Roberto. 2010. *The Power of Ideology: From the Roman Empire to Al-Qaeda*.New York: Routledge.
Ibssa, Sisai. 1992. "Implications of Party and Set for Oromo Political Survival." Paper presented at the 35th Annual Meeting of the African Studies Association. Seattle, November 20–23.
Jaarrraa, T. Adam and Muusaa H. A. Saaddoo. 2011. *Seenaa Oromo Fi Madda Walaabuu (History of the Oromo and Madda Walaabuu)*. Self-published.
Jackson, Donna Rose. 2018. *US Foreign Policy in the Horn of Africa: From Colonialism to Terrorism*. New York: Routledge.
Jalata, Asafa. 1993a. *Oromia and Ethiopia: State Formation and Ethnonational Conflict, 1868–1992*. Boulder: Lynne Rienner Publishers.
———.1993b. "Sociocultural Origins of the Oromo National Movement in Ethiopia." *The Journal of Political and Military Sociology* 21 (Winter): 267–286.
———. 1994. "Sheik Hussein Suura and the Oromo National Struggle." *The Oromo Commentary* 4(1): 5–7.
———. 1996. "The Struggle for Knowledge: The Case of Emergent Oromo Studies." *African Studies Review* 39(2): 95–123.
———. 1997. "Oromo Nationalism in the New Global Context." *Journal of Oromo Studies* 4(1–2): 83–114.

———. (ed.) 1998. *Oromo Nationalism and the Ethiopian Discourse*. Trenton, NJ: Red Sea Press.

———. 2001. *Fighting against the Injustice of the State and Globalization: Comparing the African American and Oromo Movements*. New York: Palgrave.

———. 2002. "The Role of the Oromo Diaspora in the Oromo National Movement: Lessons from the Agency of the 'Old' African Diaspora in the United States" *Northeast African Studies* 9(3): 133–160.

———. 2005. "State Terrorism and Globalization: The Cases of Ethiopia and Sudan." *International Journal of Comparative Sociology* 46(1–2): 79–102.

———. 2007. *Oromummaa: Oromo Culture, Identity and Nationalism*. Atlanta: Oromia Publishing Company.

———. 2010a. *Contending Nationalisms of Oromia and Ethiopia: Struggling for Statehood, Sovereignty, and Multinational Democracy*. Binghamton, NY: Global Academic Publishing.

———. 2010b. "The Tigrayan-Led Ethiopian State, Repression, Terrorism and Gross Human Rights Violations in Oromia and Ethiopia." *Horn of Africa* 28: 47–82.

———. 2011. "Terrorism from Above and Below in the Age of Globalization." *Sociology Mind* 1: 1–16.

———. 2015a. "Theorizing *Oromummaa*" *Journal of Oromo Studies* 22(1): 1–35.

———. 2015b. "The Triple Causes of African Underdevelopment: Colonial Capitalism, State Terrorism and Racism." *International Journal of Sociology and Anthropology* 7(3): 75–91.

———. 2016. *Phases of Terrorism in the Age of Globalization: From Christopher Columbus to Osama bin Laden*. New York: Palgrave Macmillan.

Jalata, Asafa and Harwood Schaffer. 2009. "Being In and Out of Africa: The Impact Duality of Ethiopianism." *The Journal of Black Studies* 40: 189–214.

———. 2011. "Imperfections in U.S. Foreign Policy Toward Oromia and Ethiopia: Will the Obama Administration Introduce Change? *The Journal of Pan African Studies* 4(3): 131–154.

———. 2013a. "Indigenous Peoples in the Capitalist World System: Researching, Knowing and Promoting Social Justice." *Sociology Mind* 3(2): 158–178.

———. 2013b. "The Oromo, *Gadaa/Siqqee* and the Liberation of Ethiopian Colonial Subjects." *AlterNative: An International Journal of Indigenous Peoples* 9(4): 277–295.

Jeffrey, James. 2016."Ethiopia's Smoldering Oromo,"http://www.ipsnews.net/2016/04/ethiopias-smoldering-oromo/, accessed on 7/17/2018.

Johnson, Alan. 2001. "Self-emancipation and Leadership: The Case of Martin Luther King." In *Leadership and Social Movements*, edited by Colin Barker, Alan Johnson, and Michael Lavalette. Manchester: Manchester University Press.

Jonassohn, Kurt. 1998. *Genocide and Gross Human Rights Violations: In Comparative Perspective*. New Brunswick: Transaction Publishers.

Kassam, Aneesa. 1994. "The Oromo Theory of Social Development." In *Between the State and Civil Society in Africa: Perspective on Development*, edited by T. Mkandawire and E. E. Osagahae. Dakar, Senegal: CODESRIA, pp. 19–40.

Kelly, H. A. 1992. *From Gada to Islam: The Moral Authority of Gender Relations among the Pastoral Oroma of Kenya*. Unpublished Doctoral Dissertation. University of California, Los Angeles.

Kiernan, Ben. 2007. *Blood and Soil: A World History of Genocide and Extermination from Sparta to Darfur*. New Haven: Yale University Press.

King, Martin Luther. 1967. *Where Do We Go from Here: Chaos or Community?* New York: Harper and Row.

King, Richard and Dan Stone, (eds.) 2007. *Hannah Arendt and the Uses of History*. New York: Berghahn Books.

Knight, Jack and Itai Sened, (eds.). 1995. "Introduction." In *Explaining Social Institutions*. Ann Arbor: The University of Michigan Press, pp. 1–13.

Knutsson, K. E. 1967. *Authority and Change: A Study of the Kallu Institution among the Macha Galla of Ethiopia*. Goteborg, Sweden: Ethnografiska Musset.

Kumsa, Kuwee. 1997. "The Siiqqee Institution of Oromo Women." *Journal of Oromo Studies* 4(1–2).
Ladha, K, K. 2003. *Kleisthenes and the Ascent of Democracy*. https://www.cerge-ei.cz/pdf/events/papers/031016_t.pdf, accessed on 06/09/2018.
Legesse, Asmarom. 1973. *Three Approaches to the Study of African Society*. New York: Free Press.
———. 1987. "Oromo Democracy." Paper presented to the Conference on the Oromo Revolution, Washington, DC, August 16.
———. 2000. *Oromo Democracy*. Lawrenceville, NJ: Red Sea Press.
Lepisa, Dinsa. 1975. "The Gada System of Government and Sera Cafee Oromo." LLB Thesis. Addis Ababa University.
Levine, David P. 2001. *The Capacity for Civic Engagement: Public and Private Worlds of the Self*. New York: Palgrave Macmillan.
Lewis, Herbert S. 2001. *Jimma Abba Jifar: An Oromo Monarchy*. Lawrenceville, NJ: Red Sea Press.
Lord, Robert G. and Douglas Brown. 2004. *Leadership Processes and Followers Self-Identity*. Mahwah, NJ: Lawrence Erlbaum Associates, Inc.
Lorde, Audre. 1979. "The Master's Tools Will Never Dismantle the Master's House." Comments at "The Personal and the Political" panel, Second Sex Conference. In Cherrie Moraga and Gloria Anzaldua, *This Bridge Called My Back*. New York: Kitchen Table Women of Color Press, 1981.
Luling, Virginia. 1965. "Government and Social Control among Some Peoples of the Horn of Africa." MA Thesis. The University of London.
Luther, Ernest W. 1958. *Ethiopia Today*. London: Oxford University Press.
MacKinnon, Catharine. 1994. "Rape, Genocide, and Women's Human Rights." *Harvard Women's Law Journal* 17: 5–16.
Magdoff, Harry. 1970. *The Age of Imperialism: The Economics of U.S. Foreign Policy*. New York: Monthly Review Press.
Malik, Kenan. 1996. *The Meaning of Race*. New York: New York University Press.
Mann, Michael. 1993. *The Sources of Social Power*, Vol. II. New York: Cambridge University Press.
Mannheim, Karl. 1936. *Ideology and Utopia: An Introduction to the Sociology of Knowledge*, translated from the German by Louis Wirth and Edward Shils. New York: A Harvest/HBJ Book, 1936.
Marcus, Harold. 1983. *Ethiopia, Great Britain, and the United States, 1941–1974*. Los Angeles: University of California Press.
Marx, Karl. 1967 [1932]. *Capital*. F. Engels (ed.). New York: International Publishers.
Mbembe, Achille. 2008. "What Is Post-colonial Thinking? An interview." *Esprit, eurozone*. Interview by Olivier Mongin, Nathalie Lempereur, and Jean-Louis Schlegel, original in French, translated by John Fletcher.
McAdam, Doug. 1982. *Political Process and the Development of Black Insurgency*. Chicago: University of Chicago Press.
McCarthy, John D. and Mayer N. Zald. 2001. "The Enduring Vitality of the Resource Mobilization Theory of Social Movements." In Jonathan H. Turner (ed.), *Handbook of Sociological Theory*. New York: Springer Science and Business Media, LLC, pp. 553–566.
McGovern, Seana. 1999. *Education, Modern Development, and Indigenous Knowledge*. New York: Garland.
McGregor, Deborah. 2004. "Traditional Ecological Knowledge and Sustainable Development: Towards Coexistence." In *The Way of Development: Indigenous Peoples, Life Projects and Globalization*, edited by M. Blaser, H. A. Feit, and G. McRae. London: Zed Press, pp. 72–91.
Milton-Edwards, Beverley. 2009. *The Israeli-Palestinian Conflict*. New York: Taylor & Francis Group.
Mohammed, Duri. 1969. "Private Foreign Investment in Ethiopia, 1950–1968." *Journal of Ethiopian Studies* 7(2): 53–78.

Moore, MariJo (ed.). 2003. "Introduction." *Genocide of the Mind: New Native American Writing*. New York: Nation Books.
New York Times. 1909. "Menelik Has Investment Here."http://www.africanidea.org/EmperoMenelik20II20Nov20720(2).pdf, accessed 07/17/18.
Nikuze, D. (2014), "The Genocide against the Tutsi in Rwanda: Origins, Causes, Implementation, Consequences, and the Post-genocide Era." *International Journal of Development and Sustainability* 3(5): 1086–1098.
North, Douglass C. 1995. "Five Propositions about Institutional change." In *Explaining Social Institutions*. Ann Arbor: The University of Michigan Press, pp. 15–26.
The Oakland Institute. 2013. "Understanding Land Investment Deals in Africa."https://www.oaklandinstitute.org/sites/oaklandinstitute.org/files/OI_Ethiopa_Land_Investment_report.pdf, accessed on 7/17/2018.
———. 2014. "Engineering Ethnic Conflict."https://www.oaklandinstitute.org/engineering-ethnic-conflict, accessed on 7/17/2018.
———. 2015. "We Say the Land is not Yours."https://www.oaklandinstitute.org/sites/oaklandinstitute.org/files/BreakingtheSilence.pdf, accessed on 7/17/2018.
Ober, J. 2007. "'I Besieged That Man': Democracy's Revolutionary Start." In *Origins of Democracy in Ancient Greece*, edited by Kurt A. Raaflaub, Josiah Ober, and Robert W. Wallace. Berkeley: University of California Press, pp. 83–104.
Oliverio, Annamarie. 1997. "The State of Injustice: The Politics of Terrorism and the Production of Order." *International Journal of Comparative Sociology* 38(1–2): 48–63.
Oromia Culture and Tourism Bureau. 2006. *History of the Oromo to the Sixteenth Century*. Finfinnee: Berhanena Selam Printing Enterprise. Second Edition.
The Oromia Support Group. 1997; 2002; 2003 series.
The Oromo Liberation Front Program. 1976. Originally produced in 1974 was improved and expanded.
The Oromo Relief Association, 1980.
The Oromo: Voice against Tyranny. 1980. Originally produced in 1971 and reprinted in 1980 in *Horn of Africa* 3(3).
Piven, Frances and F. Richard Cloward. 1979. *Poor People's Movements*. New York: Vintage.
Pollock, Sue. 1996. "Ethiopia-Human Tragedy in the Making: Democracy or Dictatorship?" *The Oromia Support Group*.
———. 1997. "Politics and Conflict: Participation and Self-determination." In *Ethiopia: Conquest and the Quest for Freedom and Democracy*, edited by Seyoum Y. Hameso, T. Trueman, and T. E. Erena. London: TSC Publications, pp. 81–110.
Putnam, R. "1995. Turning In, Turning Out: The Strange Disappearance of Social Capita in America." *PS: Political Science and Politics* 28(4).
———. 2000. *Bowling Alone: The Collapse and Revival of American Community*. New York: Simon and Schuster.
Quan, H.L.T. 2012. *Growth against Democracy: Savage Developmentalism in the Modern World*. Lanham, MD: Lexington Books.
Rahmato, Dessalegn. 2011. "Land to Investors: Large-Scale Land Transfers in Ethiopia." https://www.ethioobserver.net/Ethiopia_Rahmato_FSS_0.pdf.
Rajagopal, Balakrishnan. 1999. "International Law and the Development Encounter: Violence and Resistance at the Margins." *Proceedings of the Annual Meeting of the American Society of International Law* 93:16–27.
———. 2003. *International Law from Below: Development, Social Movements and Third World Resistance*. Cambridge: Cambridge University Press.
Rejai, Mostafa. 1984. *Comparative Political Ideologies*. New York: St. Martin's Press.
Reuters, May 15, 1995.
Reuters Business Briefing, July 5, 1994.
Reyntjens, Filip. 2015. "Rwanda: Progress or Powder Keg? *Journal of Democracy* 26(3): 19–33.
Robinson, William. 1996. *Promoting Polyarchy*. Cambridge: Cambridge University Press.

Robinson, William I. 2004. *A Theory of Global Capitalism: Production, Class, and State in a Transnational World.* Baltimore: John Hopkins University Press.

———. 2008. *Latin America and Global Capitalism.* Baltimore: John Hopkins University Press.

———. 2010. "The Crisis of Global Capitalism." In *The Great Credit Crash*, edited by Martin Konings and Jeffrey Sommers. London: Verso, pp. 289–310.

Rodney, Walter. 1972. *How Europe Underdeveloped Africa.* Washington, DC: Howard University Press.

Rostow, W. W. 1960. *The Stages of Development: A Non-Communist Manifesto.* Cambridge: Cambridge University Press.

Roy, W. G. 2001. *Making Societies: The Historical Construction of Our World.* London: Pine Forge Press.

Said, Edward. 1993. "The Politics of Knowledge." In *Race Identity and Representation in Education*, edited by Cameron McCarthy and Warren Crichlow. New York: Routledge, pp. 306–314.

Sambou, Joseph. 2016. *Genocide in Rwanda: Understanding Why They Died.* MA Thesis. City University of New York.

Santos, Boaventura de Sousa (ed.). 2007. "Preface." *Another Knowledge Is Possible: Beyond Northern Epistemologies.* London: Verso.

Schraeder, Peter J. 1996. *United States Foreign Policy toward Africa: Incrementalism, Crisis and Change.* London: Cambridge University Press.

Schwab, Peter. 1979. *Haile Selassie I: Ethiopia's Lion of Judah.* Chicago: Nelson-Hall.

Sen, Amartya. 1999. *Development as Freedom.* New York: Knopf.

Sharlach, Lisa. 2002. "State Rape: Sexual Violence as Genocide." In *Violence and Politics: Globalization's Paradox*, edited by K. Worcester, Sally Avery Bermanzohn, and Mark Ungar. New York: Routledge, pp. 107–124.

Shillington, Kevin. 2005. *African History.* New York: Palgrave.

Singer, Norman J. 1978. "Ethiopia: Human Rights, 1948–1978." *Proceeding of the First International Conference on Ethiopian Studies.* April 13–16, pp. 672–673.

Skocpol, T. 2003. *Diminished Democracy: From Membership to Management in American Civic Life.* Norman: University of Oklahoma Press.

Smelser, Neil J. 1962. *Theory of Collective Behavior.* New York: The Free Press, 1962.

Smith, Jackie. 2008. *Social Movements for Global Democracy.* Baltimore: Johns Hopkins University Press.

Smith, Linda T. 1999. *Decolonizing Methodologies: Research and Indigenous Peoples.* London: Zed Books Ltd.

So, Alvin. 1990. *Social Change and Development: Modernization, Dependency, and World System Theories.* London: Sage Publications.

Soltan, Karol. 1998. "Institutions as Products of Politics." In Karol Soltan, Virginia Haufler, and Eric M. Uslaner, eds., *Institutions and Social Order.* Ann Arbor: The University of Michigan Press, pp. 45–64.

Soltan, Karol, Eric M. Uslaner, and Virginia Haufler (eds.). 1998. "New Institutionalism: Institutions and Social Order." In *Institutions and Social Order.* Ann Arbor: The University of Michigan Press, pp. 3–14.

Stanton, George. 2009. "An Open Letter to the United Nations High Commissioner for Human Rights."www.genocidewatch.org, accessed April 1, 2009.

Straus, Scott. 2007. "The Order of Genocide: The Dynamics of Genocide in Rwanda." *Genocide Studies and Prevention: An International Journal* 2(3): 259–264.

Strauss, Peter L. (tr.). 1968. *The Fetha Nagast* (The Law of the Kings). Addis Ababa: HSIU.

Sturgis, Amy H. 2007. *The Trail of Tears and Indian Removal.* Westport, CT: Greenwood.

Survival International, 1995.

Ta'a, Tesema. 1986. "The Political Economy of Western Central Ethiopia: From the Mid-16th to the Early-20th Centuries." PhD Dissertation. Michigan State University.

Third World Network. (1993). "Modern Science in Crisis: A Third World Response." In S. Harding, ed., *The "Racial" Economy of Science*. Bloomington: Indiana University Press, pp. 418–518.
Thomson, Sorcha Amy and Macarena Espinar López. 2015. "Oromo Protests Shed Light on Ethiopia's Long-Standing Ethnic Tensions," http://saharareporters.com/2015/12/26/oromo-protests-shed-light-ethiopia%E2%80%99s-long-standing-ethnic-tensions, accessed on 4/14/16.
Tibebu, Teshale. 1995. *The Making of Modern Ethiopia 1896–1974*. Lawrenceville, NJ: Red Sea Press.
Tilly, Charles. 1978. *From Mobilization to Revolution*. Reading, MA: Addison-Wesley.
Trigger, B. G. (2006). "All people are (not) good." In J. Solway, ed., *The Politics of Egalitarianism*. New York: Berghahn Books, pp. 21–29.
Trueman, Trevor. 1997. "Democracy or Dictatorship?" In *Ethiopia*, edited by Seyoum Y. Hameso, T. Trueman, and T.E. Erena. London: TSC Publications, pp. 141–150.
———. 2001. "Genocide against the Oromo People of Ethiopia? Western Influence." Paper presented at the 44th Annual Meeting of the African Studies Association, Houston, November 14–18.
Turner, Jonathan H. 2003. *Human Institutions: A Theory of Societal Evolution*. Lanham, MD: Rowman & Littlefield Publishers, Inc.
U.S. Agency of International Development, Office of Financial Management. 1974. *U.S. Overseas Loans and Grants, and Assistance from International Organizations, Obligations and Loan Authorizations*, July 1, 1945–June 30, 1973. https://www.usaid.gov/sites/default/files/documents/1868/USOverseasLoansGrantstheGreenBook2013.pdf, accessed on 7/17/2018).
Van de Loo, J. 1991. *Guji Oromo Culture in Southern Ethiopia: Religious Capabilities in Rituals and Songs*. Berlin: Berietrich Reimer Verlag.
Waltzer, Michael. 1977. *Just and Unjust Wars: A Moral Argument with Historical Illustrations*. New York: Basic Books.
Welsh, Bridget. 2002. "Globalization, Weak States, and Death Toll in East Asia." In *Violence and Politics: Globalization's Paradox*, edited by K. Worcester, Sally Avery Bermanzohn, and Mark Ungar. New York: Routledge, pp. 67–89.
Winant, Howard. 1994. *Racial Conditions: Politics, Theory, Comparisons*. Minneapolis: University of Minnesota.
Wittner, Lawrence. 2017. "Can Our Social Institutions Catch Up with Advances in Science and Technology?" http://.dailkos.com.story/2017/3/26/1647554/, accessed on 06/01/2017.
Wolfe, Patrick. 1998. *Settler Colonialism and the Transformation of Anthropology*. London: Cassel.
Wood, Adrian. 1983. "Rural Development and National Integration in Ethiopia. "*African Affairs* 82(329): 509–539.
Woodson, Carter G. 1990 [1933]. *The Miseducation of the Negro*. Trenton, NJ: Africa World Press, Inc.
Worku, Kenate. 2008. "The Expansion of Addis Ababa and its Impact on the Surrounding Areas: A Preliminary Study of the Nefas Silk Lafto District." *Journal of Oromo Studies* 15(2): 97–131.
Wrong, Michela. 2005. *I Didn't Do It for You: How the World Betrayed a Small African Nation*. New York: Harper Perennial.
Zoga, Olana. 1993. *Gezatena Gezot and Macha Tulama Association*. Addis Ababa: No publisher available.

Index

Abbaa Gadaas (presidents of the assembly), 23, 32
Abbaa Muuda, 22, 24–25, 141
Abdulle, Muhammad Rashad, 111
Abyssinian Christians, 139
Abyssinians, 19, 22, 34, 57–59
Addis Ababa (Finfinnee), 75, 150
Addis Ababa Master Plan, 70–71, 161–162; master genocide in, 61, 129; opposition to, 131; Oromo protest movement and, 13; Oromo society opposing, 27; student protest movement against, 85
Adolfo, Gilly, 46
Afaan Oromoo (Oromo language), 38, 79, 109
African Americans, 110
Agyeman-Duah, Baffour, 125
Ahmed, Abyi, 7, 132, 145
Akbar, Na'im, 39, 47–49
Ali, Ayisha, 64
Ali, Tariq, 104
American Railroad Stock, 154
Amhara elites, 133
Amhara National Democratic Movement (ANDM), 126
Amhara-Tigrayan state, ix, 34, 36–37, 47
ancestral lands, 73n5
ANDM. *See* Amhara National Democratic Movement
Annuak people, 66, 67, 97n1, 128
Arab states, 29, 171
Arafat, Yasser, 170, 171
Arendt, Hannah, 170
Arffan Qallo musical group, 4
artists, 87
auto-destruction, 46

badhadha, 21

Baissa, Lemmu, 32
baliina, 21
Bari, Magarsa, 5
Barki, Lagasse, 5
al-Bashir, Omar, 66, 128
Bates, Darrel, 140
Baxter, Paul T., 23
Berberoglu, Berch, 56, 126
Biftu Ganamo musical group, 4
Biru, Tadassa, 6
Biyyaa Oromoo (Oromia), 33, 58, 132, 138
Black nationalism, 110
Bourdieu, Pierre, 89, 98n9, 151n1
Boyd, Robert, 166, 167
Breslauer, George W., 103
Buber, Martin, 170
Buechler, Steven M., 10
Bulatovich, Alexander, 22, 58
Bulhan, Hussein Abdilahi, 36–37, 43, 90
butta wars, 141

Cabral, Amilcar, 107
caffee (Oromo assembly), 138–139
capital, 123; culture, 89, 98n9, 151n1; economic, 89, 151n1; Haile Selassie government gaining, 124; social, 89; Tigrayan-led regime accumulation of, 62, 126–127, 130
capitalism, 2, 3, 56, 101; commercial, 16; global, 16, 54–55, 122, 154; socialist countries developing, 103–104; Western countries interests in, 102; Western Europe's developing, 19
capitalist globalization, 26
capitalist/socialist development, 122
capitalist world system, 8, 158; colonialism and, 45–47;

enslavement in, 122; modernization theory used by, 104; societal destruction from, 102–103; two sides of, 102; violence and terrorism from, 104–105
Chalk, Frank, 56, 123
checks and balances, 33
Chilimoo forest, 131, 151n3
China, 116n3
Christianity, 18–19, 138–139; absolutism, 104; Islam's war with, 140–141; Oromo people suppressed by, 25–26, 111
civic engagement, 115
civil rights, 112
Civil Rights Movement, 110
clan families, 35, 81
class differentiation, 141
cognitive liberation, 10, 94
Cohen, Herman, 170
Coleman, James S., 158
collective actions, 156–157
collective behavior, 8–9
collective denial, 65
collective grievances, 4
collective history, 45
collective identities, 2
collective norms, 40
collective property, 55
Collins, Patricia Hill, 46
colonial capitalism, 2, 3
colonial elites, genocidal policies of, 27
colonialism, 14; capitalist world system and, 45–47; Ethiopian settler, 3, 6, 34, 87, 97n5; Ethiopian terrorism in, 79–80; genocide and ethnocide by, 43–44; governments of, 101; indigenous lands occupied in, 81; institutions in, 36, 120; people suffering under, 102; school systems in, 98n6; terrorism from, 42, 55, 78; United States promoting, 101–102
colonization, 3, 58, 79
colonized societies, 15, 91, 158
commercial capitalism, 16
commercial farming, 61
conflict theory, 9
conflict zones, 164
consciously-designed controls, 156

Cormack, Mike, 109
crimes against humanity, 28, 65
culture, 20, 29, 48; analysis of, 84–85; capital, 89, 98n9, 151n1; Habasha, 38, 44, 88; of Oromo people, 36–37, 44, 81, 137–138; in *Oromummaa* nationalism, 70, 148–149; politics relationship with, 138; renaissance of, 107

Dache, Gobana, 19
dagaaga, 21
Dallin, Alexander, 103
democracy: crimes against humanity for, 65; egalitarian, 58, 91, 97n1, 104, 149; egalitarian Oromo, 84, 105–108; *gadaa/siqqee* system strength from, 48–49; liberal, 101; Oromo movement's transition to, 145–146; Oromo nationalism rules for, 168; of Oromo people, 75, 104; Oromo society rules for, 151; *Oromummaa* nationalism and free, 91–92; *See also gadaa* system (Oromo democracy)
democratic republic, 33
derg (military regime), 59
Desalegn, Haile Mariam, 132
de Salviac, Martial, 57, 58
development aid, from U.S., 130
divide-and-conquer strategies, 48
division of labor, 96–97
dominant society, 36
dominant systems, 16, 47, 109, 129

economic capital, 89, 151n1
economic facilities, 92, 112
economic resources, 122
education denied, 41–42
egalitarian democracy, 58, 91, 104
egalitarian multinational democracy, 91, 97n1, 149
egalitarian Oromo democracy, 84, 105–108
Einstein, Albert, 170
Ejjetto (Sidama youth movement), 144
elites, in social hierarchies, 17
emancipatory project, 103
empowerment, 47, 119

Index

ENLF. *See* Ethiopian National Liberation Front
epistemicide, 14
EPRDF. *See* Ethiopian People's Revolutionary Democratic Front
equality, socialist countries against, 103–104
Ethiopia: colonial elites of, 137–138; government of, 31; masks of, 81; ruling elites of, 3–4; standard of living in, 129; Transitional Government of, 69; U.S. aid to, 124
Ethiopian colonialism: brutal repression by, 84; capitalism maintained in, 56; colonial terrorism by, 79–80; *gadaa/siqqee* system suppressed by, 25–26; genocide from, 31, 120–121; human rights violations in, 106–107, 113; independent institutions prevented by, 160; land dispossessing by, 121–122; liberation from, 29, 87; oppression by, 39; Oromo education denied by, 41–42; Oromo identities distorted by, 39, 81; Oromo leaders killed by, 20; Oromo national institutions and, 38, 155–156, 158, 159–165; Oromo national movement challenging, 1–2; Oromo people and heavy-handedness of, 165; Oromo people empowered and, 19–20, 144; Oromo regional and religious boundaries from, 39; Oromo self attacked by, 37; politically conscious imprisoned by, 63; psychological legacy of, 39–40; savagery of, 96; terrorism from, 113, 120–121; theatre of great massacre by, 57; unfreedoms imposed by, 85, 90, 97n4; U.S. imperialism and, 124–125, 126
Ethiopian Empire, 32–33, 71, 154
Ethiopianism, ix, 78
Ethiopian-led regime, 101, 126, 164
Ethiopian National Defense Forces, 67, 128
Ethiopian National Liberation Front (ENLF), 5

Ethiopian People's Revolutionary Democratic Front (EPRDF), 6–7, 126, 144–145
Ethiopian settler colonialism, 3, 6, 34, 87, 97n5
ethnic tribes, massacres of, 128
ethnocide, by colonialism, 43–44
Eurocentrism, 15
Europe, 19; capitalist class, 37; colonialists, 73n3; Parliament, 165

Fanon, Frantz, 35–37, 38
Fatah, 170, 171
Fincila Dida Garbummaa (Revolt Against Political Slavery), 162
Finfinnee (Addis Ababa), 75, 150
finna (social and cultural development), 20
forests, Abyssinians devastating, 59
Fossati, Bruna, 63, 127
framing and construction theory, 10
free press, 62

gabbina concept, 20–21
gadaa/siqqee system, 14, 22, 148; democratic strength from, 48–49; egalitarian Oromo democracy of, 84, 105–108; Ethiopian colonial state suppressing, 25–26; levels of, 32–33; Oromo nationalism pride in, 99–100, 107; *Oromummaa* nationalism enshrined in, 114–115; peace and stability from, 159; political freedom from, 111; *qaallus* institution in, 25; restoring, 108–109, 150; rule of law in, 33, 50, 112; values required in, 83
gadaa system (Oromo democracy), 22, 75, 138–139, 151n2; global imperialism suppressing, 142; *moottii* system incompatibility of, 141–142; peace and stability from, 143; renewal and reorganization of, 140–141; rule of law in, 23, 147
Galata, Abiyu, 5
Gamson, William, 10
gang rape, 127
gangsters, 62
garden without boundary, 58

garee, 134n3, 163
Geertz, C., 4
genocide, 27, 106, 172–173; Addis Ababa Master Plan as master, 61, 129; capital dispossession by, 123; colonial elites policies of, 27; by colonialism, 43–44; from Ethiopian colonialism, 31, 120–121; master, 61, 129; Oromo people massacres of, 65; types of, 123; United Nations problem with, 56–57
Gidada, Nagasso, 5
Giorgis, Tamrat G., 61
global capitalism, 16, 54–55, 122, 154
Global Gumii Oromia, 85, 161, 167
Global Gumii Oromiyaa, 51
global hegemonic power, 124
global imperialism, 96, 142
The Glory of the Kings document (Kebra Nagast), 22
Goffman, Ervin, 10
gott, 134n3, 163
Gragn, Ahmed, 140
Gramsci, Antonio, 83, 86, 100, 107
grievance expression, 64
Gucaa Dargaagoo (publication), 5
guddina concept, 20–21
Gudina, Merera, 154
Gumii Gaayyo (assembly of multitudes), 23, 72
Gumii Oromiyaa (national assembly), 147–148
Gumuz people, 145, 174
gun holder (*nafxanya*), 120

Habasha colonialists, 106
Habasha culture, 38, 44, 88
Hadiya people, 97n1
Haile Selassie government, 4; colonial institutions consolidated by, 120; Ethiopian Empire uprisings overthrowing, 71; Menelik policies continued by, 59; Oromo nationalism suppression by, 77; overthrow of, 125, 174; U.S support of, 60, 124–125; wealth and capital gained by, 124
Halliday, Fred, 124
Harding, Sandra, 15, 16

haroomsa gadaa (renewal), 138
Harvey, David, 55
Hasselblatt, Gunnar, 59
Hassen, Mohammed, 4, 62, 65, 66
Herman, Edward S., 73n2
Herzl, Theodor, 169–170
Hoffman, Bruce, 55, 123
Holcomb, Bonnie, 5, 79
hoormata, 21
human beings, 43, 47–48, 88–93
human liberation, 15
human psychology, 158
Human Rights Experts, 165
human rights violations, 31; in Ethiopian colonialism, 106–107, 113; in military regime, 121; in United States, 98n7
Hutu people, 172–173

Ibssa, Sisai, 5
ICC. *See* International Criminal Court
ideological problems, 83–84, 105
ideologies: knowledge and, 26; national, 82, 85, 109–110; religious, 103; self-serving, 101
IMF. *See* International Monetary Fund
imperialism, 14–15; global, 96, 142; U.S., 124–125, 126; of Western countries, 116n3
independent institutions, 158, 160
India, 58
indigenous people: colonialism occupying lands of, 81; destruction of, 104; European colonialists exterminating, 73n3; knowledge of, 14–15, 16
indigenous religion (*Waaqeefannaa*), 14, 34, 138, 160
inferiority complex, 32, 36–37, 46, 85–86
Integrated Addis Ababa Master Plan, 161–162
International Criminal Court (ICC), 66
International Monetary Fund (IMF), 122, 131
international organizations, 68
Intifadas (shaking off), 172
invisible-hand approach, 156

Islam, 18–19, 138; Arab culture separated from, 29; Christianity's war with, 140–141; Oromo people suppressed by, 25–26, 111

Jewish diaspora groups, 169
Jewish state, 170
Jiloo, Walaabuu, 140
Jonassohn, Kurt, 56–57, 65, 123–124
journalism, 62–63
Journal of Oromo Studies, 93
Der Judenstaat (The Jewish State, Herzl), 170

Kassam, Aneesa, 21
kayyo, 23, 28
kayyoon deebitee (our freedom returned), 107
Kebra Nagast (The Glory of the Kings document), 22
Kedir, Muktar, 144
Kelly, H. A., 24
Khalaf, Salah, 170
King, Martin Luther, 110
knowledge: ideology and, 26; indigenous, 14–15, 16; liberation, 32, 47, 95; in *Oromummaa* nationalism, 86; scientific, 15; western countries globalization of, 18–19
Kohn, Hans, 170
Kuree, Ahmed Mohamed, 64

labor, socialization of, 54–55
land dispossessing, 121–122
leadership, 97, 144, 150
leaders (*moottii*) system, 141
Legesse, Asmarom, 159
liberal democracy, 101
liberal Enlightenment, 17
liberation, 15, 91, 94, 116; cognitive, 10, 94; from Ethiopian colonialism, 29, 87; knowledge, 32, 47, 95; mental, 32, 40, 47, 106, 107; Oromo organizations for, 149–150; of Oromo people, 42, 47, 52, 106, 107; in *Oromummaa* nationalism, 95, 105–109
lives sacrificed, 95–96
Liyu Police, 174

localized identities, 35, 81, 152n8
Luling, Virginia, 33

Macha-Tulama Self-Help Association, 53, 72, 100, 153; banning of, 5; emergence of, 143; formation of, 4; mental liberation from, 40; OPDO and attacks on, 70; Oromo nationalism and, 5, 77, 113; *Oromummaa* created by, 35; political freedoms and, 93
Madda Walaabuu, 139–140
Malcolm X, 110
Mann, Michael, 114
Mannheim, Karl, 105
Marcus, Harold, 125
Mariam, Mengistu Haile, 6, 59, 120–121
Marx, Karl, 9, 54, 89
massacres: Abyssinians ruling with repression and, 34; Ethiopian colonialism creating theatre of, 57; of ethnic tribes, 128; of Oromo people, 59, 65, 83, 120; Oromo protest movement and, 163–164
master genocide, 61, 129
McAdam, Doug, 9
McGovern, D., 16
Megersa, Lemma, 144
Menelik (Abyssinian warlord), 19, 22, 58, 154
Mengistu regime, 71
mental enslavement, 40
mental liberation, 32; Amhara-Tigrayan state preventing, 47; from Macha-Tulama and OLF, 40; for Oromo people, 106, 107
mental oppression, 47
metal production, 18
Mezhenger people, 66, 128
micro-mobilization, 10
military regime (*derg*), 59, 121
Mill, John Stuart, 9
modernization theory, 98n7, 101, 104, 125
Molyneux, Maxine, 124
Moore, MariJo, 106
moottii (leaders) system, 141–142, 149
Mosisa, Abraham, 5
Motzkin, Leo, 170

nafxanya-gabbar system (semi-slavery), 34, 59, 120–121, 159
nagaa (peace), 21, 24
Namarra, Lydia, 5, 63
Namarra, Tsegaye, 5
Nasser, Gamal Abdel, 171
National Assembly of *Gumii Oromiyaa*, 147
national *Gumii Oromiyaa*, 51, 146–147
national identities, 69
national ideologies, 82, 85, 109–110
national institutions, 166, 174
national liberation, 116
national pride, 132
natural resources, 58–59, 130
needs, of human beings, 43
neoliberalism, 55, 122–123
neo-Marxism, 9
Niggli, Peter, 63
Nilo-Saharan societies, 141
Noggo, Dima (Yohanis), 5
North, Douglass, 168
Nuer people, 97n1

Odaa Nabee, 138
Odaa Roba, 139
Ogaden-Somali people, 97n1, 128
OLF. *See* Oromo Liberation Front
one-to-five (*tokkoo-shane*), 131, 134n3, 163
OPDO. *See* Oromo People's Democratic Organization
oppression, 44, 45, 116; by Ethiopian colonialism, 39; global capitalism's aspects of, 16; mental, 47; reward and punishment and, 90; victimization by internalizing, 49
organic unity, 95, 108
Organization of African Unity, 7
Oromia (*Biyya Oromoo*), 33, 58, 132, 138
Oromia Support Group, 67, 134n2
Oromo assembly (*caffee*), 138
Oromo communities: mass shootings in, 59; natural resources of, 58–59; political mechanisms needed in, 83; refugees from, 67–68; resource mobilization for, 84; social hierarchies in, 86; Tigrayan-led regime selling minerals of, 61, 130;
town hall meetings in, 50
Oromo cultural capital, 86
Oromo democracy. *See gadaa* system
Oromo Diaspora communities, 28, 46, 133, 169; public diplomacy needed by, 51–52; self-destruction of, 50
Oromo farmers, 59, 65
Oromo intermediary elites, 35, 68
Oromo language (*Afaan Oromoo*), 38, 79, 109
Oromo Liberation Army, 97, 100
Oromo Liberation Front (OLF), 5, 31, 53, 72, 153; emergence of, 143; mental liberation from, 40; OPDO and attacks on, 70; Oromo nationalism and, 19, 77, 113; *Oromummaa* created by, 35; political freedoms and, 93
Oromo movement theory, 76–88
Oromo national assembly, 149
Oromo national institutions: absence of, 166, 174; Ethiopian colonialism and, 38, 155–156, 158, 159–165; obstacles to, 166–167; rebuilding organizations and, 143–144; self-help associations and, 161
Oromo nationalism, ix–x; challenges facing, 145–150; collective history reclaimed by, 45; critical self-evaluation of, 41; cultural analysis of, 84–85; cultural history restoration in, 48; democratic rules created for, 168; egalitarian democracy in, 84; Ethiopian elites threatened by, 3; *gadaa/siqqee* system pride of, 99–100, 107; Haile Selassie suppressed by, 77; leadership destruction in, 3; Macha-Tulama movement and, 5, 77, 113; major issues facing, 109–111; OLF created by, 19, 77, 113; peaceful protest movement for, 131–133, 151n3, 162; people killed and tortured for, 83; political consciousness gained by, 42–43, 63, 148; political organizations for, 111, 112; political refugees from, 128; politico-religious system of, 139; self-determination sought in, 1;

Index   193

terrorism against, 6; traditions of, 110; wealthy class emergence in, 142

Oromo nationalist elites: collective grievances of, 4; Ethiopian ruling elites mistreating, 3–4; identity sought by, 4; inferiority complex of, 36–37, 46, 85–86; knowledge and ideology of, 26; mental enslavement of, 40

Oromo national movement, 28, 154, 172; capitalist globalization and, 26; challenges facing, 68–69; democracy transition of, 145–146; egalitarian multinational democracy in, 91; empowerment of, 119; Ethiopian colonial state challenged by, 1–2; ideological problems of, 83–84, 105; lives sacrificed in, 95–96; national *Gumii Oromiyaa* for, 146–147; origins of, 2–7; OSA created by, 93–95; political objectives of, 138; sacrifices of, 69; self-determination of, 134; unfreedoms of, 113

Oromo peace movement, 145

Oromo people, 33; *Abbaa Muuda* and, 24; Abyssinians colonizing, 22; Amhara-Tigrayan state attacking culture of, 36–37; ancestral lands uprooting of, 73n5; Christianity and Islam suppressing, 25–26, 111; as collection of tribes, 132; collective identities struggle of, 2; collective norms of, 40; colonization resistance of, 3; crisis faced by, 31; crossroads for, 53; culture of, 36–37, 44, 81, 137–138; democracy enjoyed by, 75, 104; education denied of, 41–42; enslavement of, 34; Ethiopian colonialism and empowered, 19–20, 144; Ethiopian colonialism heavy-handedness toward, 165; Ethiopian elites destroying culture of, 137–138; *finna* concept from, 20; free press attacked of, 62; grievance expression not allowed for, 64; *guddina* and *gabbina* concept of, 20–21; Habasha culture oppressing, 44; history and culture suppressed of, 81; identities distorted of, 39, 81; internal dilemma issues of, 32; journalism and, 62–63; journalists outlawed of, 127; leadership weaknesses of, 27, 34–39; liberation knowledge needed by, 47; liberation of, 42, 47, 52, 106, 107; localized identities of, 35; massacres of, 59, 65, 83, 120; mental liberation for, 106, 107; national identity of, 69; national pride restoration of, 132; power to determine destiny of, 51; private ownership for, 92; public passiveness of, 112; regional and religious boundaries of, 39; relational identities localized of, 152n8; religions misdirecting, 111; repression of, 154; resources lacking to guide, 38; self-determination of, 44–45; status of, 57–69; Tigrayan-led regime removing farmers of, 129–130, 162; Tigrayan-led regime repressing, 127–128

Oromo People's Democratic Organization (OPDO), 81, 112, 126, 144–145; dominant society and, 36; Macha-Tulama and OLF attacks by, 70; Oromo intermediary elites and, 35, 68; puppet organization of, 60; *safuu* and, 160

Oromo protest movement, 14, 70–71; Addis Ababa Master Plan and, 13; social volcano of, 165; student protest movement, 85; Tigrayan-led regime challenged by, 168; torture and massacres from, 163–164. *See also* peaceful protest movement

Oromo Relief Association, 134n1

The Oromos (Bari, Noggo, Tolosa, Gidada, Namarra, T., and Xadacha), 5

Oromo self, 37

Oromo society, 143, 149–150, 151; Addis Ababa Master Plan opposed by, 27; class differentiation in, 141; norms and behaviors reshaped for, 146, 167; social change in, 157–158

Oromo Studies Association (OSA), 93–95, 161; division of labor in, 96–97; national problems studied

by, 87; political freedom lacking of, 77
Oromo youth. *See Qeerroo/Qarree*
Oromummaa (Oromo nationalism), 20, 28, 32, 79; civic engagement for, 115–116; conceptualization levels of, 78; culture in, 70, 148–149; free democratic society goal of, 91–92; future plans from, 86; *gadaa/siqqee* and, 114–115; global expansion of, 87; knowledge and values in, 86; leadership for, 97; liberation in, 95, 105–109; Macha-Tulama and OLF created by, 35; as national ideology, 82; national ideology of, 109–110; organic unity in, 95, 108; Oromo artists contributing to, 87; as Oromo movement theory, 76–88; political activism for, 115–116; political awareness in, 82; *safuu* concept building, 148; self-discovery in, 46; theoretical insights of, 75–76; unfreedoms of, 77, 87–88
OSA. *See* Oromo Studies Association
our freedom returned (*kayyoon deebitee*), 107

Palestinian diaspora groups, 169
Palestinian Liberation Organization (PLO), 171, 172
participatory research, 11
PDFLP. *See* Popular Democratic Front for the Liberation of Palestine
peaceful protest movement, 131–133, 151n3, 162
PFLP. *See* Popular Front for the Liberation of Palestine
PLO. *See* Palestinian Liberation Organization
political process theory, 9, 10
politico-religious system, 139
politics: activism in, ix, 115; awareness of, 82; consciousness in, 42–43, 63, 148; culture relationship with, 138; freedom in, 77, 92, 93, 111, 112; global capitalism structures of, 54; Oromo communities mechanisms of, 83; Oromo nationalism organizations for, 111, 112; Oromo national movement objectives in, 138; refugees of, 128
Popular Democratic Front for the Liberation of Palestine (PDFLP), 171
Popular Front for the Liberation of Palestine (PFLP), 171
private ownership, 92
protective security, 92, 112
psychology, 38, 39–40, 45, 158
public diplomacy, 51–52
public passiveness, 112

qaallus (spiritual leaders), 23
qaallus institution, 24, 25
Qeerroo/Qarree (Oromo youth), 7, 13, 131, 162; government reaction to, 163; leadership, 144, 150, 175n3; peaceful protest movement and, 151n3

racism, in global capitalism, 54–55
Ragassa, Hailu, 6
Red Revolutionary Terror, 73n3
Rejai, Mostafa, 114
religious ideologies, 103
repression, 34, 84, 154
resource mobilization theory, 9, 84
Revolt Against Political Slavery (*Fincila Dida Garbummaa*), 162
Richerson, Peter J., 166, 167
Robinson, William I., 73n5
Rodney, Walter, 37, 98n6
Rosenzweig, Franz, 170
Rostow, W. W., 8
rule of law, 23, 33, 50, 112, 147
Rwandan genocide, 172–173

safuu (moral and ethical order), 24, 28, 87; OPDO joined and, 160; *Oromummaa* built on concept of, 148; societal divisions influencing, 143
Said, Edward, 11
Sambou, Joseph, 172
Santos, Boaventura de Sousa, 14
Saphalo, Bakari, 111
Scholem, Gershom, 170
scientific knowledge, 15
self-actualizing powers, 43

self-clarity, 44
self-destruction, 50
self-determination, 1, 44–45, 115, 134
self-discovery, 46
self-enforcing equilibriums, 156
self-evaluation, 41
self-help associations, 161
self-image, 109
self-serving ideologies, 101
semi-slavery (*nafxanya-gabbar*), 34, 59, 120–121, 159
Sen, Amartya, 76, 92, 112
SEPDM. *See* Southern Ethiopia People's Democratic Movement
shaking off (*Intifadas*), 172
sham elections, 7
Sheko people, 66, 128
Shuqairy, Ahmad, 171
Sidama people, 66, 97n1, 128, 142
Sidama youth movement (Ejjetto), 144
Singer, Norman J., 73n3, 121
slavery, 3, 120; in capitalist world system, 122; mental, 40; Oromo elites mental, 40; Oromo farmers and, 59, 65; Oromo people in, 34; psychology of, 38
Smelser, Neil J., 8
Smith, Linda T., 18
social cancer, 170
social capital, 89
social change, 157–158
social-constructionist model, 17
social Darwinism, 157
social equality, 33
social hierarchies, 17, 86, 90
social institutions, 155–157
socialism, 18, 59, 101, 103–104, 122
socialist/communist model, 98n7, 101
social justice, 103–104
social movements, 9
social norms, 158
social opportunities, 92
social revolutions, 8–9
social theories, 17
social volcano, 165
societal divisions influencing, 143
societies, 17, 102–103; colonized, 15, 91, 158; Nilo-Saharan, 141
solidarity perspective, 156

Somali Abo Liberation Front, 81
Southern Ethiopia People's Democratic Movement (SEPDM), 126
Soviet Union, 60
spiritual leaders, 23
standard of living, in Ethiopia, 129
Stanton, Gregory, 66–67, 128
state of emergency, 164
state terrorism, 63; capital dispossession by, 123; by dominant group, 129; by Ethiopian government, 31; international organizations and, 68; United Nations problem with, 56–57
student protest movement, 85
subaltern movements, 8
sub-identities, 38
suffering, colonialism and people, 102
supernumeraries, 73n5

technology, 18
terrorism: by Abyssinians, 57–58; from capitalist world system, 104–105; colonial, 55; from colonialism, 42, 55, 78; by Ethiopian colonialism, 79–80, 113, 120–121; fear through violence in, 55–56; against Oromo nationalism, 6; state, 31, 56–57, 63, 68, 123, 129; Tigrayan-led regime and, 134; torture and, 83, 127, 163–164
Third World countries, 56
thought, organic quality of, 86
Tibebu, Teshale, 154
Tigrayan authoritarian-terrorist regime, 60
Tigrayan elites, 81
Tigrayan hegemony, 7
Tigrayan-led regime: capital accumulation by, 62, 126–127, 130; Liyu Police mobilized by, 174; Oromo farmers removed by, 129–130, 162; Oromo journalists outlawed by, 127; Oromo leadership weaknesses and, 27, 34–39; Oromo minerals sold by, 61, 130; Oromo people repressed by, 127–128; Oromo protest movement challenging, 168; rotten from inside,

71; state terrorism of, 63; as terrorist regime, 134; U.S. siding with, 56
Tigrayan Liberation Front, 82, 153
Tigrayan liberation movement, 72
Tigrayan People's Liberation Front (TPLF), 6, 60, 112, 144–145, 160
Tilly, Charles, 9
tokkoo-shane (one-to-five), 131, 134n3, 163
Tolosa, Addisu, 5
torture, 83, 127, 163–164
town hall meetings, 50
TPLF. *See* Tigrayan People's Liberation Front
Transitional Government of Ethiopia, 69
transparency guarantees, 92, 112
tribes, 128, 132
Trueman, Trevor, 129
Tulama Oromo, 140
Tumasa, Baro, 5, 110
Tumsa, Gudina, 5, 110
Turner, Jonathan H., 157
Tutsi people, 172–173

Ummata, Kifile, 5
underground activists, 162
unfreedoms: Ethiopian colonialism imposing, 85, 90, 97n4; human capability obstacle of, 88–93; of Oromo national movement, 113; *of Oromummaa* nationalism, 77, 87–88
UNHCR. *See* United Nations High Commission for Refugees
Union of Oromo in North America, 161
United Kingdom, 130
United Nations, 56–57, 165
United Nations High Commission for Refugees (UNHCR), 67, 128–129
United States (U.S.): colonialism promoted by, 101–102; country control conspiracy of, 73n2; development aid from, 130; Ethiopia aid from, 124; Ethiopian colonialism and, 124–125, 126;

Global Gumii Oromia based in, 167; as global hegemonic power, 124; Haile Selassie government supported by, 60, 124–125; human rights violations in, 98n7; modernization theory applied by, 125; sham elections and, 7; Tigrayan-led regime backed by, 56. *See also* Western countries

values, 83, 86
victimization, 49
villagization program, 130
violence, 55–56, 104–105

Waaqa (God), 21, 24, 58
Waaqeefannaa (indigenous Oromo religion), 14, 138, 160
Waaqeefata (indigenous Oromo religion), 34
Wallo Oromo, 141
al-Wazir, Khalil, 170
wealthy class, 142
Weber, Max, 9
Western countries: capitalist interests of, 102; imperialism of, 116n3; indigenous knowledge suppressed by, 14–15, 16; knowledge globalization by, 18–19; neoliberalism of, 122–123; self-serving ideologies of, 101; sham elections and, 7
Western Europe, 19
Winant, Howard, 55
Wittner, Lawrence S., 166–167
women, in prison, 127
Woodson, Carter G., 37–38, 41
World Bank, 122, 130, 131
World Zionist Organization, 169

Xadacha, Boru, 5

Zenawi, Meles, 66, 67, 71, 128
Zionism, 169–170

About the Author

Asafa Jalata is Professor of Sociology and Global and Africana Studies at the University of Tennessee, Knoxville, and the author several books, including *Cultural Capital and Prospects for Democracy in Botswana and Ethiopia* (2019) and *Phases of Terrorism in the Age of Globalization: From Christopher Columbus to Osama bin Laden* (2016).

www.ingramcontent.com/pod-product-compliance
Lightning Source LLC
Chambersburg PA
CBHW050905300426
44111CB00010B/1395